FENIANISM IN NORTH AMERICA

Fenianism in
North America

W. S. Neidhardt

THE PENNSYLVANIA STATE UNIVERSITY PRESS

UNIVERSITY PARK AND LONDON

Library of Congress Cataloging in Publication Data

Neidhardt, W. S.
Fenianism in North America.

Bibliography: p. 152
Includes index.
1. Canada—History—Fenian invasions, 1866-1870.
2. Fenians. I. Title.

F1032.N36   971.05'1   74-31392
ISBN O-271-01188-2

To My Parents and My Wife

CONTENTS

LIST OF MAPS

PREFACE

The story of the Fenian Brotherhood and its full impact on the course of Canadian history is probably not as well known as it deserves to be. A substantial amount of published material about the Fenians does indeed exist, including several important pioneering articles by C. P. Stacey and a study of the Fenian movement in the United States by William D'Arcy. However, the attention given to the Canadian aspect of the Fenian story has generally been limited to a number of brief historical articles or several highly personal memoirs by participants in the events surrounding the Fenian raids. Since both of these sources are not easily accessible, I hope that this book will cast additional light on the Canadian phase of the remarkable tale of the Fenian Brotherhood.

The rise and fall of the Fenian movement is indeed a fascinating story. The Fenians are often seen as muddleheaded, troublesome braggarts: the secretive origins and early failures of the "Brotherhood" in Ireland, its constant internal strife in the United States of America, its fantastic military schemes concocted by officers of the "Fenian Army" who had little appetite for fighting, and finally the abortive raids on British North American territory—all provide detailed evidence of utter incompetence and sheer stupidity. This picture that historical hindsight and the words of some historians have painted offers only a part of the real story.

It is my belief and contention that the activities of the Fenian Brotherhood during the mid-1860s were not seen by contemporary Canadians as the "comic opera" which many history books have tended to depict. Although Canadians were initially amused by some of the outrageous claims and ridiculous demands of the Fenian leaders, they soon grew concerned that one day the wild boasts of the Fenians might actually lead to an invasion of Canadian soil and that blood would be spilled. Thus, as the rumors of imminent Fenian raids proliferated in the months of 1866, an increasing sense of tension and alarm began to prevail, particularly in the border regions of the country.

The Fenian Brotherhood's hostility toward British North America should therefore not be treated in too cavalier a fashion, nor should Fenianism be regarded as a revolutionary movement of little or no consequence for the historical development of Canada. It would be much more realistic to consider the Fenians as an organization which created a tremendous amount of excitement and elicited a great deal of concern in most of British North America during the confederation era. The Fenian story is more than a mere sidelight in the mainstream of Canadian history.

A closer study of the Fenian activities would also reemphasize the point made by Professor Stacey several decades ago that the Brotherhood did much to create a sense of national feeling within Canadians and therefore was most influential in helping to create a more favorable political climate for the acceptance of the Confederation scheme in British North America during the 1860s. In the province of New Brunswick, for instance, the Fenian threat clearly affected the critical spring election of 1866 and helped in returning the pro-confederation party to power. In the Province of Canada, the repeated rumors of Fenian raids, and finally the raids themselves, did much to convince Canadians that "confederation," already passed and accepted by a majority of their elected representatives, was indeed most desirable and advantageous at this time. Furthermore, the defense system of Canada was greatly improved as a direct result of the Fenian incursions in the late spring of 1866.

If we are to understand the actions of Canadians during this crucial period in the country's history, we must attempt to understand their public and private thoughts and feelings toward the issues of their time. And it becomes very clear, if one consults even a small selection of contemporary sources, that the Fenian Brotherhood occupied much of the attention of Canadians during its heyday in the mid-1860s. The Fenian threat was no joke to many inhabitants of British North America, particularly those living along the lengthy Canadian-American border, and their constant vigilance and anxiety as well as their eventual eagerness to defend themselves against the Fenian raiders were living proof of their concern.

My interest in the story of the Fenian Brotherhood began while I was a graduate student at the University of Western Ontario in the mid-1960s. As this book began to take shape over the last few years, a number of institutions and individuals provided me with information and advice for which I am most grateful.

A special acknowledgment must certainly be made to the Public Archives of Canada and the Public Archives of Ontario. Their resources provided me with most of my primary materials and their staffs were always attentive and most cooperative. Professor C. P. Stacey of the University of Toronto and Professor J. Alex Edmison, Q.C., of the University of Ottawa offered several valuable suggestions, and the latter kindly provided me with some important data about the Fenian prisoners. Sincere thanks must also go to Mr. John Swettenham and his research staff at the Canadian War Museum in Ottawa for reading and commenting on my original manuscript. Some of my colleagues at Northview Heights Secondary School and my friend Barry M. Statham also offered some helpful advice and criticism. My special thanks go to Mrs. Heather McRae, who typed the original manuscript, and to my brother Ulf Neidhardt, M.B.A., who spent many hours completing many minor tasks. To John M. Pickering and Carole Schwager of The Pennsylvania State University Press, who were instrumental in the preparation of this book for publication, I am indebted.

The maps in this book are the work of the Cartographic Office, Department of Geography, York University, and my deep appreciation for their work and advice goes to Mrs. Carol Randall, Miss H. Guzewska, and Professor B. V. Gutsell.

I also wish to acknowledge the Ontario Historical Society for granting me permission to use portions of one of my articles previously published in *Ontario History* as part of Chapter 11 of this book.

My most deep-felt expression of gratitude must be reserved for my wife Anne, who, in her own special way, was indispensable to me throughout the writing of this book.

W. S. N.

1

THE FENIAN MOVEMENT:
THE FORMATIVE YEARS

Ireland in the 1840s experienced two major tragedies. During the "Great Hunger" of the mid 1840s repeated failures of the potato crops plunged the country into a period of social and economic dislocation hitherto unknown in Irish history. Famine and disease took a terrible toll among the population of the Emerald Isle, and as hope for a better future grew increasingly dim, thousands upon thousands of Irish men, women, and children left their homeland. They hoped to find a better way of life elsewhere, and the New World—particularly the shores of the United States of America and Canada—beckoned enticingly. At the same time, Ireland was the scene of a dramatic uprising against the British government, as a wave of Irish nationalism—fueled and guided by the "Young Ireland Movement"—culminated in open rebellion against British rule in Ireland. The '48 Rebellion was suppressed by the British authorities, but for Irish nationalists everywhere the "Failure of '48" merely served to increase their bitterness and hostility toward anything British. Wherever Irish nationalists gathered, whether in the New World or the Old, they talked and planned of another attempt to liberate the Irish homeland. Sooner or later, they argued, an opportunity would present itself when Ireland's freedom could be won.

Over one million Irishmen left their homeland at the height of the Famine between 1846 and 1851, and the total population of the island declined from 8,175,124 in 1841 to 6,552,385 by the time the 1851 census was taken.[1] Some of these emigrants decided to settle in Britain, but the majority chose to make the United States of America their new home. Across the Atlantic these Irish immigrants hoped to find a better and more secure way of life. Some of the new Irish settlers went as far west as California, but most settled in the growing cities of the eastern United States where they worked as semiskilled and unskilled laborers. The city of Boston, for example, received over 37,000 Irish in 1847 alone, and New York City became the home of at least twice that number in the same year.[2] By 1850, New York City's Irish population exceeded 133,000.[3]

Most of the new arrivals had come to America in search of economic survival: the New World, they believed, was a land of opportunity for those who were willing to work hard and long hours. There was cheap or free land to be obtained if one was interested and, most important, the United States was an independent nation. Any Irishman living in America had at last escaped from the hated rule of England.

Along with these hundreds of thousands of Irish who wanted little more than economic security and a fresh start in life came a small but vociferous group of Irish revolutionaries. These men had come to America not by choice but through sheer necessity, for political persecution in Ireland had forced them into exile. These Irish nationalists had escaped from British prisons or had chosen voluntary exile abroad to continue their struggle for Irish independence after the "Young Ireland" revolt collapsed in 1848.

In late February 1848, the forces of liberalism and nationalism were attempting to gain political power throughout Europe. In Ireland, the revolutionary movement, led by the Young Ireland party—decidedly anti-British and deeply concerned with the national self-regeneration of Ireland—was convinced that the moment had come to expel the English from Irish soil forever. The Young Irelanders were most enthusiastic. They even sent a delegation to revolutionary France, hoping to win French assistance for their cause. However, the mission received nothing but moral support and returned home empty-handed.

Meanwhile the British authorities in Dublin Castle, fully aware of the revolutionary activities of the Young Irelanders, decided to crush the movement.[4] The Irish Constabulary quickly arrested many of the leaders, and at their subsequent trials most of the men were given long sentences to be served in the penal colony of Australia.

The Revolt of '48 saw only one major skirmish between the revolutionaries and the British. It occurred when William Smith O'Brien, an Irish Member of Parliament at Westminster, led a small group of rebels in an attack on a much larger police force in Tipperary. The Irish nationalists were easily defeated and O'Brien was sentenced to be hanged, drawn, and quartered, a sentence later commuted to deportation for life in Tasmania. Among the few rebels who managed to escape the authorities were two young men who sought refuge in Paris. Within a decade their names—James Stephens and John O'Mahony—would become familiar to thousands of Irishmen on both sides of the Atlantic.

The hundreds of thousands of Irishmen who made America their new home during the 1840s and 1850s[6] took their bitter memories and a strong enmity toward anything "English" to the New World. Their arrival and settlement in the United States did not diminish their deep-felt love and loyalty for the homeland, and many continued to cherish the dream of Irish independence. They were convinced that one day Ireland would be free of "foreign" domination, and many were willing to play a part in the fulfillment of this dream.

When the Crimean War broke out in the spring of 1854, many Irish-Americans rejoiced, for now England's need could become Ireland's golden opportunity. Irish societies suddenly appeared throughout the eastern seaboard states of the Union. First there was John Mitchel's short-lived Irishmen's Civil and Military Republican Union, soon followed by the Emmett Monument Association, the brainchild of John O'Mahony and Michael Doheny, another "man of '48." To arouse support for its cause, the society began publishing a weekly newspaper called the *Honest Truth*. In August 1855, The Massachusetts Irish Emigrant Aid Society held its initial meeting, and one of its pledged aims was to encourage Irishmen to return to their homeland to work there for Ireland's liberation.[7]

But none of these societies managed to survive for any length of time. The traditional Irish propensity for factionalism and internal dissension seemed to make cooperation, even for the good of Ireland, a sheer impossibility. And when the Crimean War ended in the spring of 1856, the opportunity to exploit England's exposed position vanished.

There was still no thought of abandoning the dream of Irish independence. In the late autumn of 1857, O'Mahony and Doheny sent a fellow Irish-American, Owen Considine, from the United States to Ireland with a secret letter addressed to James Stephens, who had only recently returned home from exile in France. Stephens was encouraged to build an organization whose objective was to be the overthrow of British rule by means of an armed insurrection.[8]

James Stephens was a good choice as a leader. Born in 1824 in Kilkenny, he had espoused the nationalist cause early in life. He had fought with O'Brien at the barricades in Tipperary, and had managed to escape the police manhunt by fleeing to France. In Paris he had scratched out a meager living by teaching and writing for several daily and weekly journals. His main aims in life through his seven years in exile, wrote his biographer, had been "to keep alive, to pursue knowledge, and to master the technique of conspiracy."[9] No longer wanted by the British authorities, Stephens had returned to Ireland in 1856, hoping that some of the "spirit of '48" still existed.

Stephens was clever and resourceful; he excelled as an organizer, and when the offer came from America to raise once more the standard of revolt on Irish soil, he was most willing and eager to accept.[10] Yet he was also determined to undertake the great task only on his own terms. In a letter to Michael Doheny, dated 1 January 1858, Stephens expressed the conditions under which he would organize a revolutionary movement:

> I undertake to organize in three months from the date of his [Considine's] return here at least 10,000, of whom about 1500 shall have firearms and the remainder pikes. These men, moreover, shall be so organized as to be available (all of them) at any one point in twenty-four hours notice at most. . . . You must then be able to furnish from £80 to £100 a month, dating from the departure of bearer from New York. . . . I believe it essential to success that the centre of this or any similar organization should be perfectly unshackled; in other words, a provisional dictator. On this point I can conscientiously concede nothing.[11]

James Stephens clearly expected that the Irish-Americans would act as the providers of goods and money for his insurrection. He would supply the leadership and the manpower.

Stephens's personal conditions were eagerly accepted by the men in New York City, and in due course several hundred dollars were raised and sent to Dublin as the first monthly payment. Stephens, too, lost no time in carrying out his part of the bargain, and on the evening of 17 March 1858, the Irish Revolutionary Brotherhood (I.R.B.) was formed in Peter Langan's timberyard on Lombard Street in Dublin. A small group of men pledged their lives when they swore this original I.R.B. oath:

> I . . . do solemnly swear, in the presence of Almighty God, that I will do my utmost, at every risk, while life lasts, to make Ireland an independent Democratic Republic; that I will yield implicit obedience, in all things not contrary to the law of God [or "the laws of morality"] to the commands of my superior officers; and that I shall preserve inviolable secrecy regarding all the transactions of this secret society that may be confided in me. So help me God! Amen.[12]

By the summer of 1859, this original oath was revised and rewritten. The "secrecy clause" was now omitted, but the reference to obedience to the orders of "superior officers" was deliberately retained. The change was largely due to the official denunciation by the Church of all forms of secret oaths, and the personal dislike of such pledges by several I.R.B. members. The revised oath now reads:

> I, A.B., in the presence of Almighty God, do solemnly swear allegiance to the Irish Republic, now virtually established; and that I will do my very utmost, at every risk, while life lasts, to defend its independence and integrity; and, finally, that I will yield implicit obedience in all things, not contrary to the law of God [or "the laws of morality"] to the commands of my superior officers. So help me God. Amen.[13]

The Organization, as the I.R.B. was popularly known in Ireland till 1865, had a simple, systematic structure. James Stephens became the first "Head Centre" of the movement, which was composed of "circles." Each circle was commanded by a "centre" who, in turn, had nine "captains" under his command. Each of these captains was in charge of nine "sergeants," who commanded nine "privates" each. Originally this scheme was designed to limit one circle to less than 800 members, but this rule was later relaxed and several circles numbering nearly 2000 men came into existence.[14] Fenianism had finally taken root in Irish soil, and soon the branches of the movement spread throughout the island, seeking to undermine the social and political structure of Ireland.

Sympathy and support for the Irish Revolutionary Brotherhood came from many quarters. Farmers' sons, laborers, artisans, mechanics, and numerous small shopkeepers became, according to Stephens, the backbone of the movement.[15] The "Chief Organizer," as James Stephens was popularly known, eventually claimed that over 200,000 members were part of the Organization throughout Ireland and the rest of Britain.[16] The hierarchy of the Roman Catholic Church did, of course, denounce this "secret society" with its revolutionary aims and its challenge of authority and legitimacy, but the majority of the Catholic population of Ireland sympathized with the I.R.B. The British Government suspected Fenian supporters among the members of the Irish Constabulary and even feared that large numbers of British soldiers had sworn allegiance to the Fenian cause.[17]

In November 1863, Stephens became more bold, and he sought more converts by publishing his own newspaper, the *Irish People*. This paper, largely dependent on financial support from Irish-Americans, spread the Fenian doctrine and denounced everything British, from the Queen and Parliament to the Governor in Dublin Castle. It was in the editorial office of the *Irish People* at No. 12 Parliament St. in Dublin where the revolutionaries held their meetings, formulated their plans, and assembled their military arsenal. It was literally in the shadow of Dublin Castle that the insurrection against the British government was plotted.

The men who worked and planned so late at night in their small newspaper office knew that a violent clash with the British authorities was inevitable, but they were optimistic about the outcome. After all, they could choose the time and the place for the uprising, and the battle would be fought on their own home ground.

While the Irish Revolutionary Brotherhood spread its roots and branches throughout the Emerald Isle, the affairs of the Fenian movement developed in a unique way in the United States. As early as the autumn of 1858, James Stephens, to elicit greater financial support from his American sponsors, made a personal appeal in the United States, which he hoped would secure the much-needed funds for "the men in the gap" back in Ireland. On 13 October, he arrived in New York City and later, at a meeting in Tammany Hall, he installed his old friend John O'Mahony as the "supreme organizer and Director of the Irish Revolutionary Brotherhood in America."[18]

O'Mahony had become a prominent Irish nationalist after he immigrated to the United States in early 1854. Born in the little village of Clonkilla, near Mitchelstown, County Cork, in 1816, he had lived the life of a country squire until the 1848 uprising, when he became deeply involved in the insurrection and raised some 2000 men in his own district in Tipperary. However, the men were never involved in any action because the revolt collapsed so quickly.

O'Mahony then fled to Paris where he studied at the Sorbonne and met often with James Stephens. After his arrival in America, he became actively involved in several Irish-American societies, particularly the Emmet Monument Association, whose aim was the liberation of Ireland and whose members participated in weekly drill sessions. In the spring of 1856 he retired from active participation in the affairs of Irish-Americans and soon thereafter suffered a brief mental collapse. However, he soon recovered and published a scholarly translation of Keating's *History of Ireland* from Gaelic into English.[19]

O'Mahony was an impressive man. He was physically very powerful, and his commanding moustache, as well as his piercing eyes and his always immaculate clothes, gave him the appearance of a leader. Yet he was a quiet and reserved man. One of his colleagues considered him too methodic and cautious, always "keeping his likings and dislikings very much to himself."[20]

John O'Mahony was pleased with his appointment as the American "director" of the I.R.B., and there was no indication as yet that the two Head Centres would ever clash in their opinions over the structure and policy of their organization. Some years later, O'Mahony described the events of late 1858 in these words:

> I accepted the position of Head Centre of the Fenian Brotherhood, with the understanding that my duty should be to unite and organize, as far as possible, the Irish element in America, and to concentrate its moral and material forces, and to direct them systematically. The understanding was that the Irish Revolutionary Brotherhood should be organized secretly with James Stephens as its leader and chief.[21]

Stephens's personal appearance in the United States had firmly established the Fenian movement in the New World. Henceforth the American wing of the Brotherhood promised to become more actively involved in raising men, money, and supplies for the Irish insurrection. However, when Stephens finally returned home in early 1859, he carried only £600 in his billfold.[22]

Early in 1859, shortly after Stephens had left the United States, John O'Mahony changed the name of the American wing of the I.R.B. to the "Fenian Brotherhood." He took the name from the leader of the ancient militia of Ireland, Finn Mac Cumhal, who had ruled the old kingdom of Erin in the pre-Christian era and had died in A.D. 283. The "Fianna Eirionn" were specially selected and trained warriors whose physical and military prowess made them the cream of Irish manhood in pre-Norman times.[23] James Stephens did not object to this development, and in his subsequent correspondence with his American Head Centre he chose instead to reemphasize his great need for more money and arms.

In the summer of 1859, O'Mahony decided to start another weekly newspaper. The journal devoted itself almost exclusively to events in Ireland and the related activities of the Fenian Brotherhood in the United States. Before long, O'Mahony began to publish strong appeals to Irishmen in all sections of the American Union to assist in the liberation of their homeland by joining the ranks of the Fenian movement or at least to make some financial contribution to the cause.

The Brotherhood's membership grew slowly, mainly because of the well-warranted suspicions of many Irish-Americans about any "organizations" which claimed to have only the interests of the motherland at heart. There had, after all, been other Irish societies which had professed similar intentions on several earlier occasions. Eventually, however, recruitment increased steadily, and Fenian circles appeared in the New England states, New York, the Midwest, the Great Lakes region, and even in the newly created territories of Nevada, Utah, and Oregon.[24]

But as the American Fenian movement gained strength, the once friendly relationship between Stephens and O'Mahony quickly deteriorated.

Separated not only by the Atlantic Ocean but also by strongly differing personal opinions and views, the two Fenian leaders came to see themselves as rivals. O'Mahony soon began to show great dissatisfaction with his role as the Fenian Head Centre in the United States. He resented being subordinated to Stephens, and he desperately wanted a greater say in the Brotherhood's policy-making. He wished to be master in his own house and envisaged a far greater role for Irish-Americans than providers of the arsenal for the planned insurrection. Furthermore, he resented Stephens's constant complaints about insufficient funds as well as the Chief Organizer's policy of "shadowing" American envoys that O'Mahony decided to send to Ireland for a personal assessment of the prevailing political atmosphere.

To reconcile some of these differences, O'Mahony sailed for Ireland in late 1860. He arrived in time for the Christmas festivities—the first time in many years that he was able to do this on Irish soil. During his three-month stay in Ireland, O'Mahony met often with Stephens and the other leading members of the I.R.B., and during their lengthy discussions many of their differences over policy and decision-making were apparently settled. When the American Fenian leader finally returned home in March 1861, he was convinced that the planned insurrection of the Irish Revolutionary Brotherhood would succeed. O'Mahony firmly believed that Fenianism deserved to triumph, for Ireland had a right to political independence; and if violent revolution was the only means available, he was willing to do his part.

2

THE CIVIL WAR YEARS

The year 1861 became an important turning point in the Fenian movement. The death of Terence McManus, who had been a prominent figure in the abortive '48 uprising against the British in Ireland, brought new impetus to the movement. His travels in exile had finally led him to the United States, where he died in San Francisco on 15 January 1861. Now, by his death, he once again stirred patriotic memories of the recent past in the hearts of many Irish, both in the United States and back in Ireland.

The Fenian leaders hoped to exploit this fresh wave of Irish nationalism. To them, the funeral of McManus would have to be more than a mere commemoration of the past.[1] They expended great effort to identify the recent Fenian activities with the now almost sacred cause of '48. The body of the dead nationalist was placed on public view in several major American cities. The ritual took several months and aroused much sympathy for the Fenians in many areas of the United States. In early autumn the body of McManus was finally shipped "home," and the coffin arrived in Ireland on the last day of October 1861.

Thousands of Irish lined the streets and railroad tracks between Cork and Dublin as the casket was carried to its final resting place.[2] James Stephens informed John O'Mahony in a personal letter that "from 80,000 to 100,000" took part in the funeral procession in Cork alone, and that in Dublin the mourners numbered at least 150,000.[3] No amount of money from the United States, or any action of the British government, could have given the I.R.B. the momentum and popularity that the McManus funeral was able to generate.

The outbreak of the Civil War in the United States in 1861 was another critical point for the Fenian movement. In April of that year, the unity of the American republic, already hanging for years by the slender thread of various political compromises, was finally shattered when the first artillery shells exploded within the walls of Fort Sumter in South Carolina. The events of the next four years would cut the United States deeply, leaving wounds and scars that would linger for generations.

The Fenian movement, however, was able to reap some real benefits from the Civil War and the organization experienced a period of substantial growth. The Fenian leaders quickly realized that Britain's ambiguous conduct in this fratricidal struggle might draw her into an armed conflict with the Union government. The *"Trent* affair" in early November 1861, for example, could easily have led to war.

On 8 November, the American warship *San Jacinto* stopped the British mail steamer *Trent* on the high seas near Bermuda and seized two Confederate commissioners on their way to Europe in search of support for their cause. The Union vessel had openly violated the freedom of the seas, and the British government was highly incensed. Some newspaper editorials and hot-headed politicians began to talk of an imminent war. The British grew so worried that they rushed 10,000 more regulars to British North America, and Canadians were greatly alarmed that they would be the ones to suffer most in this Anglo-American dispute. The *Toronto Globe* remarked that "the cry of war rings throughout the land," and one prominent citizen of London, Canada West, remarked in her diary: "War, war, we hear of nothing but war."[4] Finally, the personal diplomacy of Britain's Prince Albert prevented a war. The two captured Confederate agents, Mason and Slidell, were released and the crisis passed.

However, normal diplomatic relations between Britain and the Union government were never restored during the remainder of the Civil War years. The British policy of permitting the Confederacy to build ships, including the *Alabama* and the *Florida*, in her ports, greatly angered the Lincoln administration, especially when these raiders soon inflicted a great deal of destruction on Union shipping. For years after the war, the *"Alabama* claims" remained a persistent issue in Anglo-American relations.

The Fenians therefore hoped that any of these international incidents would sufficiently exacerbate relations between the two nations to lead to war. Such a conflict would offer the Fenian Brotherhood an unequaled opportunity to strike at a weakened Britain in Ireland.

And even if an Anglo-American war failed to develop, important officials of the Brotherhood lost no time in suggesting that the Civil War itself would provide an excellent training ground for the sons of Eire for later exploits in the name of Irish freedom. Besides, many Fenians forced themselves to believe that their active participation in the war might well earn "the favor of the U.S. government for their later plans."[5]

The appeal "to gain military experience" fell onto willing ears. Thousands of young men of Irish birth flocked to the colors, convinced that they were performing valuable service for their homeland. It has been estimated that Irish constituted about forty percent of all foreign-born soldiers in the Union army, and nearly one-sixth of the entire Union enlistments.[6] Such almost purely Irish units as the New York Sixty-Ninth, the Massachusetts Ninth, and Thomas F. Meagher's "Irish Brigade" were merely a small sample of the Irish enthusiasm for military service.[7] At first, only individual members of the Brotherhood enlisted, but soon whole circles followed to a man.[8] It has been estimated that about 150,000 to 175,000 Irish served in the Northern army during the Civil War.[9]

Recruiting agents for the Union government also let it be understood that once the war was won, the Fenian Brotherhood, in its daring insurrection against Britain, would not only receive countenance but perhaps even material aid from the American government.[10] Some opportunistic politicians quickly offered soothing words and vague promises of support, which were interpreted as "actual support" by eager Fenians. So desperate was the North for manpower as the war dragged on that it sent recruiters to Ireland, and by granting large bounties the recruiters lured many young Irish across the ocean to fight in the Union ranks.[11]

But as the Civil War continued, further strains developed in the relationship between James Stephens and John O'Mahony. The American Head Centre became increasingly concerned about the dilatory tactics and the "dictatorial arrogance"[12] of his Irish counterpart, and Stephens complained constantly about the American's failure to provide him with adequate funds to carry out his revolutionary work.[13] Although there was never a formal break between the two sections of the organization, the constant bickering over policy and mutual suspicion of the two leaders undoubtedly were detrimental to the Fenian cause.

In addition, the Brotherhood now encountered increasingly vocal opposition from the Roman Catholic Church. High Church officials on both sides of the Atlantic openly condemned the Fenian movement. They maintained that it was an atheistic and irreligious society whose aims included the subversion of established religion and the overthrow of just and legitimate governments. Bishop Moriarity of Kerry publicly remarked that "hell is not hot enough nor eternity long enough to punish the miscreants."[14] Churchmen also attacked the Brotherhood for its alleged secrecy, although that particular charge made little sense in light of the open and undisguised conduct of most Fenian affairs, particularly those in the United States.[15]

The opposition from the lower clergy, particularly in the United States, was much less intense than that of the upper echelons of the Church hierarchy. Many Irish priests were convinced that Fenianism would at best turn out to be an ephemeral affair, and therefore refused to condemn the Brotherhood. Many priests believed that it simply made little sense to involve Mother Church in this Fenian business, particularly if members of their flock considered an open denunciation of the movement an unwanted and unnecessary religious interference with their private patriotic beliefs.

To discuss and possibly remove many of their existing difficulties, the American Fenians gathered in Chicago on 3 November 1863. There were only eighty-two delegates at this first Fenian convention, but they came from twelve states, and some arrived directly from the Union armies.[16] During the following three days, the convention created a constitution and elected its executive officers for the upcoming year. John O'Mahony was re-elected as head centre but was henceforth to be assisted by a "Council of Five," a treasurer, and an assistant treasurer, all of whom were to be elected annually.[17]

The Brotherhood also attempted to streamline its entire organization. The head centre was to be held responsible for all national activities of the movement, and he was authorized to appoint the "state centres" for each state in the Union. The individual state centres could then appoint their various "district centres," who in turn headed individual circles. Each Fenian circle was then subdivided into captain, sergeants, and privates. Responsibility always rested with superior officers, and the chain of command and obedience went all the way to the head centre.

The convention emphatically proclaimed its intention to seek "the national freedom of Ireland . . . by every honorable means within our reach, collectively and individually, save and except such means as may be in violation of the constitution and laws under which we live."[18]

Each and every member of this inaugural Fenian Congress was then asked to take this oath:

> I _____ solemnly pledge my sacred word of honor as a truthful and honest man, that I will labor with earnest zeal for the liberation of Ireland from the yoke of England, and for the establishment of a free and independent government on Irish soil; that I _____ will implicitly obey the commands of my superior officers in the Fenian Brotherhood; that I will faithfully discharge the duties of my membership, as laid down in the Constitution and By-Laws thereof; that I will do my utmost to promote feelings of love, harmony and kindly forebearance among all Irishmen;

and that I will foster, defend and propagate the aforesaid Fenian Brotherhood to the utmost of my power. [Resolution III]

The Fenians declared their "intense and undying hatred towards the monarchy and oligarchy of Great Britain," which had for "so long ground their country to the dust, hanging her patriots, starving out her people, and sweeping myriads of Irishmen, women and children off their paternal fields, to find refuge in foreign lands." And they resolved

That it is the special duty of the members of the Fenian Brotherhood to strive with all their might, and with their whole heart, to create and foster amongst Irishmen everywhere, feelings of fraternal harmony and kindly love of each other, unity of counsel, and a common policy upon the Irish question, with mutual forbearance upon all others, so that their efforts may be unanimously directed towards the common objects of their universal wishes after a common preconcerted plan. Thus will their force become irresistible, guided by one will and one purpose, in one undeviating system of action, and thus will they give shape and life, direction and movement to that love of Ireland, and that hatred of her oppressors, which are the predominant passions of every true Irish heart. [Resolution IV]

Among the resolutions adopted at this convention was one that completely disavowed any form of secrecy about the affairs of the Brotherhood. Another resolution offered support to "any enslaved land under the sun," and expressed "deep and heartfelt sympathy with the People of Poland in their war against oppressors" (Resolution XI). Finally, this small assembly of Fenians was so confident about its success that it resolved

That the Fenian Brotherhood, be declared hereby A FIXED AND PERMANENT INSTITUTION in America, and that it continue its labors without ceasing until Ireland shall be restored to her rightful place among free nations. [Resolution XII]

At the conclusion of its first session, the convention issued an "Address to the People of Ireland" wherein the delegates pledged "to labor earnestly and continuously for the regeneration of our beloved Ireland."[19]

The Fenian Brotherhood had declared itself of age. The formal organization of the society at Chicago in late 1863 had its desired effect. Fenian circles suddenly mushroomed throughout the United States during the next two years. Thousands of new supporters were recruited, particularly from the ranks of the Union army. Even ladies of Irish ancestry lost little time in creating a Fenian Sisterhood under the leadership of Miss Ellen O'Mahony.

The avowed purpose of these female Fenians was to spur their men on to renewed energy and activity.[20]

Financial contributions soon began to flow into the Fenian treasury. The money came not only from Irish men and women in civilian life but also from prominent politicians and military men. Several members of the House of Representatives contributed over $100 each and one general of the U.S. Army donated the sum of $1000 to the Fenian organization.[21] Other funds were collected by holding numerous picnics, bazaars, and dances, where good "Irish turf" could be purchased for a mere 25¢ per package.[22]

Perhaps the best-known fund-raising event held by the Fenians was their Annual Irish National Fair, the first of which was held on Easter Monday, 1864, in the city of Chicago, Illinois. Tickets for this event were $1, and their holders were told they were helping "the holiest cause that ever engaged the brain and heart of man."[23] They were now also eligible to win one of the thousand prizes ranging all the way from watches, pipes, tea sets, and cigars to a marble bust of General Michael Corcoran, the popular commander of the Sixty-Ninth Regiment of New York, who had died suddenly in December 1863. The proceeds of all the sales at this Chicago fair were meant to subsidize the Fenian military preparations.

Meanwhile, James Stephens had become increasingly perturbed over O'Mahony's independent management of Fenian affairs in the New World. Thus he decided to make another personal appearance in the United States. Stephens arrived in New York City on 23 March 1864, after a stormy thirteen-day trans-Atlantic voyage. He immediately met with O'Mahony and the two men attempted to clear up the personal differences that had begun to impede the overall progress of the Fenian movement.

Ostensibly, the visit of James Stephens was meant to demonstrate the Fenians' unity of purpose and action; and when the chief organizer was invited to speak at the Chicago fair he emphasized this point. But there was little doubt that his major concern at this time was not only public "fence-mending" but also a burning desire to re-establish his unquestioned supremacy within the Fenian organization.[24] Besides, he hoped to secure additional funds for revolution in Ireland, which he now promised would take place before the end of 1865.[25] Furthermore, Stephens was determined to personally recruit scores of young Irish lads from within the ranks of the Union army for eventual service in Ireland.

John O'Mahony fully understood Stephens's position and conduct. In a private letter to a friend, dated 25 March 1864, he made these comments about the Stephens visit:

I impressed upon him [Stephens] the ruinous effect of allowing any appearance of misunderstanding between us to be manifested in the organization. He seems fully alive to this; still I feel he would supersede me, if possible. He wants a money-feeder for the I.R.B. here, not a directing mind.[26]

Immediately after the Chicago fair, James Stephens spent several weeks touring many of the Northern states. Under the assumed name of Captain James Daly he addressed large and small groups of Irish people in New England, New York, and the Midwest. Everywhere he traveled, he sought to win converts to the Fenian cause. He paid particularly close attention to the military camps of the Union army where he was able to recruit quite openly since "someone in a high position in Washington" had apparently given him an "official" pass.[27] It was from the rank and file of the Northern armies that the Fenian Brotherhood would eventually draw its strongest support.

By August, James Stephens felt secure enough to return to Ireland. He had won much sympathy and support in cities like Chicago, New York, Buffalo, Philadelphia, Cleveland, Memphis, Toledo, and Milwaukee. He had raised nearly $50,000 for the Fenian cause, and he was now determined to make 1865 the year of "insurrection or dissolution" in Ireland.[28]

As the Civil War finally drew to its conclusion, the second convention of the Fenian Brotherhood met in Cincinnati, Ohio, on 17 January 1865. The increased strength of the movement and the enthusiasm of its supporters were now clearly visible. There were 348 delegates, representing 273 Fenian circles, some from as far away as Oregon and Utah,[29] listening intently as plans for immediate action against England were unfolded. As soon as the war was over, or so the members were led to believe, rebellion would convulse the Irish homeland. However, John O'Mahony, whose leadership was regarded as too unaggressive by some members of the Brotherhood, was stripped of some of his executive power, and the authority of the Central Council was correspondingly increased.

The Fenian Brotherhood, now nearly 10,000 strong, was on the move, and its immediate future seemed bright indeed. The war which had torn apart the American Union would soon be over, and from the demobilized armies thousands of young, militant Irish were expected to seek service within the ranks of the Fenian Army. The fatal blow could at last be struck at the British oppressor, and the freedom of Ireland seemed to be within easy grasp.

3

THE CANADIAN DILEMMA

The Civil War, which was partly responsible for the growth and expansion of the Fenian Brotherhood, had other ramifications for British North America. There is a distinct possibility that Fenianism would have encountered far greater opposition in its rise to public prominence had Britain adopted a more pro-Northern policy during the conflict. But Britain's recognition of the Confederacy's belligerence (although never its political independence) and her apparent encouragement of Southern marauding on the high seas produced a strong anti-British sentiment in the Northern states. The *"Trent* affair" in November 1861, the raids on the *Alabama* and her sister ships, and finally the St. Albans raid in October 1864 convinced most Northerners of Britain's obvious sympathy toward the Confederate cause. A feeling of hostility arose in the North, and many Union supporters hoped that an opportunity would present itself to "pay back" Britain for her unfriendly conduct during these difficult years for the American Republic.

The most obvious place for Americans to strike at the British Empire was her vast North American possessions. James Gordon Bennett's *New York Herald* editorialized as early as 26 September 1861:

Let them remember, however, when the termination of our civil conflict shall have arrived, it may be the turn of our foreign enemies to suffer the consequences of the mischiefs they are attempting to do us. Four hundred thousand thoroughly disciplined troops will ask no better occupation than to destroy the last vestiges of British rule on the American continent, and annex Canada to the United States.[1]

Although the *New York Herald* was not necessarily reflecting the unanimous opinion of the United States government or that of the majority of Americans, its words nevertheless had a sobering effect on the people of British North America. Thomas D'Arcy McGee spoke for many of his concerned fellow Canadians:

That shot fired at Fort Sumter was the signal gun of a new epoch for North America, which told the people of Canada, more plainly than human speech can ever express it, to sleep no more, except on their arms—unless in their sleep they desire to be overtaken and subjugated.[2]

Even the *Times* (London) expressed similar sentiments:

And when the time has at last arrived when, either from the termination of civil strife or the failure of money and credit, the United States are no longer able to support their vast army, what is to prevent that army from marching towards the Northern frontier, and satiating its revenge, its love of plunder and of conquest, in the rich and unwasted provinces of Canada?[3]

Most British North Americans, particularly those living in the Province of Canada, were only too painfully aware of what could happen if the large Union armies were to be wheeled around and ordered to advance upon Canada. Canadian defenses were wholly inadequate at this point to repel any massive invasions, for Canadians were still relying on the mother country to defend them and were unwilling to accept the responsibility for their own defense and safety.[4]

Yet in Britain a strong feeling had developed which insisted that Her Majesty's government should not shoulder alone the entire burden of defending the North American colonies. In 1860–61, for example, the British government had spent £295,612 to keep a force of about 4,500 British soldiers in British North America. But by the end of 1862, the tension produced by the American Civil War saw the expenditure rocket to £939,424 for almost 17,000 officers and men.[5]

It was the *Times* (London) which took the colonies to task in an editorial on 6 June 1862:

Let not the Canadians . . . believe that they have in their present connexion with Great Britain a sufficient protection against invasion without taking any trouble to defend themselves. Such an opinion is founded on a mistake both of our power and our will. It is not in our power to send forth from this little island a military force sufficient to defend the frontier of Canada against the numerous armies which have learnt arms and discipline in the great school of the present civil war. Our resources are unequal to so large a concentration of force on a single point; our empire is too vast, our population too small, our antagonist too powerful. But, if we had the power, it is quite certain that we should not have the will. . . . If they [Canadians] are to be defended at all, they must make up their minds to bear the greater part of the burden of their own defence.

Yet most Canadians thought they knew where their safest course of action would lie. The *Toronto Globe* spoke for this majority:

Neutrality is best for England, but for Canada is absolutely essential. . . . Men will differ in opinion about North and South, but our evident policy is to observe strict neutrality as a people towards both sections, and maintain as much cordiality with our neighbours as is possible.[*Toronto Globe,* 27 November 1862]

While Canadians worried about their precarious position and inadequate defenses, the British authorities urged immediate action. In late August 1862, the Duke of Newcastle wrote Governor-General Lord Monck and asked "for some better military organization of the inhabitants of Canada than that which now exists." The Secretary for the Colonies explained:

We have the opinions of the best military authorities that no body of troops which England could send would be able to make Canada safe without the efficient aid of the Canadian peoples. Not only is it impossible to send sufficient troops, but if there were four times the numbers which we are now maintaining in British North America, they could not secure the whole of the frontier.[6]

The only real possibility for Canadian defense, according to a commission of military experts, lay in a program of extensive fortifications along the entire international frontier, particularly in Montreal and Quebec City, and the establishment of naval supremacy on the Great Lakes and the major Canadian rivers.[7]

Yet in spite of all the talk about American invasion and the urgent need for a more comprehensive defense system in British North America during the early 1860s, the only action taken was a substantial increase in British regulars after the *Trent* crisis in late 1861. In the United States, the armies of

North and South were so preoccupied with their own conflict that little serious thought was given to an immediate invasion of the British provinces.

Meanwhile, many Southerners continued to arrive on Canadian soil, and some of these new arrivals, men like Clement C. Clay and the wealthy Jacob Thomson, were actually paid agents of the Confederacy. These men hoped to use Canada as a safe base from which to harass the Union goverment while promoting the Southern cause in the Northern frontier states. Other Southerners, finding their way to cities like Montreal, Toronto, London, and St. Catharines, were voluntary exiles, living in comfortable hotels or temporary homes where they "nurse[d] their wrath against the Yankees ... and sustain[ed] each other's spirits."[8] But the presence of these numerous Confederates, although conducive to additional tension in the already highly-charged atmosphere of Anglo-American relations, did not worry Canadians unduly.

Suddenly a new crisis developed for Canadians. During the early afternoon of 19 October 1864, a group of twenty-one Confederate raiders crossed the peaceful border into the United States and robbed three banks in St. Albans, Vermont, of over $200,000. While making their escape, they set fire to several wooden frame houses and accidentally shot one citizen of the village. Having seized the best horses from the local livery stable, they fled rapidly across the border back to Canada.[9]

Northern reaction to this St. Albans raid was violent and furious. Conveniently ignoring the fact that one of their own generals, Philip Sheridan, had totally devastated the Shenandoah Valley exactly one month earlier, the Northern press now screamed in uncontrolled anger. Naturally, the Canadians became the major target of these verbal assaults since the Confederates had sought safety on Canadian soil.

The *Chicago Tribune*, for example, called upon the American government "to march a sufficient body of troops to Montreal, Quebec or any other place where the St. Albans pillagers may have taken refuge."[10] And President Lincoln was compelled by a group of Radical Republicans and an aroused public opinion to give formal notice of the abrogation of the existing Reciprocity Treaty, which allowed certain goods to cross the border duty-free. The president also warned that the American government would insist on adherence to the Rush-Bagot Convention of 1817, and henceforth all travelers passing from British North America into the United States might be required to show passports.[11]

The fierce American reaction to the St. Albans raid produced a great state of excitement in the British colonies, and talk of war once again ensued. By mid-December the Canadian government felt compelled to call out 2,000 volunteers for permanent patrol duty along the frontier. These men were placed on active duty, "not for the purpose of warfare, but with the object of aiding the civil power in its efforts to prevent aggression on the territories of a friendly State, on the part of persons enjoying the right of asylum in Her Majesty's dominions, and to maintain, as regards Canada, that complete neutrality with respect to the war now existing in the United States."[12] Furthermore, John A. Macdonald, now minister of militia, appointed Gilbert McMicken and Edward Ermatinger as stipendiary magistrates whose duty it was to prevent Canadian soil from being used as a base of further operations by soldiers of the Confederacy.[13]

Yet the war fever in the provinces persisted. Mrs. Amelia Harris, a long-time resident of London, noted in her diary that "there appears to be a great probability of war with the Yankees."[14] And the sister-in-law of the governor-general, Mrs. Frances Monck, who was traveling through the colonies during the fall and winter of 1864, observed in her travel journal: "One would think that there was going to be war to-morrow from talk and fuss about the Militia."[15]

It was in this tense atmosphere that Canadian politicians settled down in Quebec City to debate the great issue of British North American Union. The idea of confederation had existed for many years and had been proposed by many men,[16] and each advocate of the scheme had advanced at least one common reason for the union: united we stand—divided we fall. The men at Quebec City, more than any others before them, were acutely aware of their position. They realized that individually the various provinces had little chance of survival; indeed, to paraphrase Alexander T. Galt, they were like a bundle of loose sticks which could be singly broken but were able to resist any pressure once bound together.[17]

The pro-Confederationists had ample ammunition for their "unity is strength" argument. They merely had to point to the speeches of annexationists like Charles Sumner or Zach Chandler, or to the number of American newspapers, particularly the *New York Herald* and the *Chicago Tribune*, whose pages continuously printed vigorous annexationist sentiments.

Hence it was not too difficult to demand immediate action. George Etienne Cartier commented on the problem in these simple terms when he observed during the "Confederation Debates": "The matter resolved itself into this, either we must obtain British North American Confederation or be absorbed in an American Confederation."[18] J.M. Cameron, fearing that "we might be plunged into hostilities at any moment," argued for immediate union of all the provinces and called for a much greater defense budget.[19] And Thomas D'Arcy McGee, the most eloquent of all the parliamentarians, sought to rally support with this emotional appeal: "I repeat now that of the 2,700 great guns in the field, and every one of the 4,600 guns afloat, whenever it opens its mouth, repeats the solemn warning of England—prepare —prepare—prepare."[20]

But as the winter months of 1864–65 dragged on, the tension and excitement slowly diminished. It soon became obvious that neither the United States nor Great Britain had any desire to become involved in an armed conflict. In early March 1865, Secretary of State W.H. Seward wrote the American minister at the Court of St. James, Charles Francis Adams, that the United States "did not contemplate war with Great Britain whether for Canada or any other object."[21] And Prime Minister Palmerston expressed his own firm conviction in the House of Lords shortly thereafter when he stated, "there is no danger of war with America."[22]

Meanwhile America's great domestic tragedy neared its bitter conclusion and all attention was being focused on the final acts of the great drama. Few persons talked of annexation now. The Civil War had been so long and costly that thoughts of another military campaign would have seemed preposterous. Then, completely unexpected, came the assassination of Abraham Lincoln in Ford's Theatre. Although the president had his enemies, and not only in the Confederacy, his murder outraged most Americans. In Canada, too, Lincoln's death was marked by open displays of mourning by the government, in the public press, and by private citizens everywhere. In Windsor, Ontario, for example, Mayor Macdonell asked that all stores be closed on Tuesday, 18 April, as a mark of respect and sympathy for the slain President.[23]

These genuine expressions of sorrow throughout Canada did not go unnoticed in the United States, and even the usually hostile *New York Herald* was forced to admit that "These evidences of the appreciation in which our late lamented Executive was held will go far to wipe out any causes for resentment that we may have had against the people of the provinces."[24]

During mid-July 1865 a final attempt was made to save the Reciprocity Treaty of 1854. It now seemed doomed, and business interests from almost all major American cities assembled in Detroit, Michigan, and argued either for or against retention of the treaty.[25] But the abrogationist forces were victorious, and reciprocity between the United States and Canada was lost for decades to come.

The *New York Herald*, the *New York Tribune*, and the *Chicago Tribune* rejoiced over the possibility that economic pressure would eventually lead to political absorption of the British colonies.[26] Had not John S. Potter, the American consul at Montreal, urged cancellation of the treaty at the recent convention and promised that as a direct consequence "in two years from the abrogation of the Reciprocity Treaty the people of Canada themselves will apply for admission to the United States"?[27]

But those Americans who believed that the termination of reciprocity would push the British provinces into the arms of the American Republic were greatly mistaken. Although the twelve years of free trade had meant previously unknown prosperity for most Canadians, the sudden cancellation of this arrangement merely supplied the pro-Confederationists with another compelling argument for the immediate union of British North America.

As the summer months passed, less was heard of the American desire to incorporate the British provinces into the American Union. Even such "northward ho" advocates as the *Herald* and the *Tribune* became increasingly concerned with the postwar problems of their own country. The reconstruction of the prostrate South, the rebuilding of the war-torn economy of the Republic, the much-needed development of the West, and the struggle between President Andrew Johnson and radical members of his party quickly overshadowed any preoccupation with the annexation of British North America.

The point should be emphasized here that there never existed a majority in the United States which sought to use force to bring the British colonies into the American Union. Nor was there one major political figure who seriously felt that if economic necessity brought about a North American Union, so much the better for everyone. The use of force was advocated only by a small, although vociferous, minority.[28]

When Lieutenant-General Ulysses S. Grant visited Quebec City in August 1865, he suggested quite frankly that there would never be an attack on Canada unless Great Britain chose to support France in Mexico.[29] An interesting and somewhat different view of the annexationist specter, which kept haunting British North Americans, can be found in an editorial in the *New York Times* of 22 July 1865:

> We beg the people of Canada not to get unduly excited about the subject of annexation—or, rather, about our desire to annex their territory to the Union. We do not know anybody on this side of the lines who gives a thought to the matter.... They [Canadians] are protesting, through their papers and otherwise, that they don't desire annexation ... that they are loyal to the Queen, and satisfied with their institutions; that they dread democratic rule, and are appalled at our national debt; that they are happy as clams with the present condition of things.... All we have to say is, "all right." Be not excited. We will not and would not annex you. We should not, in fact, know that such a thing was ever thought of by anybody, if we did not from time to time learn of it from the Canadian papers.

Thus by the autumn of 1865 most Americans had become deeply concerned with their own affairs and had little interest in seeking expansion to the north. The Civil War had exhausted the nation, and the time had now come to bind up its wounds.

Yet it was precisely during this period that the Fenian Brotherhood decided to launch its great effort. It hoped to benefit from the anti-British sentiment that was still smoldering beneath the surface of American society. The Fenian leadership was convinced that the time for action had come at last. Promises made in the past had to be fulfilled, and the liberation of Ireland was finally to become a reality.

4

THE FENIANS PREPARE

The Civil War was still raging when the Fenian Brotherhood began recruiting men from the Union ranks for its own private army. Now that the war was over, most war-weary Americans were eager to return to their peacetime pursuits, but the more adventurous types in the Union Army were easily enticed to join their comrades in the Fenian movement. Recruiting agents of the Brotherhood made liberal promises. Each recruit was not only promised military glory and the gratitude of Irishmen everywhere, but each was also assured a £100 bounty on enlistment in the Fenian Army. Since a mere $6 enabled every veteran to purchase his gun and equipment from United States government quartermasters, there was no lack of enthusiasts. The British consul in New York City, Edward Archibald, sent several reports concerning these dangerous developments to Sir Frederick Bruce, the British Minister in Washington.[1]

As early as 5 May 1865, the activities of the Fenian Brotherhood made the front pages of at least one major American newspaper: the *New York Herald* carried a full account of the Fenian organization, its leaders, and their objectives. The resulting publicity was enthusiastically received by the Fenian leadership.[2]

Meanwhile the demobilization of the Union forces had proceeded swiftly. By early August nearly two-thirds of the men had left military service,[3] and a substantial number were eager to escape the drab and shiftless life that probably awaited them as returning veterans. Thus they willingly joined the ranks of the Fenian Brotherhood.

The Fenians had become topical and at times even sensational news in British North America as early as the autumn of 1864. In the first few days of November that year, reports appeared in the city of Toronto that the local branch of the Orange Order, whose members generally suspected that any good Catholic was a Fenian, would launch a major demonstration against all Catholics in the city on Guy Fawkes Day. Rumors spread that Orangemen would burn effigies of Guy Fawkes and Daniel O'Connell, and that loyal Catholics would fight them. But when 5 November came, the Orange Order failed to appear for the demonstration. Instead, large groups of men—many strangers to Toronto—were reported to be seen wandering in public places. Nobody seemed to know for certain who they were and what their intentions might be. Later in the day, about four hundred of these men, most of them apparently Irish, assembled in Queen's Park. After a few speeches the group proceeded to parade briefly, and then they dispersed. No violence took place between Protestants and Catholics that day.

Yet by nightfall large groups of men, some "armed with guns, pistols, swords, and weapons of other descriptions," began to appear in the downtown area along Queen and College streets. When some shots were fired about 2 A.M. in the west and east ends of the city, the more timid souls in the neighborhood thought that violence was about to break out. But the only real trouble during the night of 5 November was a small fire in the back of a house along Yonge Street.[4]

George Brown of the *Toronto Globe*, however, was convinced that the Fenian Brotherhood was deeply involved in these happenings. In an editorial on 8 November, he maintained: "It is certain we have in our midst an armed, secret organization. . . . We fear that there can be no moral doubt these Hibernians are identical with the Fenians in the neighbouring States."

This type of journalism created much excitement in the city and in the rural areas of southwestern Ontario where the *Globe* was most influential. One worried reader was so carried away by the apparent threat of Fenians that he wrote this warning letter to Magistrate Gilbert McMicken: "There is an organised band of Fenians on the Seventh Concession of Howard. They received four boxes of Pikes and Pistoles [*sic*] last Sunday night. The Preists [*sic*], two in number, are drilling them nightly. There will be a general massacre of the protestants [*sic*] in Morpeth and this place either next Sunday night or the following."[5]

D'Arcy McGee sought to calm Canadians. At the annual meeting of the

St. Patrick's Society, of which he was a member, he commented on the recent rumors of Fenian activities. McGee had publicly stated his view of Fenianism several years earlier when he told another Montreal audience that "we have no right to intrude our Irish patriotism on this soil; for our first duty is to the land where we live."[6] Now, on 11 January 1865, he once again denounced the Fenians as "a seditious Irish society, originating at New York, whose founders have chosen to go behind the long Christian record of their ancestors, to find in days of Pagan darkness and blindness an appropriate name for themselves." Fenianism, McGee concluded, was "a foreign disease" and its presence was akin to "political leprosy."[7]

Yet nothing seems more difficult to squelch than a rumor; and rumors of imminent Fenian raids on Canadian territory continued to spread. The Fenian problem now not only became part of official government correspondence but also appeared in the letters of private citizens. "I hope and trust we shall not have any trouble with the Fenians," wrote Mrs. Sydney Jones to her son Beverley on 7 June 1865, "but the constant talk about their coming is very shameful."[8] As the summer months passed, the talk increased about Fenian incursions for the sake of plunder or in order to divert Britain's attention from the Irish political scene. In mid-September, Governor-General Monck received an urgent dispatch from Consul Archibald in New York City.[9] Archibald, among whose several secret informers were "Red" Jim McDermott and Rudolph Fitzpatrick, the assistant secretary of the Fenian Brotherhood,[10] first reported "increasing activity on the part of the Fenians," and then continued:

> I have . . . reason to suspect that an attempt will shortly be made to create [a] disturbance on the Canadian frontier. From the reports which have been communicated to me, and which are not very definite, I incline to believe that a number of outlaws, men who have been in the U.S. Military service, and who are probably Fenians, will organize a raid or raids for the purpose of plundering Banks and committing outrages in Canadian towns near the frontier.[11]

Henceforth the Canadian authorities, particularly John A. Macdonald, minister of militia, followed every Fenian movement south of the border with increased attention. Macdonald, as during the aftermath of the St. Albans crisis in late 1864, once more relied on Gilbert McMicken's small "detective force" to provide him with all the necessary information about hostile movements south of the border. He authorized McMicken to hire more men so that the magistrate could carry out his duties more thoroughly, for he had no wish "to be caught napping."[12] Macdonald also informed the governor-general about his policy with regard to Fenianism, and concluded by saying: "I am watching them [Fenians] very closely with his [McMicken's] assistance and think that the movement must not be despised, either in America or Ireland. I am so strongly of that opinion that I shall spare no expense in watching them on both sides of the line."[13]

Meanwhile in Ireland disaster had struck the Irish Revolutionary Brotherhood. In Stephens's words, 1865 was to have been "the year of insurrection or dissolution." The Chief Organizer of the I.R.B. had claimed mounting support for his movement throughout the year. Sworn members of the Brotherhood were reported to number several hundred thousand, and with adequate funds arriving from the United States, the uprising seemed well under way.[14]

Then on the night of 14 September the British authorities in Dublin Castle struck at the Organization. The offices of the *Irish People* were raided, the staff arrested, and the paper suppressed. Incriminating documents were seized by the Constabulary, and the Brotherhood's nerve center was now completely destroyed. James Stephens managed to escape and hide for several weeks under an assumed name in a Dublin suburb, before he surrendered himself in the early morning hours of 11 November.

The much heralded "Movement of '65" was dead. The ranks of the I.R.B. were now in disarray and many of its leading members were under arrest and awaiting trial. The Royal Navy also seized the *Erin's Hope*, an American sailing vessel which was carrying arms and men from the United States to supplement the Irish force in the planned insurrection.

The raid had been the work of a double agent by the name of Pierce Nagle, who had gained the trust of James Stephens but worked for the authorities in Dublin Castle. Nagle had been employed in the offices of the *Irish People* for the last six months and thus had gained much valuable information about the activities of Stephens and his movement. When Nagle managed to secure a letter from James Stephens to the Fenian circle at Clonmel stating that "this year . . . must be the year of action," he delivered it to his British employers. The authorities then decided to break up the I.R.B. and Stephens's dream of liberating Ireland had come to an abrupt end.

James Stephens managed to escape from Richmond Jail during the night of 24 November. The British government immediately offered a reward of £1000 for his capture, or £300 for any information regarding his whereabouts. But Stephens wasn't betrayed again. He continued to scheme for another few months while in hiding, but eventually he decided to go abroad for assistance. In March 1866 he sailed for France where rumor had it that he would see the Emperor Napoleon III in person and ask for his advice and support. Stephens received only sympathy in France, therefore he resolved to make another voyage across the Atlantic to America. He explained his position and plans in this short sentence: "I am going to America for an army of 250,000 men who are expecting me, and I will return with them to deliver Ireland, my country, from the British yoke!"[15]

Yet in spite of Stephens's optimism, the harsh truth was that open revolution in Ireland had now become totally unrealistic. The task of winning Irish independence was now placed squarely on the shoulders of the American wing of the Brotherhood.

In the autumn of 1865 the American Fenians met for their third national convention in the "city of brotherly love," Philadelphia, Pennsylvania. The recent events in Ireland had created intense excitement in Fenian circles, and their enthusiasm was slowly reaching its peak.

Over six hundred delegates from all over North America, including a representative from Canada by the name of J. McGrath, assembled on 16 October and loudly cheered a message from James Stephens, who was then still in hiding. They then settled down to serious business and as a result the organization in America emerged from this third congress drastically altered.

Head Centre John O'Mahony was confronted in Philadelphia with a serious challenge to his power and authority from within the organization itself. A group of militant Fenians, calling themselves "men of action," had become dismayed with O'Mahony's cautious policies and his apparent reluctance to commence actual hostilities against England. These Fenian rebels were now successful in securing a number of important constitutional changes within the Brotherhood, thereby giving a new direction to the Fenian movement.

Henceforth the organization would be modeled on the American congressional system. The position of head centre and the central council were completely abolished, and a president, a senate, and a house of delegates took their place. The president of the Fenian Brotherhood would thereafter be elected annually by the Fenian Congress and his powers would be limited to making appointments to various offices within the organization. Party policy was henceforth removed from his hands and placed with the fifteen-member senate, whose president thus became as powerful as the president of the Fenian Brotherhood himself. Thus, although John O'Mahony was easily elected to the presidency, he had been shorn of most of his policy-making power. The loss of this prerogative brought this quiet but proud man into a bitter conflict with William Randall Roberts, the newly elected president of the Fenian Senate and the leader of the "men of action."[16]

William R. Roberts had been born in Ireland. In 1849, at the age of nineteen, he had come to the United States and worked in a large dry goods store in New York City. Eventually he opened his own business in Brooklyn, called the "Crystal Palace," and became involved in the affairs of the Fenian movement in America.[17] Roberts became the rallying point of the anti-Mahony faction, and with the constitutional changes at the Philadelphia congress, he became a virtual "vice-president" of the organization. Henceforth the Senate had to approve any major policy by a two-thirds majority, and if President O'Mahony were ever unable to be at a policy meeting, Roberts could take his place.

The president of the Fenian Senate was not popular. Many members of the Brotherhood considered him a vain and ambitious man who liked to make a "showy" impression. He was particularly loathed by Fenians in Ireland, who talked of Roberts and his followers as "men of whom we knew little and for whom we cared less."[18]

The "men of action" had their own ideas about how they could best serve the cause of Ireland. They felt that an invasion of British North America would be more effective in bringing about Irish independence than any uprisings on Irish soil. Consequently, Roberts's followers put forward Brigadier-General Thomas William Sweeny, a distinguished officer of the U.S. Army, who was preparing a master plan for invading Canada.

Thomas W. Sweeny, born in Ireland, had emigrated to the United States as a boy of twelve in 1832. Growing up in New York City, he worked as a printer and enrolled in a local militia unit. He joined the army in 1846 and during the next two decades saw action in the Mexican War (where he lost his right arm), the American West (in various campaigns against the Indians), and finally in the Civil War. He rose through the ranks to become a brigadier-general, and when mustered out of full-time military duty in August 1865, he joined the Fenian Brotherhood. At the Philadelphia convention, Sweeny was elected "secretary of war" for the organization and appointed commander-in-chief of the fledgling Fenian Army. "Fighting Tom," as he was nicknamed, had joined the Fenian movement because he believed in a free Ireland.[19] His honesty, his military skill, and his energy were greatly admired by Roberts and his supporters. They were convinced that they had the right man to carry out their Canadian invasion scheme.

Britain's North American provinces, Sweeny argued, could be captured without too much difficulty; all that was required was an ample supply of men and arms.[20] Once the Fenian Army had solidly entrenched itself on Canadian soil and the population of Canada had been won over to the Fenian cause, the territory could be used as a military base from which quick forays could be carried out against Britain. Thomas Sweeny had visions of a fleet of Irish privateers eventually forcing the British government to bargain with the Fenian leaders for the independence of Ireland. And if this scheme did not work, the Fenians hoped that they could create enough friction between Britain and the United States to cause war between the two countries. From this conflict, the Fenians argued, Ireland could only profit.

The newly reorganized Brotherhood also lost little time in issuing proclamations of its sincere determination to liberate Ireland from "British thraldom." In fact, before the Philadelphia convention had dispersed, the delegates proudly gave notice that "the Irish Republic was now in existence," and that the new headquarters of the Brotherhood were now located in New York City's Union Square at the old Moffatt mansion, which had been newly furnished with green and gold upholstery and beautiful mahogany furniture.

However, Consul Archibald's continuous vigilance over all these Fenian proceedings made it nearly impossible for Sweeny and his "general staff" to formulate any invasion plan without the British and Canadian authorities being informed about the most minute details.

The British government finally asked its minister in Washington, Sir Frederick Bruce, to approach the American authorities and discuss the hostile and illegal activities of the Fenians. Bruce met with little success, for it appeared that no one in a responsible government position felt at all uneasy about the Brotherhood. Secretary of State Seward told a surprised Bruce that "he thought the Fenian affair was much exaggerated, and that nothing would serve so much to give it importance as that it became the subject of official correspondence."[21]

The attitude of the American government toward the Fenian Brotherhood was at best ambiguous. During the recent Civil War the Union government had allowed Fenian agents to travel unimpeded among the Northern armies, and W.H. Seward was well known for his pro-Irish sympathies.[22] In fact, members of the Illinois State Circle wrote a lengthy letter to Seward in September 1865, reminding him of the great contributions made by the Irish during the Civil War and expressing the hope that "when the day of Ireland's trial came . . . America would not forget the many brave Irish hearts who marched to death beneath the starry banner."[23]

The Fenians sought to convince the Secretary of State that their "organization contemplates no breach of American Law, nor the dragging of America into any imbroglio for the sake of Ireland, but we do need the sympathy and material aid of the American men. . . . We appeal to you then for your aid; we want money."[24]

Secretary Seward did not reply immediately, but in late November he wrote a brief note to Bernard Dorion Killian, the Fenian treasurer, explaining that he would not find it "compatible with the public interest" to engage in any form of "official" correspondence with the Fenian organization.[25]

Although Seward was probably quite eager to use the Fenians as a political lever to force the British government to reopen negotiations on a whole range of unsettled Civil War claims, he did make it clear to the Brotherhood that "this Government expects to maintain and enforce its obligation and perform its duties towards all other nations . . . as those obligations and duties are defined by our own municipal law and law of nations."[26]

The British government, however, began to take more careful notice of the Fenian movement. On 16 November, the British colonial secretary, Lord Clarendon, instructed Sir Frederick Bruce to approach the American authorities once again to convey very strongly "Her Majesty's great displeasure" with regard to "the Fenian agitators in the United States."[27] Several weeks later Bruce wrote a strongly worded letter to William Seward asking him to clarify the status of Thomas Sweeny, who, although the Fenian Secretary of War, was still permitted to retain his reserve officer's rank in the U.S. Army. Bruce suggested that "the effect of his acting as Secretary of War, is to confirm the Fenian dupes in the belief that the Gov. [sic] of the U.S. favours the movement."[28]

Meanwhile the Canadian government and people had become excited about the latest Fenian movements. On 1 November Consul Archibald had sent a hurried dispatch to Sir John Michel, commander-in-chief of all British forces in North America, stating that a Fenian attack was imminent. The consul reported that one of his informers, a man who had been a member of a New York Fenian circle for some time, had told him that "they [the Fenians] have received an order from OMahony [sic] . . . for Volunteers to hold themselves in readiness at short notice."[29]

Soon rumors of the expected Fenian raid spread throughout the Province of Canada. A mild panic ensued in many frontier towns and villages, and in at least one area a number of banks removed their money to more secure surroundings in the interior.[30] The *London Free Press*, noting a sudden movement of troops in the southwestern corner of the province, remarked on 11 November that "this movement may be looked upon as a precautionary one, in view of the Fenians."

The Canadian authorities, who had been fully aware of these proceedings within the Fenian movement, had already acted to insure the safety of the frontier population. On 9 November nine companies of volunteers had been called out for frontier duty. The Canadian government, believing that "raids or predatory incursions on the Frontier of Canada, may be attempted during the winter, by persons ill disposed to her Majesty's Government," was unwilling to take any chances, and was determined to keep the volunteers on duty "for as long a period as may be thought necessary."[31]

The volunteer units were under the general supervision of Sir John Michel, who, in turn, gave the eastern section command to Major-General James Lindsay and the western command to Major-General George Napier.

The Canadian militia had received some basic training already and was eager to serve.[32] Any Fenians planning to cross the international border in such places as Prescott, Niagara, Windsor, or Sarnia would receive an unwelcome reception. But no Fenians were sighted on this occasion anywhere along the Canadian-American frontier.

Throughout the winter of 1865–66, many Canadians swayed back and forth, sometimes worrying that "the Fenians were coming" and sometimes sure that the whole thing would turn out to be overly inflated rumors. Consul Archibald kept the Canadian authorities constantly informed about the latest Fenian movements in New York City,[33] and Gilbert McMicken's spies followed closely all Fenian activities in other major northern cities. But nothing happened. Not one hostile Fenian appeared along the guarded frontier, and not one shot was fired in the defense of Canada.

Internal dissension continued to weaken the unity of the Fenian Brotherhood. O'Mahony never forgave his opponents for curtailing his powers so drastically at Philadelphia, and he drifted farther away from the Senate wing of the organization. He strictly opposed a Canadian invasion as the best means of securing Ireland's freedom. For him, the orthodox path of revolution still lay in an insurrection on Irish soil. And to raise money for this purpose, O'Mahony issued a series of bonds in late 1865. These "bonds of the Irish Republic" were printed in valuations from $5 to $500 and were redeemable with an interest rate of six percent per annum six months after the Irish Republic was formally and legally established.

The printing of these Irish bonds precipitated the long-expected split between the two Fenian factions in the United States. The Fenian Senate quickly accused O'Mahony of violating the Fenian constitution because he had failed to obtain the Senate's necessary consent in printing and selling the bonds.[34] When O'Mahony ignored them, the senators called a hurried session and quickly deposed O'Mahony. He retaliated by excluding all supporters of the Roberts faction from his Union Square headquarters.

Henceforth there was no cooperation and very little communication between the two rival groups, as each leader firmly adhered to his own convictions. Even the personal intervention of James Stephens could not alter this situation. Stephens addressed himself in a special letter, dated 23 December 1865, to all members of the Brotherhood in America:

> Countrymen and Friends: Aware that certain members of the Fenian Brotherhood, and notoriously the "Senate" of that association, have, madly and traitoriously moved to a mad and traitorous end, raised the cry of "to Canada!" instead of the cry "to Ireland!" and aware that John O'Mahony, known as Head Centre and President of the Fenian Brotherhood, has wisely and firmly, as in duty bound, opposed this mad

and traitorous diversion from the right path—the only path that could possibly save our country and our race. I in consequence hereby appoint the said John O'Mahony Representative and Financial Agent of the Irish Republic in the United States of America, Canada, etc., with ample and unquestionable authority to enroll men, raise money, and fit out an expedition to sail for Ireland and reach Ireland on the earliest possible day, and in all other ways in which, to the best of his judgment, he can serve Ireland—that land to which he has devoted life and honor—I hereby authorize and call on him.[35]

Stephens failed to heal the breach in the ranks of the Fenians, and finally O'Mahony, in a desperate search for approval of his own policy, called for another national convention of the Brotherhood.

On 2 January 1866 the O'Mahony supporters met in New York City's Clinton Hall. The only representative to appear from the Roberts faction was Thomas Sweeny, who once more talked of his invasion plans and called for "deeds not words" and an immediate end to the Brotherhood's "disgraceful squabble."[36] But the convention was packed with supporters of O'Mahony, and Sweeny's scheme was unceremoniously rejected and the old dogma of revolution in Ireland was overwhelmingly reaffirmed. Furthermore, the old constitution of 1863 was reinstated and the changes made in Philadelphia were completely scrapped. Sweeny left the convention in dismay, and soon was seen touring the midwestern states with William Roberts, seeking support for the Canadian scheme and promising that "before the summer's sun kisses the hill tops of old Ireland, a territory will have been conquered on which the green flag, the sunburst of old Ireland, shall float in triumph, and a base be formed for some glorious operations there."[37]

The Roberts-Sweeny wing of the Brotherhood, in reply to O'Mahony's New York convention, held its own meeting in Pittsburgh on 19 February. John O'Mahony, deeply concerned about the existing schism, made a feeble attempt at reconciliation, but the proffered olive branch was rudely rejected and his representatives had to leave among sneers and insults from Roberts's supporters. It was in Pittsburgh that T.W. Sweeny's master plan for the invasion of Canada was finally unveiled. Basically the plan called for a multipronged invasion of British North American territory stretching all the way from Vermont in the east to Illinois in the west. The right wing of the Fenian Army was to assemble at St. Albans, Vermont, and launch a major offensive against the Missisquoi frontier. The center of the Fenian attack would come from Malone and Potsdam, New York, and would see thousands of Fenian soldiers descending on Cornwall and Prescott before heading toward Ottawa and Montreal. The left wing of the Fenians would advance eastward from Illinois, cross Lake Michigan and Lake Huron, and then land at Goderich and Sarnia. From here this army would move toward London via

Stratford, after having seized control of the western terminal of the Buffalo and Lake Huron Railway. In the meantime, smaller detachments of Fenians were to cross the Canadian border from such American cities as Ogdensburg, Cleveland, Detroit, and Buffalo, which was particularly important because the Fenian targets from there would be the Welland Canal, the eastern terminus of the Buffalo and Lake Huron Railway, Hamilton, and eventually Toronto.

Sweeny felt he could conquer Canada with an army of 10,000 men and $450,000 worth of arms and supplies.[38] He made no allowance whatsoever for the possibility that such quantities of men and money might never be obtained. Nor, apparently, did he realize that the Province of Canada still had a substantial force of British "regulars" and could muster three or four times as many volunteers as he had Fenian soldiers. The Fenian general paid only limited attention to such vital matters as transportation and a commissariat system, fully expecting Canadians to provide both. He was convinced that "with the single exception of Quebec . . . the whole of the British provinces will fall in a single campaign."[39]

The Fenian strategy also rested on several other questionable assumptions. Sweeny fully expected American neutrality while his armies descended on the Province of Canada, and he firmly believed that the existence of a Fenian Republic in North America would be formally acknowledged by the United States. Furthermore, he supposed that a quick military success in Canada would rally thousands of Irishmen, on both sides of the border, around the green and gold flag of the Brotherhood.

Thomas Sweeny and William Roberts were confident of victory, and their time was now taken up with constant strategy meetings at which the great invasion plan was continuously "perfected." Ever-increasing numbers of young Irishmen enlisted in the Fenian Army, fully expecting the Canadian venture to be an easy military success. Had Thomas Sweeny not told them as early as late January 1866 during a speech in Buffalo that "before the sun of May shines, they [the Fenians] will have conquered a territory, over which the Irish flag will float, and which will serve as a base from which to operate against the British power in Ireland itself"?[40]

On 5 February the *Buffalo Courier* printed a lengthy column, signed by the local Fenian leader, Patrick O'Day, who called upon all the Irish in the United States to prepare for an impending conflict. O'Day claimed that

> a veteran Irish officer of unsullied honour and a brilliant military reputation, who has spent eighteen years in the military service of the United States, has volunteered his services to lead the hosts which are now about to be marshalled under the green flag of Ireland. The time for action has arrived. The plans of action are perfected, and all that is now required is arms to place in the hands of the thousands of brave men who

are today ready to take the field and fight for their country's liberation. [*Toronto Globe*, 6 February 1866]

The author of the letter concluded by saying he was certain that "our American fellow citizens . . . will not be deaf to the call which the Fenian brotherhood of America now makes on them to aid the work of winning Irish independence."

Thus as the winter months passed Fenian enthusiasm waxed and reached a new level of strength and confidence. And soon a song gained popularity among the members of the Roberts wing of the Brotherhood:

We are the Fenian Brotherhood, skilled in the arts of war,
And we're going to fight for Ireland, the land that we adore,
Many battles we have won, along with the boys in blue,
And we'll go and capture Canada for we've nothing else to do.[41]

The time for talk appeared to be over; the time for action seemed to have come at last.

5

THE MARCH SCARE OF '66

On 17 February 1866 the British Parliament, in a special emergency session, suspended the right to *habeas corpus* in Ireland. This drastic curtailment of civil liberties was taken to prevent any further violence between British troops in Ireland and members of the I.R.B. This was a potential danger as long as James Stephens directed the I.R.B.—even from hiding. The British government was convinced that this policy was the only possible alternative to domestic unrest and violence in Ireland, and thus the suspension bill passed Parliament easily.[1] Immediately hundreds of Fenians, including a group of about one hundred and fifty Irish-Americans, were arrested by the British authorities.

When the news of these developments reached North America, the Fenians were furious. O'Mahony issued a proclamation calling on all Fenian circles to immediately send men to assist their Irish brothers.[2] Soon mass meetings were held in numerous cities and towns, and the Fenian offices in New York City "were thronged with visitors, and there was an appearance of renewed activity among the officers of the Fenian Brotherhood."[3] On Sunday afternoon, 4 March, thousands of supporters and sympathizers flocked into Jones' Wood in New York City, despite Archbishop John McCloskey's admonition to his parishioners "to take no part in what must be regarded as an open profanation of the Lord's day, an act of public scandal to religion and an outrage to the feelings of all good Catholics." O'Mahony himself addressed the vast throng and harangued "the foul tyrants of our race," while pleading for more money "to put munitions of war in the hands of the Irish army. . . [and] to put Irish ships upon the sea."[4]

The action of the British Parliament had indeed stirred up a hornet's nest in North America. The Fenian Brotherhood was spurred on to increased activity, and soon the British North American provinces were affected by the repercussions of the measure taken by their mother country.

On 28 February the *Toronto Leader* and the *Globe* printed a dispatch from the *New York Herald* which reported that General Sweeny was ready "to make a demonstration against Canada about the middle of March." And soon thereafter Gilbert McMicken received further information from his detectives that trouble was indeed brewing. He quickly notified John A. Macdonald that "a desperate advance and attack will be made along the whole of the Frontier on or about the 17th instant."[5] Meanwhile Lord Monck had sent the following dispatch to Edward Cardwell, the Secretary for the Colonies:

> . . . information has reached me from many quarters tending to shew [*sic*] an intention on the part of the Fenians to make an inroad on Canadian territory. This information was further supported by Police reports, announcing that parties of suspicious looking persons were observed entering Canada from the United States, and were recognized in the streets of our large towns. These reports . . . had induced a feeling of great uneasiness and insecurity amongst the people.[6]

Canadians anxiously awaited St. Patrick's Day, 1866. The government had taken every possible precaution in light of the pending invasion. On the afternoon of 7 March, Macdonald had telegraphed Colonel Patrick MacDougall, the Adjutant-General of the Militia, and ordered him to "Call out ten thousand (10,000) men of the Volunteer Force. . . . They must be out in twenty-four (24) hours, and for three (3) weeks and whatever further time may be required."[7] Obviously the minister of militia was not taking a chance on being caught "napping," thereby risking further censure from his constant tormentor, the *Toronto Globe*.

The public response to the call for volunteers in the Province of Canada was not only quick but also overwhelming. Thousands of men from every walk of life rushed forward to serve their country.[8] Anti-Fenian meetings and patriotic rallies were held all over the province. By midnight, 8 March, 14,000 volunteers had been enrolled, and Colonel MacDougall later admitted that he could have mustered at least 32,000 men within 24 hours if the necessity had arisen.[9] Each man seemed ready and eager to defend his country against "the threatened piratical attacks of lawless men, who use the territory of a neighboring power for the purpose of openly organizing enterprizes against the Sovereign rights of our Queen and the security of her subjects."[10]

The next few days were filled with considerable tension. Some frontier towns developed nerves to a point that soon approached absurdity. St. Catharines, for example, organized its volunteer units with "the ringing of the town bells, the sounding of bugles, and the firing of artillery—at about 1 a.m." when a false rumor was circulated that the Fenians were coming. Its home guard performed sentry duty day and night, and a number of cannons covered the roads leading into the town.[11] In London Mrs. Harris noticed "a great scare about the Fenians" and felt certain that an attack would definitely be made "before the 20th of the month."[12]

Most Canadian newspapers took the opportunity during this public furor to castigate the American government for allowing the activities of the Fenian Brotherhood to go unchecked. The *Toronto Globe* (9 March 1866) suggested impatiently that the time had finally arrived when the United States authorities "are bound to interfere and bring to an end the proceedings of the Fenian Society throughout the Union." The *Toronto Leader* (9 March 1866) demanded that the American government "do all that could be done to prevent threatened raids across the border," and the *Niagara Mail* (7 March 1866) deplored the American government's "professed sympathy with Fenianism" and feared that the movement had already grown so powerful that the authorities "may not be able to stop it with a proclamation." An editorial in the *London Free Press* (19 March 1866) perhaps expressed most accurately the feelings of many Canadians:

> It is very unpleasant that we should be put to the expense and annoyance for preparing for a state of war when Great Britain and the United States are at peace. It inflicts a serious injury upon us, by alarming our people, swelling our public expenditure, and deranging our trade and commerce, which the citizens of no friendly power should do.

Meanwhile in Toronto trouble was brewing over the upcoming St. Patrick's Day parade. On 9 March the *Globe* published an appeal to the local Irish Roman Catholic community to refrain from parading on the seventeenth, since that was the day the Fenian invasion was expected. The editorial added that a public demonstration of this sort at this particular time would only increase the already inflamed passion of the local Orange Order. The next day, the *Toronto Leader* joined its rival and also demanded cancellation of the annual parade. Leading citizens even sought to induce Mayor Francis H. Medcalf to forbid the event in the interests of public safety.

As the critical day drew closer, almost everywhere along the frontier, as well as in the capital, tension mounted.[13] In cities and towns the Church attacked the Fenian movement. Bishop Joseph Lynch of Toronto advised his flock that it was "their duty as loyal subjects to repel invasion and defend their homes; for loyalty is a virtue, as it is also a duty towards the Government under which we have liberty, protection, and just laws."[14] Bishop Farrell of Hamilton called the Fenian Brotherhood "a treasonable and contemptible organization" and maintained that "no man who was a good Catholic could possibly countenance the proceedings of . . . an unholy, unlawful, and illegal association."[15]

Several American newspapers editorialized somewhat irresponsibly about the imminent Fenian raid. The *Rochester Union and Advertiser*, for example, took it upon itself to castigate Canadians for their recent "misconduct" during the Civil War, which had caused, according to the editorial, many sleepless nights for American citizens. The paper concluded its comments with unabashed sarcasm:

> Let them understand how it is to be alarmed. Let their men walk the streets in arms—let their women and children pass a few sleepless nights, as did ours. Nay more; let their citizens in some peaceful village, like St. Albans, be shot down by some Fenian band—if need be, to show them that justice is sure to overtake the guilty.[16]

Alexander McLeod, one of McMicken's spies who had infiltrated the Fenian organization, informed John A. Macdonald on 12 March that large numbers of Fenians were being drilled and equipped in the Buffalo area, and that "ammunition, military accoutrement and wagons are now ready in the city for an invading force of 5,000 men." However, McLeod was not certain if St. Patrick's Day was to be the day of the planned invasion, and he added: "I don't think the time to advance is fixed yet. Some say in about a week, others not until May."[17] Another Canadian spy, Patrick Nolan, had earlier informed his employers of his recent experience while staying in a hotel filled with American Fenians: "I slept in one room with three [Fenian] Senators and Congressmen every night. Their full determination is to organize immediately and make a strike for Canada. If they can arrest the Governor General and D'Arcy McGee and other Government officers they will do it."[18]

But St. Patrick's Day, 1866, came and went without any incident along the Canadian-American frontier. Nowhere were there any signs of Fenian soldiers attempting to cross into Canada. Although most Canadian towns did not hold parades, Toronto did have a march by the Hibernian Society. There were, however, no outbursts of violence anywhere along the parade route.

In many American cities the local Irish population, including considerable groups of Fenians, marched in honor of its patron saint, but the only excitement was created by Fenian orators who harangued the British government for its conduct in Ireland.[19] The great "March Scare" had been merely another Fenian rumor. The *Detroit Free Press* (18 March 1866), having followed Canadian military preparations during the last few weeks, could not refrain from remarking somewhat caustically: "St. Patrick's Day, 1866, having passed, we trust that the assembled martial host of Her Majesty's British North American Provinces will return to their homes and firesides, and laying aside their trusty armour, again betake themselves to the paths of peace."

Consul Archibald was firmly convinced that Canadian military readiness had prevented an invasion. "I do not think," he wrote on the day of the expected assault, "Sweeny will trouble you [Canada] for some time to come. Your preparations have evidently dampened the Fenian ardor."[20]

Yet it was not until late March that most of the province's volunteer units were disbanded.[21] The events of the last few weeks, however, were not without some beneficial aspects for Canadians. The *Toronto Globe* (30 March 1866) in a lengthy editorial, summed up the affair:

> The events of the last fortnight have not only shown unmistakeably [*sic*] that the true British spirit beats universally throughout our country— that the people of Canada are ready, as one man, to defend their homes and firesides—but they have established the fact that the military system of the Province works efficiently. . . . The Fenians have unwittingly done an essential service to the Canadian people, by inspiring them with a degree of confidence in their defensive strength which they did not before possess. They have, moreover, given our Republican neighbours an opportunity of seeing how earnest and unanimous is the love of the people of British North America for British alliance, and how utterly groundless has been the impression so diligently propagated, that the desire for annexation to the United States was general in Canada.

This kind of loyalty toward the British connection encouraged the North American correspondent of the London *Times* to write to his editor on 7 April: "The hearts of the Canadians beat true and steadily for England. This Fenian conspiracy will make the proposed Confederation of the Provinces quite certain.

The loyalty of Canadians was never in doubt and the Fenian Brotherhood was unable to win any substantial support in British North America. Fenianism was apparently introduced in the city of Toronto, Canada West, in 1859 by one Edward O'Meagher Condon.[22] But its initial strength of sixty members was probably never surpassed in the early years of organization.

Not until Michael Murphy assumed the presidency of the Hibernian Society of Canada did the movement gain additional supporters. There were many Canadians who were convinced that the Hibernian Society was merely a front for the Canadian Fenian movement and Michael Murphy emphatically denied this contention.[23] But even the Canadian government felt that there was a strong connection between the two groups.[24] There can be little doubt, however, that many members of the Hibernian Society supported or at least sympathized with the Fenian movement. President Murphy took the opportunity offered him at the annual St. Patrick's Day celebrations in 1864 to air his personal views on the subject of Irish freedom and the Fenian Brotherhood. "All that Irishmen asked," cried Murphy in a passionate and well-received speech to the assembled throng of Irish supporters, "was justice . . . to be relieved from the oppression and tyranny under which they suffered in their native land." Murphy then praised the Fenians, maintaining that "the society was a noble and good one, and had a glorious object in view—the liberation of Ireland." He then concluded his speech by appealing to all Irishmen in the province "to be ready when the time came" to work for Ireland's freedom.[25]

Michael Murphy was a Fenian, but it did not follow that therefore all members of the Hibernian Society or of the Irish community in the city were also members of the Brotherhood. In fact, Gilbert McMicken was told by his spy, Patrick Nolan, that it was a great mistake for the government to think that the whole Hibernian Society was Fenian. "There are not half of them Fenian," he wrote in late December 1865.[26] Nolan, who used the alias of Erastus Burton, also reported that there were seventeen Fenian "circles" in Canada West at this time—nine in Toronto alone, and others in the towns of London, Hamilton, Stratford, Whitby, and Cobourg. Toronto's Fenian membership was estimated at "about 650" by Nolan.[27] At a later date, D'Arcy McGee assessed the strength of Fenian supporters and sympathizers in Canada as follows: Quebec City 200, Montreal 355, and Toronto 800.[28] These figures are probably reasonably accurate, and they show that the Fenian Brotherhood was certainly never a massive organized movement in Canada.

The American members of the Brotherhood mistakenly believed they would find support for their cause in British North America, particularly in the Province of Canada. After all, the province had 241,423 persons of Irish background either by birth or descent, according to the 1861 Census Report. Several cities had large Irish populations: Montreal had 14,179 persons of Irish origin, comprising fifteen percent of the city's total population, and Toronto was home to 12,441 Irish men and women, totaling twenty-seven percent of the city's inhabitants.[29] But the calculations of the American Fenians were quite inaccurate, since they were based on completely false assumptions. For example, although nearly 250,000 persons of Irish background lived in the Province of Canada, a large number of them were not Roman Catholics but Protestants from Northern Ireland. In fact, most Irish citizens of Toronto were from Ulster,[30] and some of the most prominent were Protestants. Nor could it always be assumed that all the Irish Catholics of Canada would rally to the Fenian side merely because of their shared religious faith, although many members of the anti-Catholic Orange Order liked to think so. For Canada offered the Irish a reasonably good government, a fair legal and adequate educational system, and an opportunity to maintain a decent standard of living. Few of the Irish-Canadians, who had come by the tens of thousands during the "Hungry Forties,"[31] were prepared to jeopardize these conditions.

Those few Irish-Canadians who sympathized with the Fenian movement generally supported the O'Mahony camp. When the American Fenian organization had held separate conventions in early 1866, a Canadian delegate, Father Curley, attended O'Mahony's congress in New York City,[32] but no Canadian attended the Roberts-Sweeny convention in Pittsburgh. In fact, some Canadian sympathizers became so irate at the idea that a Fenian raid might be carried out in Canada that they published an open letter in several American newspapers strongly condemning the proposed scheme of the Roberts-Sweeny wing.[33] When the O'Mahony wing of the Brotherhood attempted its Campobello venture in April 1866, a group of Toronto Fenians, led by none other than Michael Murphy, sought to travel to the Atlantic coast to assist in the invasion. This entire group was arrested in Cornwall, and instead of fighting for the Fenian cause, its members found themselves in Canadian jails for the next few months.[34] The American Fenian movement would find great difficulty in securing Irish-Canadian assistance in its grandiose plans for the liberation of Ireland.

6

CAMPOBELLO: O'MAHONY'S CATASTROPHE

While the inhabitants of the Province of Canada worried about a raid by Roberts's supporters during the days prior to St. Patrick's Day, the leadership of the other wing of the Brotherhood was scheming to attack British North America in the Maritime Provinces.

The O'Mahony followers, trying to re-establish their claim as leaders of the American Fenian movement, suddenly begun to display an entirely unexpected degree of militancy. Bernard D. Killian, an able New York lawyer and the Fenian treasurer, sought to persuade John O'Mahony to carry out a quick military raid against Campobello, an island located at the western entrance of Passamaquoddy Bay near the Maine-New Brunswick border. Killian argued that the island was actually neutral territory and that it would provide the Fenians with an excellent base for naval operations against the British fleet and might even provoke an Anglo-American crisis from which the Fenians could benefit. Furthermore, a military success at this time was absolutely necessary, according to Killian, for only "by striking a blow and making a fight" could Fenianism's reputation be revived.[1]

By mid-March O'Mahony had succumbed, against his own better judgment, to the constant entreaties of his treasurer. What apparently convinced the Fenian president were Killian's assertions that the American authorities had given every verbal indication they would not interfere in any harmful way with the plans of the Fenian Brotherhood. The word had been spread that Secretary Seward was sympathetic to Killian's plans and had seemed "favourable to an attack on the British possessions in America by the Fenians."[2]

It is doubtful that Seward would ever have committed himself openly to the Fenian cause. But when the *Detroit Free Press* reported on 9 April that Killian and other top Fenians had been granted an interview with President Andrew Johnson, many members of the Brotherhood seemed convinced that the United States government would not hinder their plans. Apparently some Canadians thought the same, for John A. Macdonald received a warning letter from a friend informing him that "there is a perfect understanding between Mr. Seward and two of the Fenian Chiefs."[3]

The Fenian Brotherhood's activities had not been ignored by the Canadian and New Brunswick governments. As early as 11 November 1865, Colonial Secretary Edward Cardwell had informed New Brunswick's Lieutenant-Governor Arthur Hamilton Gordon of possible Fenian raids on the province. This warning to Gordon was repeated by Sir Frederick Bruce in early December.[4]

Lieutenant-Governor Gordon took these dispatches seriously and over the next few months increased militia enrollment and created a home guard. In addition, a large British naval squadron was anchored in Halifax harbor for use if the situation became too difficult for the volunteer defenders to handle.

Unfortunately, the rumors of a Fenian raid brought about a revival of much anti-Catholic feeling in the province. Just as in the Province of Canada, there were enough people, not necessarily all members of the Orange Order, who rashly believed that because most Fenians were Catholics, all Roman Catholics were members of the Brotherhood. But Archbishop Thomas Connolly of Halifax assured Lieutenant-Governor Gordon that there was no danger of disloyalty from the Roman Catholic Irish of British North America. In these colonies, he argued, Roman Catholics possessed a social and political freedom that they could find nowhere else, and he concluded by saying "there has been no period since the days of the emancipation, at which Catholics [in British North America] have not possessed that influence in the community to which their number and position fairly entitled them. . . . The great government of the United States has nothing more tempting to offer."[5] Archbishop Connolly's assessment was quite accurate, for when the Fenians did at last appeal to their co-religionists in New Brunswick, their pleas for aid fell on deaf ears. Yet during the time of the crisis, anti-Catholic sentiment continued to persist.

Although Lieutenant-Governor Gordon was annoyed by this sentiment,[6] there was good reason for local people to worry. In early March several small shipments of arms and ammunition were shipped to Eastport, Maine, a small town located on Moose Island in Passamaquoddy Bay. A small number of Fenians began to appear in both Eastport and Calais in late March. To win the support of the inhabitants of the province, the following circular was posted in several locations in St. John, New Brunswick:

> CITIZENS OF NEW BRUNSWICK
> Republican institutions have become a necessity to the peace and prosperity of your Province. English policy, represented by the obnoxious project of Confederation, is making its last efforts to bind you in effete forms of Monarchism. Annexation to the United States is not, necessarily, the only means of escape. Independence for the present is the best one, and will assure you the supreme and sole management of your affairs. Mercenary bayonets cannot—shall not prevent you asserting this independence if you desire it. Signify your wishes and you become the founders of a Free State, untrammeled by Royalty, unchecked by Misrule and certain to secure all the lost benefits of Reciprocity.[7]

On 5 April the *New York Herald* reported a force of 5500 Fenians sailing in five ships for Bermuda, but the *New York World* quickly explained that this was merely a diversionary tactic and that the expedition would change its course very soon and head toward Campobello.[8]

Bernard Killian and three aides arrived in Eastport in early April. Within another few days four hundred to five hundred fellow Fenians made their appearance. Killian now rented a large meeting hall, chartered three small sailing vessels, and purchased several kegs of powder which his men quickly converted into cartridges.

Despite the fact that the province had its defenses well prepared, the actual appearance of this substantial number of Fenians created much unrest among the inhabitants of Campobello, St. Stephen, and St. Andrews. John A. Macdonald was quite accurate when he wrote this brief note to Peter Mitchell, a leading pro-Confederation member in the New Brunswick Assembly: "At the moment I am writing this letter you are, I fancy, in great excitement about the Fenians. I really would not be surprised if these rascals gave you some trouble. . . . They have found that we are too strong for them and therefore they will make a dash at you."[9] Not even the presence of two small British warships, the H.M.S. *Pylades* and the H.M.S. *Rosario*, seemed to allay the fears of the populace.

The Fenians continued to await more men and supplies. But their mere presence, as well as the tough appearances of some of them, increased the tension in the border towns. The *St. Croix Courier* described some Fenians as

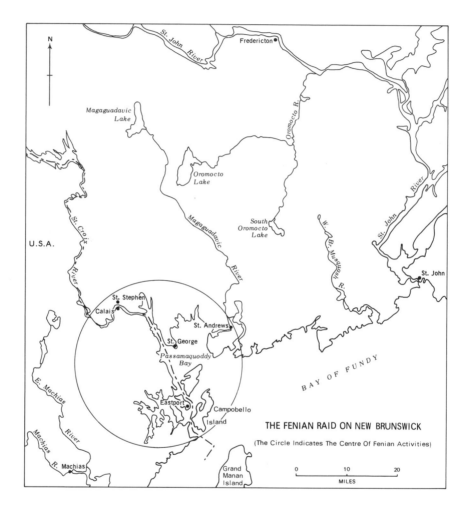

N

St. John River

Fredericton

Magaguadavic
Lake

Oromocto R.

Oromocto
Lake

Magaguadavic

South
Oromocto
Lake

W. Br. Musquash R.

St. John River

U.S.A.

St. Croix River

St. John

St. Stephen

Calais

St. Andrews

St. George

Passamaquoddy
Bay

E. Machias River

BAY OF FUNDY

Eastport

Campobello
Island

THE FENIAN RAID ON NEW BRUNSWICK

(The Circle Indicates The Centre Of Fenian Activities)

Machias River

R. Machias

Grand
Manan
Island

0   10   20

MILES

"seedy looking fellows" who appeared to be "the most villainous cut throat individuals we ever laid eyes on, men who would just be in their native element in the midst of rapine and murder."[10] And when the news spread that the Fenians had arranged to secure some old recast cannons from a nearby ironworks, consternation ran high.

The British vice-consul in Eastport, Robert Kerr, became increasingly worried and asked American authorities to intervene. As a result, Washington sent Commissioner L.G. Downes and Deputy U.S. Marshal B.F. Farrar to Eastport to enforce the neutrality laws of the United States. Secretary Seward also notified Attorney-General James Speed on 12 April about the imminent border troubles, and Speed replied that he would take all the necessary steps the situation warranted.[11] Finally, the town of Eastport was closely watched at night by a company of soldiers from nearby Fort Sullivan.

Nevertheless, the Fenians succeeded in carrying out a number of small and noisy raids.[12] On the night of 14 April, a small band managed to occupy Indian Island close to Campobello. They shouted wildly, brandished their revolvers, and managed to "capture" the Union Jack flown by the local customs inspector before rowing back to the mainland.

Inhabitants of the Canadian border towns now became alarmed. Many residents of St. Stephen fled across the St. Croix River to Calais to spend a few days in the homes of American friends. More militia and home guard units were called up for active service, and a full regiment and two artillery batteries of British "regulars" were moved to the scene. Lieutenant-Governor Gordon arrived in St. Andrews on 17 April, and on the next day a large naval squadron under Major-General Doyle arrived from Halifax. Doyle wanted to abandon the border towns temporarily and try to entice the Fenian forces to pursue the Canadian defenders into the interior of the province, where he could destroy them. Lieutenant-Governor Gordon did not agree to this plan, fearing that the morale of the residents of the abandoned areas would be too seriously affected. Consequently, a strong defensive position was established at St. Andrews. Here the Fenians were confronted by a formidable array of defenders.

The marauding Fenians had other problems. On 17 April, their long-awaited supply of arms arrived on the *Ocean Spray* in Eastport. But the vessel was immediately detained by the captain of a United States revenue cutter acting on orders of the local customs collector, Washington Long. The Fenians had their hopes raised momentarily when the district attorney in Portland ordered Long to release the 129 cases of arms unless he could prove they were destined for a foreign land. Their hopes were short-lived, however, for Commander Cooper of the U.S.S. *Winooski* decided he would impound the arms until he received final instructions from his superiors in Washington.

But Commander Cooper's good intentions left his superiors acutely embarrassed. There seems little doubt that the American government intended ultimately to enforce the neutrality legislation on its statute books, but political considerations stemming from the forthcoming congressional elections made instant enforcement of these laws extremely difficult. President Johnson explained this sensitive political position in an interview with the *London Times* when he stated that the United States government was "determined and fully prepared to put down any overt act or enterprise by land or sea. That the state of the law did not allow more to be done." But Johnson also frankly admitted that his administration was "surrounded by difficulties in its internal policy, and anxious to obtain support from any quarter . . . [and] we are desirous of avoiding if possible any collision with the popular sentiment of the Irish masses."[13]

The dilemma of the leading Republicans in Washington is further illustrated in the diary entries of Secretary of the Navy Gideon Welles. The entry of 17 April noted the reluctance of both Secretary Seward and Secretary of War Edwin M. Stanton to act decisively against the illegal activities of the Fenian Brotherhood. "I observe," Welles wrote, "that these men are very chary about disturbing the Fenians and I do not care to travel out of the line of duty to relieve them. I therefore sent word that I was content to leave the subject with Cooper till to-morrow, when General Meade would doubtless be at Eastport; if not, the civil authorities were there, with whom the Navy would cooperate, or whom they could assist."[14]

However, not all members of the Johnson administration were reluctant to act against the Fenians. Secretary of the Treasury Hugh McCullough, for example, sent immediate instructions to Customs Collector Long at Eastport ordering him to detain the vessel and its cargo of arms until further orders arrived.[15]

Finally, on 19 April, General George Meade arrived with several aides and a small artillery unit. Meade, who had won military fame at the battle of Gettysburg in 1863, had instructions from Secretary of War Stanton to "cool out" the Fenians with as little publicity and force as possible.[16]

Meade found only 300 Fenians left in Eastport. To avoid any further incidents, he immediately removed the impounded arms to Fort Sullivan. Then he told several Fenian leaders that "any breach of the neutrality laws would be instantly followed by the arrest of every one of them."[17] Meade visited Calais and even St. Andrews, where he met and talked at length with his old friend General Doyle. His commanding presence and firm action quickly assured the worried citizens of the border towns that peace and order would prevail.

The Fenians were at first perplexed by this sudden reversal in their fortunes. No one had expected this stern reaction from the American government. Killian and a small group of determined followers remained in Calais for several days, hoping desperately that their luck would change. They strolled unmolested about town and even walked across the international bridge to St. Stephen. These Fenians now became something of a curiosity for New Brunswickers, and several of the more daring citizens crossed over to Calais and actually chatted with assorted members of the Brotherhood—much to the concern of Mayor Williams of Calais who feared more incidents and asked state authorities for further assistance.[18]

The next two weeks saw a number of minor disturbances in the vicinity of St. Stephen and Calais. Dennis Doyle, the Fenian centre in Calais, and a small remnant of the Fenian Army ignited a number of wood piles one night and fired some wild shots into the air. Momentary panic and confusion set in again among the people of St. Stephen, and some timid citizens once more fled with their most treasured belongings to American friends in Calais. Meanwhile two small boats loaded with Fenians began to cross the St. Croix River a short distance below St. Stephen. They were noticed, and "Old Joe" Young, a resident of the town, apparently jumped on his horse and rode through the countryside yelling: "Arm Yourselves! The Fenians are upon you!"[19] But no more Fenians came that or any other night in New Brunswick.

Time now began to run out on the remaining members of the Fenian force in Calais. Many of their "brothers" had already left for home, some even using free railroad tickets provided by the American government. Others, being less fortunate, were constantly being harassed by angry landlords who had not been paid rent or food bills. So, after raiding Indian Island for a second time and burning several warehouses—including one filled with liquor—the remnant of the Fenian host departed. The whole affair was accurately summarized by one observer in this little piece of doggerel: "General Killian and all his men, marched up to Maine, and then—marched down again."[20]

The New Brunswick-Maine frontier soon became quiet again, and the towns of St. Stephen, St. Andrews, Calais, and Eastport returned to their quiet ways of life, but many disappointed New England Fenians soon turned up at John O'Mahony's headquarters in New York City. They were angry. Not only did they want an explanation of what had gone wrong, but they also demanded full financial compensation for their lost time and wages. O'Mahony could not offer them either. Therefore many of his old supporters left him and joined the ranks of the Roberts-Sweeny wing of the Fenian Brotherhood, for it was there that some "real action" seemed to be in the making.

The Campobello fiasco had turned into a complete catastrophe for O'Mahony; it had depleted his organization's already dangerously low treasury by over $35,000,[21] and the total failure of the venture cost him the last remains of his prestige and influence in the American Fenian movement. It was a sad ending for a man whose intentions were basically altruistic and patriotic but who had allowed himself to be pushed into a course of action that he neither believed in nor could control. Henceforth the "Canadian wing" had the field to itself, and both William Roberts and Thomas Sweeny lost no time in preparing their long-planned assault upon the Province of Canada.

For the province of New Brunswick, however, the Fenian failure at Campobello proved to be a blessing in disguise. It was the Fenian threat in the spring of 1866 which, more than anything else in New Brunswick politics at this time, helped to swing the province into the pro-Confederation column.

In early March 1865, the supporters of Confederation in New Brunswick suffered a decisive defeat at the hands of the anti-Confederation forces led by A. J. Smith. On 6 March Premier Samuel Tilley resigned and handed over his duties to Smith, who had left no doubt that he would seek to keep New Brunswick out of the proposed confederation scheme. And since Lieutenant-Governor Gordon also appeared hostile to confederation at this point, the whole plan of British North American Union was jeopardized.

But both times and men change. First, the British government informed Gordon that confederation was considered desirable at Westminster. To emphasize this point, the "uncooperative" lieutenant-governor of Nova Scotia, Sir Richard MacDonnell, had been replaced by the more "responsive" Sir William Fenwick Williams. Gordon understood the message and its implication perfectly well, and henceforth became a strong supporter of Canadian confederation.

Moreover, the Fenian raid had convinced most inhabitants of New Brunswick that their best guarantee for peace and security rested with a British North American Union. The *St. Croix Courier* summarized this argument in an editorial on 19 May 1866:

> If there is one argument in favor of Union stronger than another it is the necessity that exists for a good and efficient system of mutual defense. We have sometimes regarded this as one of the weaker points in favor of Union, invasion or trouble seemed to be at so great a distance, but now when we see how soon sudden danger can threaten us, and how our enemies may concentrate within a gunshot of our very doors, the man must be blind, infatuated, or prejudiced who can fail to recognize its force.[22]

Even the most ardent anti-Confederationist in the Maritimes, Joseph Howe of Nova Scotia, admitted during the height of the Fenian crisis that "when message after message is rushing over the wires to inform us of the gathering of raiders upon our frontiers . . . when every soldier and militia man awaits the summons . . . it has been determined to launch this Confederation scheme."[23]

The constant political bickering over confederation in the New Brunswick Assembly during the spring of 1866, as well as the uproar caused by the Fenian activities, forced another provincial election. On 9 May, Lieutenant-Governor Gordon dissolved the twentieth provincial parliament of New Brunswick, and the second election campaign over confederation was under way.

Once again the election results were decisive, but this time the pendulum of power had swung back toward Samuel Tilley. The pro-Confederationists won thirty-three seats, while A.J. Smith was left with a minority party of eight. It is not surprising to find that the only seats won by the "antis" were far away from the scene of the recent Fenian troubles. The border areas voted overwhelmingly pro-Confederation.[24] The Fenian affair had been largely responsible for this development. Tilley admitted this point in the Assembly when he told Smith that the effect of the Fenian raid had been "a most decided one, for when they came and said they were prepared to assist the Antis in preventing Confederation, the feeling in favor of Union at once became more general, for the people saw that in that alone was safety."[25]

Thus defense against a common foe, the Fenian Brotherhood, had become a decisive factor in persuading the people of the Maritime provinces, particularly those of New Brunswick, to enter the Confederation scheme. A federal union of all the provinces would offer a sense of security to all that none could provide individually.

Meanwhile the O'Mahony wing of the Brotherhood had completely disintegrated. O'Mahony had tried to extricate himself from the Campobello fiasco by ousting Bernard Killian from his position in the movement and blaming him for the abortive military venture. But on 10 May, James Stephens arrived in New York and bitterly criticized O'Mahony for "sanctioning this late most deplorable divergence from the true path." Stephens concluded his harangue by accusing his American lieutenant of weak and even criminal conduct which was "less excusable in you than in any other man."[26] O'Mahony, his influence and ego completely shattered, offered his resignation as president of the Fenian Brotherhood in the United States. Stephens accepted without hesitation.

The North American press now began to announce the obituary of the Fenian organization. The *New York Times* (5 May 1866) suggested that "Fenianism [was] dead and altogether beyond resurrection. Not only does it exhibit no signs of life, but its renewed vitality would be against the established nature of things, and the fixed laws of humbug." And the *Sarnia Observer* (11 May 1866) commented: "The failure of the CampoBello [*sic*] invasion has brought the Fenian conspiracy into universal contempt, while it has produced a row among the brethren themselves, which will not soon be quieted. They are now engaged in the interesting work of abusing each other like blackguards and pick-pockets, as they are; so that the honest peace-loving people of the Provinces are likely to be allowed to live unmolested." And Governor-General Monck, in a private letter to his son Henry, wrote: "I think the Fenians are nearly 'used up.' . . . My opinion is that we shall very soon hear no more of them."[27]

The Roberts-Sweeny wing of the Fenian Brotherhood, however, had other ideas. The Fenian snake was far from being dead and the "peace-loving" people of the Province of Canada would soon feel its bite.

7

THE FENIANS MARCH

The Province of Canada had scarcely recovered from its own "March scare" when reports arrived that Fenians were heading for Campobello. This latest news of Fenian action created renewed excitement in the province, particularly after the word spread that Michael Murphy and six companions had been arrested while heading for Eastport, Maine.[1]

Yet as new information arrived from the Maritimes, saying that the Fenian raid had completely collapsed, Canadians once more relaxed. Most provincial newspapers, with the exception of the *Toronto Globe* and the *Toronto Irish Canadian*, soon devoted fewer articles and editorials to Fenianism, and whenever new rumors of threatening Fenian movements were reported, they were disregarded. The province had been exposed to so many false alarms in the past that few people were prepared to give full credence to any more "Fenian tales." Most Canadians felt certain the Brotherhood had played its last hand. The *Sarnia Observer* (24 May 1866) noted that "so far as any fear of a Fenian invasion is concerned, the whole [frontier] force might be disbanded; for we do not believe the Fenians will venture across the border." And John A. Macdonald wrote Gilbert McMicken: "I imagine that the Fenian war may be considered as over."[2]

The Canadian conviction that the Fenians had ceased to be a danger was reinforced by comments from south of the border. The *Toronto Globe* (16 April 1866) reprinted this editorial from the pages of the *Chicago Tribune:*

Amidst the atmosphere of falsehood, deception and fraud that envelopes the whole Fenian humbug, it is difficult to tell what that organization may or may not be doing. We only know that the leaders connected with it are without brains, and the followers are very generally without character. From such a motley and dangerous crew, no good is to be expected. Incapable of working together under any organization, their own 'brotherhood' is a house divided against itself, a living testimony known and read of all men, that being unable to rule themselves they are unfit to rule Ireland.

Meanwhile the London *Times* (22 May 1866) was suggesting that "the Fenian Conspiracy [was] rendered harmless for the present by the proved imbecility or roguery of some of the ringleaders . . . who are eating green turtle and drinking madeira at the expense of stupid servant girls and waiters of New York and other cities."

Even James Stephens's personal appearance in New York to make urgent pleas for unity and money at another "mass rally" in Jones' Wood received a lukewarm reception. Less than 2000 supporters paid the 50¢ admission price to listen to the Chief Organizer of the I.R.B. in his final attempts "to conciliate and to win, if possible, every true Irishman over to a common centre."[3]

The *New York Times* (20 May 1866) commented on these latest developments within the Fenian movement on its editorial pages: "The enthusiasm gotten up here on the arrival of Head Centre Stephens [on 10 May] was very feeble in its quality, and very narrow in its range. He has not healed the factious dissensions. . . . We hear of very bitter denunciations of him by the Roberts party, and it is even attempted to transfix him as a 'British-spy.'" Yet it was only the O'Mahony-Stephens wing of the Fenian Brotherhood that faded from the scene. And while Canadians were basking in a false sense of security during late April and May 1866, the "Canadian wing" of Roberts and Sweeny was ready to try its hand at "liberating Ireland" in its own unique fashion.

The Roberts-Sweeny supporters had rejoiced over O'Mahony's failure, for now the moment had come when they could implement their own program. General Sweeny's great invasion scheme of British North America could finally be put to the test. The Roberts headquarters on Broadway Avenue began to take on a martial appearance during the last few days of April. The *New York Herald* reported that "President Roberts and General Sweeny are closeted together for many hours each day. The arms and sinews of war have aggregated to immense quantities."[4] Furthermore, the large influx of former O'Mahony supporters increased the enthusiasm of the Roberts-Sweeny camp. John O'Mahony's final attempt to create a united Fenian organization was rudely rebuffed in early May by William Roberts. Finally, on 10 May, the day that Stephens had arrived in America to heal the Fenian split, Roberts decided the time had come to move against the Province of Canada.

As early as 1 May, Thomas Sweeny had ordered such faraway Fenian contingents as the New Orleans circle to move northward to Cincinnati, but now on 10 May the rest of the Fenian Army was mobilized. By 12 May, Sweeny received a telegram informing him that "thirty canal boats and five steam tugs were secured at Buffalo."[5] The Fenian arsenal for the invasion of Canada was being built up, and soon hundreds of Fenian soldiers were arriving at their designated rendezvous points all along the Canadian-American frontier. For example, Colonel John O'Neill and his force from Tennessee were ordered to move to Cincinnati on 17 May. Thus by the end of the month, several thousand Fenians were expected to be strung out along the Canadian border. On 31 May, General Sweeny finally appointed his three major area commanders for the invasion: Brigadier-General C.C. Tevis received the command of the left wing of the invasion force, which would move from Chicago and Milwaukee twenty-four hours in advance of the center wing attack, cross lakes Michigan and Huron, and then head toward its military objective, London, Ontario; meanwhile Brigadier-General W.F. Lynch was to lead the center assault from the Lake Erie and Niagara region with headquarters located in Cleveland, Ohio; finally, Brigadier-General S.P. Spear would be in charge of military operations on the Fenian right wing covering all the territory from Ogdensburg, New York, to St. Albans, Vermont.

Sweeny had purchased about 10,000 firearms and 2.5 million ball cartridges from several United States government arsenals. He still lacked any artillery, but he hoped that the necessary heavy guns could be captured by "the gallantry of my soldiers."

The Fenian forces and their military equipment were being amassed quickly, but the total still fell far short of what Thomas Sweeny had considered absolutely necessary for certain military success. In his original campaign plans he had talked of a minimum of 10,000 men, three artillery batteries, 200 rounds of ammunition for each man, and 500 rounds of fixed ammunition for each gun. Furthermore, Sweeny had warned that unless the invasion took place when the St. Lawrence River and other waterways into Canada were still covered with ice, his force would have to be doubled in strength. The cost of the entire affair was placed at about $450,000.

Reluctantly Thomas Sweeny now prepared to risk everything, even though his plans had not been followed to the letter; neither the men nor the supplies ever reached the stipulated totals. Why then did Sweeny go ahead?

The Fenian Commander-in-Chief offers an explanation in his "Official Report," written after the failure of the invasion. Apparently he had appeared before the Fenian Senate on 16 April and was urged in the strongest possible terms to take "immediate action." The Senate was unanimous in expressing its fear that unless Sweeny "took the field at once, the dissolution of the Brotherhood would be inevitable." So he agreed to commence operations against Canada, "preferring the chances of an honorable failure in the field, to the disintegration of the organization."

Canadians had become so accustomed to "Fenian preparations" that many began to ignore these latest hostile developments south of the border. Little or no concern seemed to exist anywhere over another Fenian raid on British territory. Gilbert McMicken informed his chief, the attorney-general of Canada West, that "I cannot conceive it within the bounds of a reasonable probability that Sweeney [*sic*] will attempt any demonstration upon Canada now. I can gather nothing from any quarter at present of anything being done indicative of a movement of any kind unless we take the absence of bluster and the usual quiet every where as an indication."[6] Even the most bitter enemy of Fenianism in Canada, D'Arcy McGee, suggested sarcastically to an American friend that "we have almost ceased to take an interest in those redoubtable heroes, the Fenians."[7] And Richard J. Cartwright, a prominent Canadian politician, received a letter from the United States in early April when his correspondent informed him: "I have no fears for the Fenians attempting a Raid on Canada before next winter—when I believe they will certainly make the attempt."[8]

Even though dispatches describing serious Fenian activity were sent to the Canadian government by British consuls in New York City and Buffalo, the reports were not considered serious enough to warrant any official action.[9] When Colonel George T. Denison, one of the province's most respected military men, informed Colonel Patrick MacDougall, adjutant-general of the militia, that an American friend had informed him that the Fenians were about to move against Canada, MacDougall refused to become alarmed.[10] The repeated false rumors of earlier Fenian raids had conditioned Canadians—government and military authorities as well as private citizens—to turn a deaf ear to such reports. The Province had been lulled into a false sense of security.

Then suddenly isolated news flashes were received in Canada. The Fenians were reported on the march and were apparently heading toward the Canadian border. On 29 May the *Cincinnati Commercial* stated:

> There is a movement of the Fenians now going on. Quite a number of them left this city yesterday, bound for Canada. Large shipments of arms

have been made northward within a few days. There is an appearance that an extensive raid is about to be made on Canada. Movements of men and transportation of arms have been in progress for some days with a degree of secrecy that indicates business.[11]

And on 30 May the *Buffalo Courier* carried this interesting advertisement by P. O'Day:

Peremptory sale of muskets, rifles and commissary stores by P. O'Day, at his auction and commission house, Nos. 20 and 22 Pearl Street. Friday, June 1, at 10:00 A.M., will be sold on account of whom it may concern without reserve—muskets, rifles, carbines, swords, knapsacks, habber-sacks, tents, caldrons, frockcoats, navy white blankets, U.S. grey blankets, 23 halters, bridles, 50 horse collars, wrappers and drawers, 400 overcoats. Terms cash.[12]

Patrick O'Day, of course, was the local district centre of the Fenian Brotherhood, and his store was the hub of most of the Fenian activity in the Buffalo area.

Still the Canadian press seemed scarcely alarmed. The *Toronto Globe* (30 May 1866) expressed its confidence that if any raid were to take place, "the American and Canadian Governments will be equal to the emergency." The *London Free Press* on the same day ridiculed the reports and remarked: "It would seem as if this was but another bid for the dimes." On the morning of 31 May the editor of the *Globe* wrote: "We await with calmness the development of the Sweeney [*sic*] plan, sure that it will be the last sputter of Fenianism." Even the *New York Times* (1 June 1866), being in the midst of all the Fenian activities, scoffed at the latest Fenian moves and wrote with unmistakable sarcasm:

The Fenian ghost is walking again, although dead these past few months, and supposed to have been decently buried. . . . Within two days, however, there has been a fluttering of sensation. Some self-appointed prophet has gone down into the valley of dry bones, and succeeded in giving the semblance of life to that which has practically been long since defunct. . . . We [a]wait in feverish anxiety the great news of the Conquest of Canada and the raising of "the green above the red" on the battered and subjugated citadel of Quebec.

Finally, the editor of the *London Free Press* (1 June 1866), taking note of the recent activity in the Buffalo area, could no longer restrain himself, and after calling the Fenians "thieves" and "rogues" and "a herd of refuse of the Irish-American scum," he wished the citizens of Buffalo "joy of the set of drunken wretches who are congregated in their midst." However, the editorial concluded with the hope that "this last sensation may die out without the country being put to the cost and inconvenience of a call of the volunteers."

But during the night of 31 May 1866 the Fenians struck. A force of almost 1000 men, led by Colonel John O'Neill, crossed the Niagara River near Black Rock and invaded Canadian soil. The unexpected had happened and Canadians hastily called out their forces and prepared to defend their country.

8

RIDGEWAY

During the final days of preparation before the invasion of Canada, the Fenians had finally found "a fighting general." John O'Neill was born in Drumgallon, Ireland, on 8 March 1834. Fourteen years later he immigrated to the United States and settled in Elizabeth, New Jersey. After unsuccessful ventures in the publishing and bookselling business, he enlisted in the U.S. Army in 1857 and saw active duty in the Indian wars in the west. During the Civil War he served with great distinction and eventually reached the rank of colonel. Having been passed over for an expected promotion, O'Neill resigned his commission and soon thereafter left military service completely. After the war he worked as a land claims agent in Tennessee, and it was in Nashville that he became interested in the "Canadian plan" of the Roberts-Sweeny wing of the Fenian Brotherhood. O'Neill was a "fine looking man," according to the British spy Henri le Caron,[1] who knew him well. He was nearly six feet tall and "he combined an undoubted military bearing with a rich sonorous voice, which lent to his presence a certain charm."

O'Neill arrived in Cleveland on the night of 28 May. He had joined forces at Louisville, Kentucky, with another Fenian officer, Colonel Owen Starr, but on their arrival they found neither orders nor anyone who appeared to be in command. It was not until 29 May that Secretary of War Thomas Sweeny sent orders from the Fenian headquarters asking General W.F. Lynch, who commanded the area, to cross Lake Erie from Cleveland. Lynch, however, had apparently disappeared, so the Fenian forces gathered in Cleveland were ordered to move on to Buffalo without him; there Captain Hynes, the Fenian assistant adjutant-general, would have further instructions.[2]

Hynes was now confronted by a serious dilemma. General Lynch was still missing and Sweeny's orders had to be carried out promptly. Reluctantly Hynes made his decision and gave the command of the Fenian expedition in the Niagara peninsula to John O'Neill, the senior ranking officer in the area.

Captain Hynes gave Colonel O'Neill his written orders at 11 A.M. on Thursday, 31 May. The instructions gave O'Neill command over a force of about 800 men: his own Thirteenth Tennessee Regiment from Nashville, the Seventeenth Regiment from Kentucky under Colonel Owen Starr, the Eighteenth Ohio Regiment under Colonel John Grace, the Seventh Regiment from New York under Colonel John Hoey, and two companies of Indiana Fenians under Captain Hagerty. Most of the Fenian officers wore proper military uniforms, although many of these were unmistakably Union Army issue. Most of the rank and file, however, wore only green shirts and black belts over their civilian dress. Each Fenian regiment carried its own green battle flag embroidered with either a gold harp or a sunburst.

Shortly after midnight, Colonel Starr and a small group of Fenians marched down the American side of the Niagara River to Black Rock where they boarded a canal boat towed by a tug. Shortly thereafter the small raiding party landed at Freeburg's Wharf, less than two miles below the village of Fort Erie. At 3:30 A.M., 1 June, the main body of the Fenian expedition left American soil in four additional canal boats and was towed to the Canadian shore. Within another half hour Fenian flags flew on Canadian soil. The Province of Canada had at last been invaded.

Late evening of the last day of May now brought considerable excitement to the Province of Canada, particularly the citizens of Toronto. The latest Fenian movements were being taken seriously, and great concern was shown by both the government and the public. "Since early morning," wrote the *Toronto Daily Telegraph* on 31 May, "our office has been crowded with citizens eager to hear the latest news."

Meanwhile the Canadian government acted very quickly. On 1 June, Governor-General Monck proclaimed:

> The soil of Canada has been invaded, not in the practice of legitimate warfare, but by a lawless and piratical band, in defiance of all moral right, and in utter disregard of all the obligations which civilization imposes upon mankind. Upon the people of Canada the state of things imposes

the duty of defending their altars, their homes, and their property, from desecration, pillage and spoliation. [*Toronto Globe,* 2 June 1866]

The order was given to call out 14,000 volunteers to meet the emergency, and within 48 hours 20,000 men had come forward to serve their country.[3] They came from every walk of life: lawyers, doctors, clerks, farmers, and even students. For example, the Eighth and Ninth companies of the Queen's Own Rifles Regiment were made up completely of students from Toronto's University and Trinity colleges. Some volunteers eventually came from as far away as Chicago, Illinois.[4]

Meanwhile, in Toronto, General Napier's headquarters, responsible for the defense of Canada West, mustered its forces, for news of the Fenian border crossing had come "like a bolt from the blue."[5] Buglers were sent out into the streets of the city sounding the assembly, and N.C.O.'s personally knocked on the doors of their men and roused them from their sleep. All available troops were assembled in the early morning hours of Friday, 1 June.[6]

Toronto's Union Station and its harbor became the hubs of the city's activity even before the sun rose. A great throng of excited citizens had gathered to encourage the troops as they left by train or boat for the Niagara frontier.

The next few days produced "scenes of unparalleled excitement"[7] in the capital of Canada West. Men and women crowded into the streets at all hours of the day, seeking the latest scrap of information about events at the front. The local newspapers published numerous "extras," only to have them snatched up within minutes. "Never in the history of Toronto," observed the *Toronto Leader* on 2 June, "were there such manifestations of public feeling, such demonstrations of anxiety and such a complete harmony of sentiment." Volunteer relief committees were hurriedly organized, gathering food, money, and clothes for the brave men fighting at the front and the families they were forced to leave behind.

The Canadian volunteers, however, bubbled with enthusiasm as they approached the Niagara frontier. Not even such "culinary delicacies" as bread and red herring for breakfast[8] could deter their optimism, and their voices shouted over and over again this patriotic song:

Tramp, tramp, tramp, our boys are marching,
Cheer up, let the Fenians come!
For beneath the Union Jack, we'll drive the Fenians back
And we'll fight for our beloved Canadian home.[9]

Meanwhile, events had moved quickly at Fort Erie. This small village of 600 people was the immediate target of the Fenian advance force under Colonel

Starr, for the Fenians hoped to seize the Erie and Ontario Railway yard located in the village. The citizens of Fort Erie, however, reacted quickly as the Fenians were spotted marching toward the village. Farmers hurriedly dispersed their livestock, particularly their horses, and alert railway officials hastily assembled all their rolling stock into one long train and had four locomotives pull it to safety in the interior of the province. Some villagers fled with their most treasured personal belongings, often including cumbersome bedding and heavy furniture.[10]

Colonel Starr was thus cheated of what he thought would be an easy prize. The disappearance of the horses in particular became a serious matter to the Fenians. They had no animals of their own, having expected to be able to obtain enough horses from Canadian farmers to mount a small cavalry unit. The Fenian commander finally managed to find some horses, and adequate provisions for his men were requisitioned from the local reeve and his village council.[11] Colonel Starr then ordered his men to cut the telegraph wires and burn Sauerwine's Bridge before returning to the Fenian main camp located at Newbigging's farm, on the left bank of Frenchman's Creek. It was here that the Fenian invaders now issued this proclamation signed by T.W. Sweeny:

TO THE PEOPLE OF BRITISH AMERICA.
We come among you as the foes of British rule in Ireland. We have taken up the sword to strike down the oppressors' rod, to deliver Ireland from the tyrant, the despoiler, the robber. . . . We have no issue with the people of these Provinces, and wish to have none but the most friendly relations. Our weapons are for the oppressors of Ireland. Our bows shall be directed only against the power of England. . . . We do not propose to divest you of a solitary right you now enjoy. . . . We are here neither as murderers, nor robbers, for plunder and spoliation. We are here as the Irish army of liberation. . . . To Irishmen throughout these Provinces we appeal in the name of seven centuries of British iniquity and Irish misery and suffering . . . to stretch forth the hand of brotherhood in the holy cause of fatherland, and smite the tyrant where we can. . . . [12]

But aside from foraging for more provisions and burning another bridge, the Fenians remained inactive until late Friday afternoon, 1 June, after they had received additional arms and supplies just before noon. But the belated appearance of an American gunboat, the S.S. *Michigan*, prevented any further reinforcements of men or supplies from the American side. Then O'Neill was told that two columns of Canadian defenders were moving in his general direction. His reaction was quick. To prevent a union of the Canadian forces, O'Neill decided to meet them separately.[13] He left the camp on Newbigging's farm and moved about three miles farther down River Road until he reached Black Creek. Here he anxiously awaited the first Canadian column.

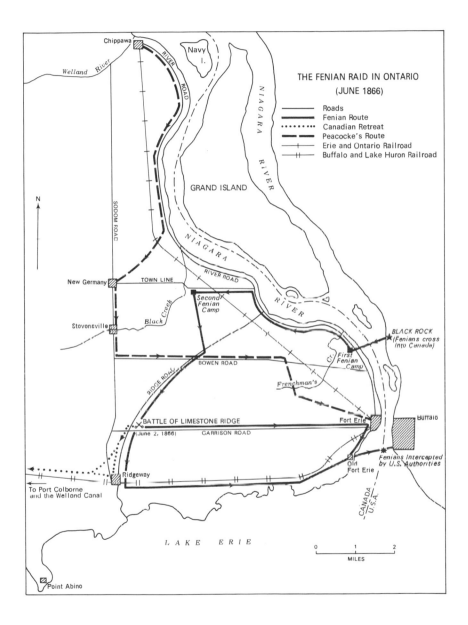

THE FENIAN RAID IN ONTARIO
(JUNE 1866)

Roads
Fenian Route
Canadian Retreat
Peacocke's Route
Erie and Ontario Railroad
Buffalo and Lake Huron Railroad

Chippawa

Welland River

Navy I.

RIVER ROAD

NIAGARA RIVER

GRAND ISLAND

N

SODOM ROAD

NIAGARA

RIVER ROAD

New Germany

TOWN LINE

Black Creek

Second Fenian Camp

Stevensville

RIVER

BLACK ROCK
(Fenians cross into Canada)

Cr.

First Fenian Camp

RIDGE ROAD

BOWEN ROAD

Frenchman's

BATTLE OF LIMESTONE RIDGE

Fort Erie

Buffalo

(June 2, 1866)

GARRISON ROAD

Ridgeway

Old Fort Erie

Fenians Intercepted by U.S. Authorities

To Port Colborne and the Welland Canal

CANADA
U.S.A.

LAKE ERIE

0   1   2
MILES

Point Abino

The Canadian defenders meanwhile had responded quickly to the Fenian invasion of the province. Major-General George Napier had received official word of the Fenian attack from Consul Hemans of Buffalo at 6 A.M, 1 June. He immediately ordered all available regular and militia units to mobilize and rush to the Niagara frontier.

Lieutenant-Colonel George T. Peacocke was sent to St. Catharines with three companies each of the Sixteenth and Forty-Seventh infantry regiments, as well as a battery of the Royal Artillery. Having learned that the Fenians were advancing along River Road in the general direction of Chippawa, Peacocke hurriedly set his own force in motion. He tried to reach the village before the enemy to prevent the main locks of the Welland Canal from being captured. Fortunately, his column managed to reach Chippawa by 9 P.M, and since no Fenians appeared, he decided to rest his men until the next morning.

Meanwhile a force of about 900 Canadians had assembled in Port Colborne under the command of Lieutenant-Colonel Alfred Booker [14] and Lieutenant-Colonel J. Stoughton Dennis. The two officers decided to catch the invaders from behind, thereby cutting off all possibilities of a successful retreat.

First, they sent eighty-seven men of the Welland Canal Battery and the Dunnville Naval Brigade on the steam tug *W.T. Robb* to Fort Erie. This force was to patrol the Niagara River off Fort Erie while the main force used the Buffalo and Lake Huron Railway (part of the Grand Trunk system) to head to Fort Erie by land. Booker remained under the impression that O'Neill's force was still encamped at Newbigging's farm.

While these battle plans were being drawn up, Captain Charles Akers of the Royal Engineers arrived in Port Colborne with an urgent message from Colonel Peacocke at Chippawa. Peacocke, the senior officer in the area, had his own ideas on how to do battle with the Fenians. His orders for Booker asked the latter "to move his whole force by rail not later than 5:30 A.M, and march to join him at Stevensville at 10 A.M. next day."[15] Peacocke was convinced that their combined forces could easily defeat the Fenian Army.[16]

But Peacocke's orders were not followed by Lieutenant-Colonel Booker, who instead persisted with his own improvisations, which he telegraphed to Colonel Peacocke at 3 A.M., 2 June. He then sent off the *W.T. Robb* under Colonel Dennis. Meanwhile Peacocke's own messenger, Captain Akers, joined this group, for he was most anxious to see some military action.

At 3:45 A.M. a telegram arrived from Colonel Peacocke, ordering Booker to adhere to the original plan. Booker was annoyed but had to obey his superior, and the train, already loaded with men and supplies for Fort Erie, was delayed. But Booker was so anxious that he left earlier than stipulated, and at 5 A.M. the train headed east to Ridgeway where the entire force was to detrain and march north to Stevensville.

It was shortly after 6 A.M. when Booker's force arrived in the village of Ridgeway, a small, quiet village consisting of a flour mill, a few stores, about twenty houses, and two taverns. Booker decided to inspect his "army." He had about 840 men carrying a limited supply of ammunition, inadequate clothing, no blankets or water bottles, and even less food. Although there were three doctors in the force, there was no one capable of assisting them in preparing and staffing a field hospital. And the only mounted soldier in the outfit was Colonel Booker himself.[17]

As he made his final preparations, Booker was informed by several local farmers that the Fenian force was fast approaching. But he did not believe them, for he still thought that the enemy was encamped at Newbigging's farm. So in the early morning hours of Saturday, 2 June, his column began to march along the dusty Ridge Road toward the village of Stevensville where he was to meet with Peacocke's troops at 10 A.M.

The Fenians, however, had been marching since the earliest sunlight, and they were now within striking distance of the Canadian volunteers. When O'Neill heard the sounds of train whistles and bugle calls, he knew the confrontation was finally at hand. The following account of "The Battle of Ridgeway" was left years later by one of the Canadian participants:

> We marched along the Ridge road for about two miles, the Queens Own leading. No. 5 Company formed the advance guard. This company had just been supplied with Spencer repeating rifles. The rest of the force were armed with muzzle-loading Enfields. Just as we reached the summit of a gentle rise, we saw the advance party standing with their shakos on the end of their rifles—a signal which meant "the enemy is in sight, in force."
>
> From the slight elevation where we were standing we could see the road stretching before us for nearly a mile. Near us were woods, but in front, to the right and left of the road, were open fields, bordered on both sides and at some distance in front by woods. It was a beautiful day—the trees were clothed with the tender, delicate foliage of early summer, and the fields were green with young crops. From where we stood we could see nothing of the enemy, but we saw the advance guard extend from its centre and push on in skirmishing order. Nos. 1 and 2 Company were ordered to move up and extend on their left and right flanks respectively, and Nos. 3, 4 and 6 advanced in support. In a few minutes puffs of smoke from the skirmishes and from the woods and fences in front of them told that the action had begun.
>
> Before long we heard the whistle of bullets in the air and No. 7 Company was extended to the left in skirmishing order, with No. 8 (Trinity College Company) in support. This brought the University Company to the front of the column, but we did not long remain there. We were marched off to the right, extended, and told to lie down on a

low, pebbly ridge, behind which grew some fine maple trees. Here we lay for a while, the bullets singing over our heads, and cutting off branches from the maple trees. In a few minutes Major Gillmor came up and ordered us to clear the woods on the right from which these bullets seemed to be coming. We jumped up and advanced in skirmishing order, supported by No. 10 Company, the Highlanders, from whom, however, we soon became separated in the thick woods, through which our course at first lay. After clearing the woods we came out into an open field. Behind the fence on the other side of the field we saw some men kneeling, and puffs of smoke showed them to be in action. It was not at first clear whether they were friends or foes. Some of our men were about to fire on them, but Ensign Whitney, who was in command, called out, "Don't fire, they may be our own men. Lie down and wait till I find out." We lay down as directed, and watched him as he quietly walked forward for a hundred yards or so. Then he stopped, took a leisurely observation through his field glass, and turning round to us, called out, cheerfully, "All right, boys! They are the enemy. Fire away." We ran up to him. Till we reached him he stood watching the enemy, apparently absolutely indifferent to the bullets that were whistling round him. We then crossed a road, where the Fenians had made a barricade of fence rails, and entered a field of young wheat, studded at intervals with black stumps. Here we could see no Fenians, but from behind fences, and from the woods in front of us, they kept up a hot fire. Our advance across this field was the most exciting part of the fight, and was conducted in this fashion: having selected a desirable stump at a convenient distance in front, we made a dash for it at full speed, and the moment we reached it we fell flat on our stomachs behind it. This was the signal for a shower of bullets, some of which whistled over our heads, some struck the stump, and some threw up the dust in the field beside us. As soon as our opponents had emptied their rifles, we fired at the puffs of smoke, reloaded, selected another stump, and so on, *da capo*. In this way we crossed the wheat field and entered another wood, through which we advanced under the cover of the trees. Here we were a good deal annoyed by the fire of some of our own friends, who, not knowing our whereabouts, were firing into the wood from behind us. Sergeant Bryce—now the Rev. Professor Bryce, of Winnipeg—had taken post behind a fine, thick maple tree. Before long it became doubtful which side of the tree was the safest, and Bryce settled it by saying, "I'd rather be hit before than behind," and deliberately placed himself in front of the tree. Beyond this wood was a recently-cleared field, and beyond that another wood in which we could plainly see the Fenians. We had begun to climb the fence into this cleared field, and indeed some of us were already there, when we heard the bugle sounding the retire. Whitney gave the word to us, and called back those who had crossed the fence. When we turned our backs on the Fenians, we had not the faintest suspicion of defeat. We had, up to the moment when we got the order to retire, steadily driven the Fenians before us, but we could see them in greatly superior numbers—there were only twenty-eight of us. We knew we had lost touch with our supports, and we supposed we were merely falling back to restore communications with them. Whitney had already sent back a sergeant to see what had become of the rest of the command to ask for orders, but he had not returned, and we thought the bugle was a summons to us to rejoin our comrades, of whose success no doubts had entered our minds. All the same we soon found out the astonishing difference on the mental, moral and physical condition of the soldier under fire which is produced by the simple rotation of his body through an angle of 180°. The first sensation was of intense disgust at having to turn our backs on the enemy; the second the acute realization that we had had no breakfast that morning, and no supper nor sleep the night before, and that we were nearly dead beat. Up till that moment the thought of fatigue had never occurred to us, and we had felt as fresh as paint. Now it seemed as if it was impossible to drag one leg after the other. But then we felt that it would not do to be left behind, for there were the Fenians. Upon them our change of position had a precisely opposite effect and they followed us cheerfully with much shooting. When we reached the crossroad a number of us stopped, and kneeling behind the fence opened a brisk fire upon the enemy, and for a time checked their advance. But there were too many of them and their fire was too fatal. Mackenzie had fallen before the retreat began, shot through the heart, and now others were dropping fast. . . . About this time Tempest and Newburn were killed, and Vandersmissen, Paul, Kingsford and Patterson were wounded. In the crossroad Tempest was next to me. Just after firing a shot he rose to his feet. He was a very tall fellow, and presented a conspicuous mark above the fence. Next moment I heard the sound of a dull, heavy blow, and saw him fall forward on his face. I ran to his side and found a small round hole in his forehead. He had been shot through the head, and the bullet, after penetrating the brain, had broken the bone at the back of the skull. Of course he died instantly. As soon as I saw that nothing more could be done for him, I looked about me and found that I was alone on the road. A little farther to the right was a brick house and orchard, and as this promised better cover than the open field, I made for it. It stood at the crossing of this road with the Ridge road, along which we had been marching before the fight, and when I reached it I saw a body of troops in the orchard, which, from their dark clothes, I took to be the Queen's Own. I hastened to join them, but they turned out to be a column of Fenians, who saluted me with a volley. An attempt to fire my rifle proved that it was empty, and while in the act of reloading I was surrounded and made prisoner. I was placed in the brick house, under charge of a guard. As soon as I was there, the fatigue, which had been forgotten during the stand in the road, returned with redoubled force, and I lay down on the mattress completely exhausted.[18]

The Battle at Limestone Ridge, as this skirmish was also known, continued throughout the morning of Saturday, 2 June. Ironically enough, about 9:30 A.M., just as his men began to exchange fire with the Fenian outposts, Colonel Booker received two further telegrams from Colonel Peacocke informing him that Peacocke's force had left Chippawa two hours late, and asking Booker to delay his own departure. Furthermore, Peacocke warned his fellow-officer to "be cautious in feeling his way, for fear obstacles should prevent a junction."[19] The messages had followed Booker's trail from Port Colborne right to the battlefield. But Booker, sensing imminent victory over the Fenians, did not break off the action; instead he sent a messenger to Peacocke asking for speedy assistance.

The Canadian volunteer force continued to fight bravely against the Fenians, soon forcing the enemy to retreat to a new line of defense.[20] But suddenly the vanguard of the Canadian militiamen saw several Fenians on horseback galloping around a bend in Ridge Road. The Canadians did not know that the Fenians had failed to secure enough horses to form a large cavalry unit, and the sight of a few isolated horsemen created a sense of panic among them. The cries of "Cavalry! Look out for Cavalry!" raced through the ranks of the volunteers, and several men swiftly retreated.

Colonel Booker immediately gave verbal instructions to Major Charles Gillmor, commander of the Queen's Own Rifles, to "look out for cavalry" and prepare his men accordingly. Gillmor ordered his bugler to sound the "prepare for cavalry," and the volunteers now rushed from their locations and tried to "Form Square" in the middle of the road in order to repel the expected "Fenian cavalry." But no cavalry materialized; instead a deadly hail of bullets began to descend upon the Canadians as they huddled in clusters on the road and nearby fields.

Booker, inexperienced in battle as he was, nevertheless quickly realized his mistake and ordered the bugler to sound the signal to "retire." Unfortunately the troops on the far side of the action mistook the signal as a sign for a general retreat, and within seconds the ranks broke and total confusion set in. Booker was left with no alternative but to sound a full retreat.

The rout of Booker's men was compared by one eyewitness to another "Battle of Bull Run."[21] The militiamen retreated all the way to Ridgeway, pursued by a group of jubilant Fenians led by Colonel Starr. By three that afternoon, most of Booker's remaining force re-entered Port Colborne, which it had left only ten hours earlier.

John O'Neill was pleased with his success, but, not wishing to be confronted with the large force of "regulars" that was now advancing toward him, he decided to retreat to the scene of his initial conquest at Fort Erie.

Colonel Booker later received heavy criticism for his poor performance at Limestone Ridge. His fateful order to "Form Square" had clearly turned the tide,[22] and soon the provincial press began to crucify him. Eventually an official inquiry was held in Hamilton at Booker's own request, and he was found completely innocent. The military tribunal was in unanimous agreement in its report that "there is not the slightest foundation for the unfavorable imputations cast upon him in the public prints." The court of inquiry also noted his personal courage and conduct and his immediate attempts to correct his error of judgment. Furthermore, it explained that many of the volunteers were inexperienced youths under twenty years of age who were too poorly drilled for such harsh battle action, most of them having been only "for a very short time accustomed to bear arms" and some having "not even been exercised with blank cartridge."[23]

While Booker's command suffered its unexpected setback at Ridgeway, Colonel Dennis arrived, as planned, in front of Fort Erie. Dennis had the Welland Canal Field Battery under Captain Richard King and the Dunnville Naval Brigade under Captain Lachlan McCallum in his command, but the total force was only eighty-seven men. Nevertheless, Dennis decided to stretch his orders a little, and instead of merely patrolling the waters in front of Fort Erie until Colonel Booker arrived, he decided during the early morning hours of 2 June to land his small force at the village's ferry landing.

Having disembarked his force, Dennis proceeded to arrest every stranger who could not account for his presence in Fort Erie. About two hours later he boarded his steam tug again and headed downstream to Freeburg's wharf. Here he landed but found only an abandoned Fenian camp and several Fenian stragglers whom he easily arrested. It was from these prisoners that Dennis heard of the Fenian advance toward Ridgeway. He now decided to return immediately to the ferry landing at Fort Erie.

That afternoon, Colonel Dennis and his men were warned by a retired officer, Captain Lewis Palmer, who had ridden at great speed from his home two miles west of Fort Erie, that a large body of Fenians, numbering between 600 and 800 men, was heading toward the village. But Colonel Dennis found this remarkable turn of events difficult to believe. So, instead of withdrawing his small detachment of men on board the *W.T. Robb*, he chose to confront the reportedly larger Fenian force and ordered his troops to "dig in" along the river road near the ferry docks.

The Fenians came within the hour and descended in overwhelming numbers on the small force of Canadian defenders, whose better guns and ample ammunition were now of little value. The Fenian troops charged with fixed bayonets and Dennis had to order a hasty retreat. It quickly became "sauve qui peut." The *W.T. Robb*, having taken on as many men as possible, hurriedly cast off from shore and drifted with the river current. Some of the men left behind ran down River Road in frantic pursuit of the steam tug and finally managed to scamper aboard.

Colonel Dennis escaped the initial Fenian rush and found a hiding place. After he shaved his moustache and disguised himself as well as possible, he succeeded in slipping by the enemy and at three Sunday morning reached Colonel Peacocke's camp, a mere three miles north of Fort Erie. Meanwhile the men on the *W.T. Robb* decided to return to Port Colborne "on account of being encumbered with so many prisoners on board . . . and so very few men left to guard them."[24]

Captain King and a few volunteers from the Welland Canal Field Battery resisted the Fenians for some time. But when a bullet shattered King's ankle, he fired the last bullets in his revolver and rolled from behind the woodpile that had protected him into the cold waters of the Niagara River, where he grasped the wooden support of a wharf until he was rescued. Unfortunately his wounded leg had to be amputated at the knee in a Buffalo hospital. Some time later, the officers and men of the Welland Canal Field Battery and the Dunnville Naval Brigade received special silver medals from the grateful people of Welland County. Captain King was presented with a beautiful ceremonial sword from the citizens of Fort Erie.

It was now Saturday evening, 2 June, and the Fenian raiders had been on Canadian soil for nearly forty-eight hours. They had fought one major and one minor engagement against courageous but inexperienced Canadian volunteer units, but now they were tired and hungry as they encamped in the ruins of the old Fort Erie. Here John O'Neill waited for the promised reinforcements from Buffalo, while sending messages to Captain Hynes informing him that by the next morning 5000 Canadians would have him surrounded. But he also explained somewhat boastfully that he was "perfectly willing to make the old fort a slaughter-pen" on the next day if orders called for it.[25]

Colonel Peacocke's troops finally left Chippawa much later than he had anticipated. A dismally poor commissariat system was largely to blame for this delay, and an inaccurate field map further impeded the column's progress. When Booker's messenger, Detective Armstrong, reached Peacocke at 10:30 A.M., his troops were still four miles from the scene of the battle. They could hear the sounds of distant gunfire but were helpless to intervene. Not being able to alter the situation, Peacocke decided to encamp his men for the night, fully expecting to meet the Fenians in the decisive battle for Canada on the next morning. The Fenian raiders, however, now in an untenable position, were unwilling to continue the struggle. In the early hours of Sunday, 3 June, they hastily abandoned their camp, including over 100 of their comrades, and embarked on two large canal boats pulled by two tugs which had crossed the Niagara River at a prearranged signal to bring the Fenian force back to the American border.

But when the entourage reached midstream, an armed American tug, the *Harrison*, steamed up and overtook the returning raiders and forced them to surrender to the American authorities. Everyone was placed under arrest, and the U.S.S. *Michigan* dropped anchor beside the floating prisons filled with Fenians and anchored in midstream, thereby effectively preventing any massive escapes. In all, about 700 Fenians were taken into custody by the authorities.[26] The American government had finally decided to intervene, with some reluctance, in the affairs of the Brotherhood. Attorney-General for the Northern District William Dart had already ordered American officials along the Canadian-American frontier to limit harbor activity to certain hours of the day and to inspect all cargos for hidden arms. The *Michigan* and the *Harrison* were now enforcing this order when the Fenians sought to return to the safety of American shores early Sunday morning, 3 June.

Furthermore, Lieutenant-General Ulysses S. Grant, who had passed through Buffalo on 2 June, instructed General George Meade, commander of the Northern military district, to inform the state authorities along the frontier "to call out the militia on the Frontier, to prevent hostile expeditions leaving the United States, and to save private property from destruction by mobs."[27]

General Meade, already familiar with the Fenians from the Campobello affair, ordered Brevet Major-General Barry to take command of the troubled Niagara frontier and directed him

> to use the force at your command to preserve the neutrality by preventing the crossing of armed bodies, by cutting off reinforcements or supplies, by seizing all arms, munitions, etc., which you have reason to believe are destined to be used unlawfully—in fine, taking all measures precautionary and otherwise to prevent violation of law.[28]

Finally, President Andrew Johnson belatedly issued a "Neutrality Proclamation," which was made public on 6 June—one full week *after* the Fenians had openly violated America's neutrality laws. The proclamation referred to the latest Fenian machinations as "proceedings which constitute a high misdemeanour, forbidden by the laws of the United States," and it warned all American citizens "against taking part in or in anywise aiding, countenancing or abetting such unlawful proceedings."[29] In conclusion it called for the arrest of all lawbreakers and empowered General Meade to use all the land and naval forces necessary to carry out the letter of the law.

The Neutrality Proclamation was definitely the most serious blow to the fortunes of the Brotherhood. "The appearance of the President's Proclamation yesterday morning threw much of a damper upon the spirits of the Fenians congregated in our city," wrote the *Buffalo Express* on 8 June, and the

New York Times on 7 June had observed: "The Fenian war now assumes a new form. It is an insurrection against the power, authority, and majesty of the Government of the United States." No longer could the Fenians hope for an Anglo-American conflict, for the United States government had at last openly denounced the Brotherhood's activities as illegal and undesirable.

This late but decisive action by the American government deeply incensed the Fenian leaders, for the full power and authority of the federal government were now brought to bear against their movement.[30] All along the frontier vast quantities of Fenian arms and ammunition were seized by federal marshals and the military personnel of General Meade. During an interview with a Fenian "general" at Malone, New York, Meade was told with much bitterness and resentment: "We have been lured on by the Cabinet, and used for the purpose of Mr. Seward. They encouraged us on to this thing. We bought our rifles from your arsenals, and were given to understand that you would not interfere."[31] Another Fenian officer, M.W. Burns, echoed these sentiments in his farewell address to his followers in Buffalo: "It was the United States and not England that impeded our onward march to freedom."[32] And Thomas Sweeny was later quoted as saying that only the power of the United States government had prevented success, for had it not been for the interference of federal officials, "no power which England could bring to bear could impede the triumphant advance of our brave boys."[33]

Thus although all Fenian prisoners were soon released by an executive order from Washington,[34] the Canadian invasion had been a complete disaster. Few newspapers on either side of the border lamented the fact. The Providence Daily Journal (5 June 1866) remarked that "the invasion of Canada ended as sensible men generally supposed it would end,"[35] and the St. Paul Pioneer on the same day observed that "However much we may delight to see the English ox gored . . . justice demands that the United States authorities shall prevent further movements in our borders to attack a nation with whom we are at peace."[36] The New York Times (June 1866) expressed the hope that "every ruffian that crossed the frontier might be straightway caught and hung." Even the pro-Fenian organ of Toronto's Irish population, the Irish Canadian (6 June 1866), was forced to admit the absurdity of recent events and concluded that "the possession of Canada by the Fenian followers of General Sweeney [sic] and President Roberts, could not advance an iota the cause of Ireland's freedom from misrule."

But in spite of these efforts by the American authorities to curb the illegal activities of the Fenian Brotherhood, there can be little doubt that their efforts were at times dilatory. The Republican party, now in power, was fully aware of the voting power of the American Irish, and since the movements of the Fenians were watched with sympathy by most Irish-Americans, any excessively stringent government action might lead to serious repercussions at the polls; the Congressional elections of 1866 were not far away.

The Fenian invasion of the Niagara Peninsula had produced a great deal of drama and excitement for Canadians. The generation which experienced the Fenian raid would always remember it, for a heavy price had been paid by the Canadian defenders.[37] Seven men had been killed in action at Ridgeway and two others soon died of their wounds. Three young college students were among the dead, and a dozen others had been severely wounded. The fact that the Fenian raiders had sustained similar losses did little to alleviate the sorrow and anger felt by Canadians everywhere.[38]

On 5 June, thousands of citizens flocked to the funeral of five members of the Queen's Own Rifles who were buried in Toronto. Business was suspended and church bells were rung throughout the city. The following day, the *Globe* delivered its eulogy:

> We have buried our dead, but the lesson which they have taught us in their fall, will live long after all who were present at the ceremonies of yesterday have followed them to the tomb. It is a lesson of devotion to country, which, when deeply learned by people, produces glorious results. Our brave fellows died to save our country from being overrun by a horde of robbers; but beyond that to preserve to us institutions and laws, attachments and sympathies, hopes and aspirations, all in fact that is dear apart from family ties, to an intelligent population. [*Toronto Globe*, 6 June 1866]

On 11 June the *Daily Telegraph* commented: "Around the graves of those who gave up for us their young lives we may stand and know that we have become more united as a people; and as our hearts beat in unison over a common loss, we shall feel that the covenant of our nationality has been sealed with blood."

It was, indeed, most unfortuitous for the first group of Fenian prisoners to arrive in Toronto on the same day as the funeral for several of the fallen "heroes of Ridgeway." The *Leader* (5 June 1866) had already demanded the extradition of the Fenian leaders, and wanted them tried before Canadian courts and summarily hanged, preferably at Fort Erie, "as a warning and an example" to those who might still entertain further plans of invasion. Fortunately for the captured Fenians, the Canadian authorities were well aware of the public temper with its present demand for blood. They decided to postpone the public trials until a later date, when the need for revenge would be replaced by a sense of fairness and objectivity.[39]

In spite of the violence, the Niagara campaign did have its lighter moments. Private R.W. Hines of the Queen's Own Rifles reported that he had been partially responsible for the shooting of at least one Fenian officer.

Apparently—so the story went—the officer took the captured private's rifle and smashed it against a nearby rock while shouting it would never shoot another Fenian. But the gun, which was still loaded, went off and killed him on the spot.[40] And during the night of 4 June, Private Billy Cordingsly was apparently so nervous while performing sentry duty that he mistook a wandering cow for an enemy scout and shot the poor animal, thereby throwing the entire camp into great and prolonged excitement.[41]

There also is the story of young Patrick O'Reilly, a Fenian from Buffalo, who was wounded in battle and sought aid at a nearby farmhouse. He found not only aid but comfort as well, for the young daughter of the farmer cleaned and bandaged his wounds and then proceeded to hide him in the nearby barn for one whole week until he was ready to make his escape. A short time later O'Reilly returned, disguised as a peddlar, and eloped with his young samaritan. The couple was married in Buffalo.[42]

Another sidelight of the Fenian raids is the tale told by a resident of Chippawa, who for years entertained his listeners with the story of the Canadian militia unit that passed by John Kirkpatrick's general store in Chippawa on its way to the front. The commanding officer apparently was an old friend of "Kirk" and therefore stopped his column, dismounted, and entered the store. Soon the two friends were seen standing beside an open keg of whiskey and drinking toasts to victory, the Queen, the brave lads at the front, to each other, "one for the road," and then some. The eyewitness swore that neither man did much else on this particular day, and thus at least one small force of volunteers failed to reach the front.[43]

There is also the open letter to the editor of the *Toronto Daily Telegraph* from a slightly annoyed volunteer who inquired on 25 June about the whereabouts of all that beer, brandy, and tobacco that various Relief Committees were supposed to have collected. Perhaps the young man should have bought the "Fenian telescope" that one enterprising Toronto optician on King Street advertised, claiming that the instrument was guaranteed "to see a Fenian five miles off."[44] Perhaps the militia man would have seen his missing brandy.

Finally, free enterprise decided to capitalize on the recent events, and as early as 12 June, the Grand Trunk Railway advertised that normal service would resume to the Niagara frontier. One immediate result was that a steady stream of sightseers appeared in the area of Fort Erie and Ridgeway, eagerly surveying the scenes of the recent conflict. This influx of visitors, and the presence of the various militia units, apparently also produced a sudden boom in liquor outlets and alcohol consumption in the neighborhood.[45]

The Fenian raid in Canada West ended as abruptly as it had begun. The

Fenians had come quietly, by night, and left in the same manner. Yet their presence had been felt throughout most of the province, even though the only actual fighting took place in the Niagara Peninsula. There were some horses and equipment stolen, some railroad property and telegraph lines destroyed, but there were few incidents of looting and violence involving the civilian population.[46] The Battle of Ridgeway was the most violent military action of the Fenian raids. It not only made but also destroyed some military reputations in the ranks of both protagonists.

John O'Neill emerged as the only impressive fighting Fenian officer. His success gave him enough prestige to propel him into the foreground of the Fenian movement in the United States; it culminated in his winning the Fenian presidency in 1868. The hopes of the Brotherhood would soon rest on his shoulders.

The Canadian Militia emerged with a fair reputation. The men and boys of the various volunteer units had fought courageously, and it was not their fault that an ill-timed order triggered the defeat at Ridgeway. The people of the province certainly made known their feelings about their militia units. They returned home from frontier duty amid cheering crowds and official receptions. The volunteer force had become "the symbol of a new national pride."[47] On the other hand, a number of high-ranking Canadian military men found the luster of their past reputations severely diminished. Officers like Booker, Peacocke, and even Napier had hardly exhibited the strength, firmness, and wisdom that people expected during a time of crisis.

The invasion of Canadian territory, however, did not only take place in the Niagara Peninsula. Even though one part of the Fenian pincer movement had disintegrated during the first week of June, there was still another Fenian commander in readiness to implement another phase of General Sweeny's master plan.

9

THE RAID IN CANADA EAST

As the Fenian invasion of Canada West failed, an increasing number of reports were received by Canadian authorities that additional Fenian concentrations were taking place along the St. Lawrence frontier. Several American newspapers recorded large movements of Fenians, all heading to the eastern Canadian border.[1] On 4 June William R. Roberts, although fully aware of the failure of the Niagara raid, publicly called upon all Irishmen in the United States to continue the fight for Irish liberation. "Pay no attention to what may seem defeats," he declared, "everything is working gloriously; and if you discharge your duty to your native land, our final triumph is certain."[2]

By the end of the first week of June, the *Quebec Morning Chronicle* made this observation about what was happening in Canada East: "Fenianism continues to be the all absorbing topic of the day. Nothing else is heard on any side. In the hotels, in the streets, on the public promenades, groupes [*sic*] of persons may be seen seriously discussing the situation."[3] Rumors soon circulated that O'Neill's Niagara venture had merely been a diversionary tactic to allow the main Fenian force to enter Canada along her eastern border. Meanwhile the Fenian leaders used American newspapers sympathetic to their cause to whip up Irish support for the Brotherhood by issuing false reports that some Fenian prisoners had been summarily shot in Canada and others had actually been scalped by bloodthirsty Canadian troops.[4]

Thomas Sweeny had expected the arrival of at least 16,800 men for the successful invasion of Canada East. By 2 June at least half of these men were to be at their designated assembly points along the border, from which they could then converge on Montreal and other provincial towns and villages. Military equipment, bought from various American army arsenals, had been forwarded to such rallying points as Potsdam, Malone, and St. Albans. Everything was supposed to function smoothly, but when the Fenian commander-in-chief traveled to the front on 4 June, he found that only 1000 men had arrived.

The American government had begun to impede the Fenian activities even before the formal Neutrality Proclamation of 6 June.[5] First, General Meade ordered the seizure of all shipments of arms along the frontier if there was any shred of evidence that these were intended for illegal purposes and the violation of American neutrality laws. Then he personally headed for the troubled frontier, visiting Buffalo on 2 June and Ogdensburg on the following day. Finding his own personal staff inadequate to prevent any actual crossing of the international frontier by Fenian troops, Meade issued strict orders to all his subordinate commanders in the area to prevent any Fenian reinforcements from joining the main body. Meanwhile they were to seize arms and ammunition wherever they found them.

General Sweeny had not anticipated these developments and saw his hopes of invading Canada East fading very rapidly. Before he could make any major alterations in his plans, he too fell victim to the zeal of the federal authorities. At midnight on 6 June he was arrested in his hotel room in St. Albans, together with his chief of staff, Colonel John Mechan. Only Brigadier-General Samuel Spear, being momentarily away from the "temporary headquarters," escaped arrest. The authorities now desperately tried to find Spear, for he was the last major Fenian officer still at large. On three separate occasions, government detectives thought they had Spear in their grasp, but each time he managed to elude them.

In the early morning hours of 7 June, General Spear decided to leave St. Albans. He already had written orders from Thomas Sweeny in his pocket, and he hastily joined the command awaiting him at Franklin, a small village less than an hour's march from the Canadian frontier.

Spear found his men hungry but still eager to invade Canada. So the Fenians marched, and by 10 A.M. they had "raised the Green Flag and [taken] a strong position" on Canadian territory.[6] However, the inhabitants of the village of Pigeon Hill, in whose vicinity the Fenian soldiers were encamped, did not welcome their "liberators" in the manner the Fenians had expected.

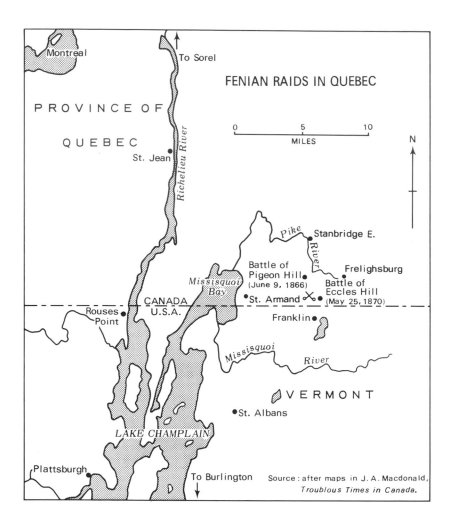

FENIAN RAIDS IN QUEBEC

Montreal

To Sorel

PROVINCE OF

QUEBEC

Richelieu River

St. Jean

0   5   10
MILES

N

Pike

Stanbridge E.

River

Battle of
Pigeon Hill
(June 9, 1866)

Frelighsburg

Missisquoi
Bay

Battle of
Eccles Hill
(May 25, 1870)

St. Armand

CANADA
U.S.A.

Rouses
Point

Franklin

Missisquoi   River

VERMONT

LAKE CHAMPLAIN

St. Albans

Plattsburgh

To Burlington

Source: after maps in J. A. Macdonald,
Troublous Times in Canada.

Consequently, Spear's men had to forage for food and supplies. The Fenian Army's "right wing" now numbered less than 1000 men, and there were guns for only half that number. Ammunition for the muskets was extremely scarce, and the 300 carbines in the camp had no proper cartridges. And the Fenian war chest contained the paltry sum of $20.15. Nevertheless, Brigadier-General Spear decided to stay for the night, for "to remove to-night would be more destructive than to remain in my present position till morning."[7] He hoped that new orders would reach him by early next morning.

Late that night a small detachment of Fenians under Captain O'Hara, while reconnoitering the area around their main camp, clashed with some Canadian defenders in the little village of Frelighsburg and won the skirmish easily. The Fenians then marched into two other Canadian villages, and now they occupied Pigeon Hill, Frelighsburg, St. Armand, and Stanbridge. At last, Spear could show some signs of optimism about his position. "Hurry up those arms," he wrote Colonel Mechan on 8 June, and then he added: "I feel in most excellent spirits and if I can hold my own until the 500 muskets and 100,000 rounds arrive, I shall have no doubts of success."[8] At this moment, the Canadian government had not yet taken any measures to counteract the presence of the Fenian enemy. In fact, the whole Missisquoi frontier was practically unguarded, as the closest army camp was at St. Jean in the Richelieu Valley.

The inhabitants of the occupied villages had, however, become increasingly concerned. News of the Fenian approach led many to send their families from the border area carrying their belongings and valuables with them. Farmers had driven their cattle into hiding places and made certain that their horses were safely dispersed.[9] Whereas the men of John O'Neill had caused very little physical damage to civilian property, the forces of Samuel Spear apparently were not above pilfering supplies and wrecking property.

The Canadian government finally began to move against the Fenian invaders on 8 June. A relief column was quickly assembled and left St. Jean for the Missisquoi frontier by train early that morning. By noon it reached St. Armand. However, the village had already been vacated by the retreating Fenians, some of whom had decided to return to the United States. The remaining Fenians had barricaded the roads leading to Pigeon Hill and were apparently prepared to make a last stand against the fast-approaching Canadian force.[10]

As the Canadian volunteers and British regulars neared the Fenian position, the Royal Guides, a cavalry corps from Montreal under the command of Captain Lorn Macdougall, were sent to the front of the massive marching column so that they might make first contact with the Fenians, who possessed no cavalry whatsoever. What happened from then on is colorfully described in the reminiscence of one of the participating members of the Royal Guides:

> I can remember as though it were yesterday...how we went galloping by the regulars and militia, and how they cheered us. Soon afterwards we came to barricades made of brushwood across the road, and we got down off our horses and took them away. There was not a Fenian to be seen; their hearts had failed them at the pinch and they had fallen back towards the frontier. We rode along and soon came upon a mob of the enemy, perhaps a couple of hundred all told, racing for the boundary. Up on the crest of the hill the Royal Artillery was unlimbering its guns ready for action; and the sight added a poignancy to the yearning for home which was at that moment afflicting the Fenian breast. As we neared them our captain ordered a charge, telling us to use only the flat side of our swords; and in a minute we were in among them slashing right and left. I saw fellows tumbling head over heels as they were struck. Quite a number of Fenians emptied their guns, and I heard the zip, zip of bullets about my head. In this running fight we soon reached the boundary line. There a company of United States regulars was stationed, and as fast as a Fenian tumbled over the line he was seized and disarmed. We came charging right up to the boundary, but were warned by the American officer in charge not to cross it. Of course we had nothing to do but obey, but our commander took advantage of the occasion to express very vigorously his opinion of the United States Government for not having prevented the raid. The American officer merely shrugged his shoulders.
>
> We captured quite a few prisoners—a dozen or so. We galloped along the frontier for some distance and invested a barn in which we were told Gen. O'Neill [who had been set free on 6 June] was hiding. We surrounded it and then carried it with a rush, only to find it was quite empty.[11]

Samuel Spear and his personal staff decided to surrender to Lieutenant-Colonel LaRhett L. Livingston of the U.S. Army, who had kept a watchful eye on the Fenian activities. The Fenian commander of the "eastern section" realized that the game was over and he had lost. His men had been so pitifully ill-equipped with arms, ammunition, and supplies that success was impossible. Moreover, the American government had impeded the progress of the raid considerably by a rigid enforcement of its Neutrality Laws. General Meade made certain that the Fenian invasion of Canada East would fail by issuing the following order at Malone on 9 June: "All persons assembled at this place in connection with, and in aid of the Fenian organization for the purpose of invading Canada, are hereby ordered, in compliance with the President's proclamation to desist their enterprise and disband."[12]

Thus the Fenian raid on Canada East also proved to be an ephemeral affair. And while the citizens along the Huntingdon frontier were kept in a state of tension and uneasiness for another fortnight, no more Fenians appeared on Canadian territory.

Nevertheless, the continued presence of several Fenian detachments across the American border did keep the local militia units busy marching, often in rainy weather along muddy country roads. There were some false alarms, and on several occasions rumors of new Fenian incursions sent Canadian defenders scurrying toward the frontier lines. But the only reward for their patriotism seemed to be mud, cold, and material deprivations. One private of the Victoria Rifles stationed in the area left this personal comment about the prevailing conditions:

> We are lying in mud around the camp fire. We have been half starved since we came here. My feet are wet, and I have not another pair of socks. If I had I could not put them on, for if I took off my boots I could not get them on again. All boys are troubled with colds, rheumatism and sore throats. We have been soaked with mud and water ever since our arrival.[13]

In fact, the only violent episode during these two weeks was a private fight between a member of the Victoria Rifles and a soldier of the Prince of Wales Rifles. The incident occurred when the latter had accused his comrade's outfit of being nothing but "feather-bed soldiers."[14]

Thus General Thomas Sweeny's elaborate invasion scheme of Canada had come to an abrupt and inglorious end. However, President William Roberts, now also in jail, continued to issue proclamations full of promises and exhortations for the future. "Stand by the cause," he wrote from the Ludlow Street Jail in New York City on 11 June. "Be not dismayed by obstacles you meet; you must surmount them, and you will. ... There is no turning back for us, my countrymen. Our movement must and will advance."[15] But his followers had encountered more obstacles than they cared to surmount. General Meade's actions had completely deflated their enthusiasm and most of them were now anxious to return home.

Within the next few days the frontier was almost depleted of Fenians,[16] most of them utilizing the free railroad tickets provided by the government or sympathetic private American citizens. As early as 8 June, Governor-General Monck had informed Colonial Secretary Cardwell that the United States government was "exerting itself in an energetic manner to arrest the further progress of the Fenian movement, within its territories." Six days later he echoed his initial dispatch when he wrote: "The determination of the Government of the United States to stop the transportation of men and supplies to the places of assembly, rendered even the temporary success on the part of the Fenians impossible."[17]

The raid in Canada East had been a futile attempt that provided the Fenian movement with little glory. Nevertheless, in spite of its failure, the members of the Brotherhood managed to romanticize their most recent exploits. One Fenian song soon became popular among the veterans of "Spear's army":

> Oh Canada is a purty [*sic*] place, of gold there is no lack,
> So I trudged from St. Albans with a musket on my back;
> We were five hundred Fenians, who never knew a fear,
> While we followed the brave leader, whose name is General Spear.
> And we trod the British soil, and we braved the British Queen,
> And we flaunted in their eyes the brave old flag of Green.[18]

The news of the Fenian raids on British North America did not arrive in Britain until mid-June. And it was not until 22 June that the London *Times* commented on the recent events in North America. But London was already caught up in the excitement of the Austro-Prussian war, and the Fenian story made as much of a splash as a raindrop falling into a large bucket of water. Commented the *Times*: "In the midst of such storms of war as are now gathering around us, the story of the Fenian raids into Canada reads like some absurd burlesque or discordant caricature."[19]

On 8 June the Canadian Parliament had reassembled in Ottawa. As its first order of business, the government had procured the temporary suspension of the *habeas corpus* act, thereby providing Canadian authorities with a convenient legal weapon should any further Fenian incursions take place.[20] The *Toronto Daily Telegraph* (9 June 1866) quickly commented on this action by suggesting that "it will provide a ready and fitting punishment for the wretches who try to cover with the cloak of patriotism deeds of violence and murder." President Roberts meanwhile had urged his followers to "return to their respective homes" on 13 June, "until such time as a fresh campaign can be inaugurated at a not far distant day."[21]

But the Fenians had exhausted themselves for the present. On 11 June the *Globe* declared: "Thus ends the most exciting event which we have had in Canada since the rebellion of 1837, and, probably, the most exciting that we shall have for thirty years to come." And the *Stratford Beacon* (16 June 1866) remarked: "They came, they saw, but they skedaddled. . . . Their fiasco was, we hope, too miserable and absurd to be repeated." Even the pro-Fenian *Buffalo Courier*, noting the departure of about 1500 members of the Brotherhood from the city on 15 June, admitted that "the Fenian excitement is virtually at an end."[22] By 12 June the Grand Trunk Railway, whose cars had been used to move men and supplies during the last ten days, once again ran its regular route into southwestern Ontario. By the middle of the month, most of the volunteer units were returning home.

Yet peace did not return immediately to all citizens of the province. The invasion of the Fenian Brotherhood created a sudden resurgence of anti-Catholic sentiment, largely fostered by the Orange Order. This had occurred on a number of earlier occasions, most notably during the recent visit of the Prince of Wales to British North America in the early autumn of 1860.

As early as the evening of 1 June, while Mayor Medcalf and other civic leaders had organized a Home Guard in Toronto's St. Lawrence Hall "to protect their homes from the threatening raid by the Fenians,"[23] one Andy Fleming had openly accused the entire Catholic population of Toronto of being "unfaithful and disloyal" to the British government. Although some of the citizens present had openly frowned upon Fleming and what he said, there were others who loudly echoed his sentiments.[24]

The first two weeks in June were uneasy ones for Catholic Irishmen in Canada West. In many parts of the province, suspicion was cast on innocent Catholics, and some arrests were even made.[25] The *Stratford Beacon* (8 June 1866) described the unfortunate situation in these words. "We regret to see a disposition in some quarters to seize upon the invasion of the Province by a band of armed ruffians as the occasion for covert attacks on resident adherents of the Catholic church. With some narrow-minded people the idea appears to prevail that if a person is a Catholic, he must necessarily be a Fenian."

Later in the year, John A. Macdonald wrote to Rolland Macdonald, a politician from St. Catharines, expressing his great concern over the practice of "allowing illiterate Magistrates to arrest every man whom they chose to suspect."[26] Macdonald added that this would mean every Roman Catholic in rural districts and he feared that such conduct would soon drive many harassed Irishmen out of the country straight to the American Fenians.

Nevertheless, the Fenian threat had vanished within weeks of its appearance on the Canadian frontier. On 21 June 1866 Governor-General Monck wrote to Secretary of State Edward Cardwell: "I have the honor to report that the bands of Fenian conspirators ... have dispersed and returned to their homes."[27] The grand invasion scheme of General Sweeny, so carefully and minutely planned, had failed. Internal causes contributed much to the disaster: unrealistic estimates of Fenian strength in men and arms, a virtually non-existent transportation system, flagrant disobedience of orders, and even several instances of cowardice. In addition, the Fenian leadership underestimated the patriotism of the Canadian people and very unwisely relied too heavily on vague promises of neutrality by American authorities. In his "Official Report," Thomas Sweeny remarked that "the immediate cause of our failure is attributable to the seizure of our arms and ammunition by the Government authorities." But he also admitted that "the misrepresentations made by the colonels of the [Fenian] regiments respecting their effective force, and their failure to report promptly when the orders were issued" did much to bring about "failure in those critical June days of 1866."[28]

Without sufficient manpower, and confronted with a substantial force of British defenders and eventually a declaration of American neutrality, the Fenian attempt to establish a power base in British North America resulted in a complete and inevitable failure.[29] Thus retreat and reorganization became the temporary watchwords of the Brotherhood. Canada had not heard the last of these idealistic but impractical Irish patriots.

10

THE LONG SUMMER OF 1866

The immediate threat of the Fenian Brotherhood had disappeared from the Canadian-American frontier by late June. Most militia units and regular forces were slowly returning to their homes and regular bases, leaving only a small force on frontier duty. When the Queen's Own Rifles returned home to Toronto on 18 June, for example, a public holiday was declared in their honor, and thousands lined the streets of the city as the volunteers marched in to the tunes of "God Save the Queen," "The British Grenadiers," and "See the Conquering Hero Comes." Soon letters to the editor recommended that special medals be struck and distributed to the participants of the Fenian raids, and that a monument be erected "to do honour . . . to those who have fallen in the defence of their country."[1]

Although there seemed to be no imminent danger from the Fenians, the recent events were not quickly forgotten. The legislators of the province were quick to grant vast increases in defense expenditures.[2] In a speech in the Legislative Assembly, Finance Minister Alexander Tilloch Galt asked for more than a $1,500,000 "to maintain our independence and safety." Galt also told his audience: "The Fenian Snake is scotched but not killed . . . it may revive at any moment."[3] The *Globe* endorsed this view, and throughout the summer of 1866, the paper kept clamoring for immediate military reform and reorganization to be fully prepared to meet the Fenians should they ever again venture across the border.[4]

The constant clamor of the *Globe's* publisher and editor, George Brown, for a better defense system did produce some results in the summer of 1866. In late August a military training camp was opened at Thorold, Canada West, where volunteer units received one week of basic training. Problems still persisted, however, and the camp commander, Colonel G. J. Wolseley, bitterly complained to his superior, the adjutant-general of the militia, about the poor state of the military equipment in the camp.[5]

In spite of this, Camp Thorold still provided a badly needed basic training for the 6000 volunteers who passed through its gates. Many undoubtedly gained valuable military experience, although some did complain "that they were treated more like dogs than persons."[6]

Furthermore, seven new field brigades were created, three in Canada West and four in Canada East. Each brigade consisted of one battalion of regulars, three volunteer battalions, one field battery, and one cavalry troop. A permanent general staff was also appointed to direct military affairs in the province. However, it was Canada West which received most of the attention of the Canadian authorities. Canada East had no counterpart to Camp Thorold and little was being done to prevent another attack on the lower Canadian frontier.

By mid-July almost all volunteer units had been recalled from the frontier. Many of the men were disappointed that there had been no further fighting, but their frustration was quickly relieved when they received some financial compensation from the vast resources of the Volunteer Relief Fund.[7] Before long their attention was fastened on the news arriving from Europe via the new trans-Atlantic cable, completed on 27 July of that year. The Austro-Prussian War and Garibaldi's march up the Italian peninsula received complete coverage in all major Canadian papers, creating great interest in European problems. Calm set in after the recent Fenian excitement, and few men—perhaps with the notable exception of George Brown—worried about the continuing intrigues of the Fenian Brotherhood.

Yet the "Fenian snake" was still very much alive in the United States. "I don't think that Fenianism is dead or that the invasion of Canada has been finally abandoned," wrote a Canadian expatriate living in New York City.[8] The arrested Fenian leaders, without exception, had been set free by the American authorities and were continuing to crisscross the country to revive the Brotherhood from its nearly fatal blow of early June.

As early as 18 June William Roberts met with several influential politicians in Washington and was promised further moral support for the cause of Irish freedom. On the last day of June he spoke in Buffalo, where he denounced the United States government for its rigorous enforcement of the neutrality laws. But he still exuded optimism as he looked into the future:

We are not one particle dismayed; we are more determined than ever.... Our organization will be less open, and much more determined in character than the old one. We are going to keep within the bounds of American law, and make such preparation that when we do move it will be like the lightning flash.[9]

The *New York Times*, which had pronounced Fenianism on the decline earlier, again observed the continuing activities of the Fenians. The paper's Chicago correspondent noted on 23 June that "notwithstanding the failure of the first Canadian campaign, there are many who are yet sanguine of ultimate success. Drilling is still going forward at several places in this city, and recruits are arriving from the interior."

Meanwhile James Stephens was still desperately trying to unite the American Fenians. He planned another mass rally in Jones' Wood. But on this occasion the New York city fathers felt it unwise to issue him another speaking permit, and he was forced to address his supporters outside the park on 24 June. Stephens's rally was sparsely attended but his small audience enthusiastically applauded his denunciation of the Roberts-Sweeny followers, whom he called "traitors" for deviating from the orthodox plan of a Fenian uprising on Irish soil. The Chief Organizer of the Irish Republic again promised to carry on with his sacred cause and pledged that "the Sunburst shall be raised again, and we shall smite once and forever the long hated foe of our race."[10]

In late July isolated rumors began to circulate that the Brotherhood was once more on the move. In fact, the first alarm of another Fenian raid was raised from Fort Erie on 27 July when Reeve Kempson telegraphed General Napier that "Fenians were crossing near Fort Erie in considerable numbers."[11] The authorities in Toronto, who received this startling news about midnight, were preparing to call out the volunteers when another telegram arrived explaining that there was no actual danger.[12] Yet this small episode clearly demonstrated that in some frontier areas nerves were still raw.

Four days later the *Buffalo Express* stated that "another and more formidable invasion than the last is in preparation against the Canadian provinces."[13] Soon rumors of imminent raids began to circulate, and once more alarmed Canadians, particularly frontier newspaper editors, began to echo the *Globe's* constant demands for military preparedness. The *London Free Press* immediately complained about the irritating and unsettling effect that these "rumors" had upon the country, and the *Grand River Sachem* hoped for an early raid by "these miserable skalliwags" so that they could be administered "such a drubbing, as they little dream of."[14] Even the little town of Berlin (today Kitchener), which had been bypassed by most of the excitement in June, decided that there must be some truth to the latest rumors, and hastily formed a volunteer company.[15]

Canadians were particularly worried because Fenian leaders continued to make inflammatory statements throughout the United States and talked incessantly of another raid on Canada. The Canadian newspapers reported numerous Fenian meetings and described in great detail the various activities of the Brotherhood as it sought to reactivate its cause. Perhaps the most disturbing news came from Chicago where another large "Fenian picnic" had been held on 15 August. The number of participants had been estimated at between 10,000 and 15,000, and the list of guest speakers who courted the Irish vote at this event was headed by Illinois' Governor Richard Oglesby, Speaker of the House Schuyler Colfax, Congressman John A. Logan and Senator Lyman Trumbull of Illinois, and the popular "hero of Ridgeway," John O'Neill.[16]

As the reports of this Chicago picnic and others similar to it arrived in Canada, the civil and military authorities reacted promptly. Under no circumstances did they want to be caught unprepared. The small force of soldiers still performing frontier duty was immediately increased, and the military training camp at Thorold suddenly became active. The Great Lakes and the St. Lawrence River were patrolled by no less than seven gunboats, three on Lake Ontario and the St. Lawrence River and the remainder on Lake Erie and the upper Lakes region, thus making any hostile crossing into Canada an extremely hazardous affair. The Canadian Parliament also passed a law making it illegal to hold "meetings and assemblies of persons for the purpose of training or drilling themselves . . . or for the purpose of practising military exercises, movements or evolutions, without any lawful authority for so doing."[17] Canadians once again were beginning to suffer from another "state of nerves."

On 23 August the *Globe* published a news item which stated that Fenians from such southern cities as Louisville and Nashville were heading north, and that an attack was to be made from the American Middle West via Lake Michigan. Shortly thereafter word was received that Thomas Sweeny was ready to make final military appointments in the reorganized Brotherhood. On 25 August the *Toronto Leader* printed a copy of Sweeny's order to all Centres of his organization, dated 24 August 1866.

> Centres of circles are requested to forward immediately to these headquarters the name of a competent military man from each circle for the purpose of appointment to reorganize the military branch of each circle. Care must be taken that none but experienced and tried officers are selected.

The *Toronto Globe* of the same day was thoroughly convinced that definite trouble was in store for Canadians and demanded government action.

The *Toronto Leader*, as early as 23 August, refused to become excessively alarmed over these latest "rumors" and suggested they were the work of the "amateur generals . . . (and) excited gentlemen" of the *Globe*, maintaining that "there is no good cause for alarm." And the minister of the militia suggested privately that "the *Globe's* idea about calling out all the Volunteers is all nonsense, and no one knows better than Brown that it is so, but he desires to make a fuss and cause discontent."[18] Yet only one day later, Governor-General Monck cabled the British government for three more regiments of infantry and additional cavalry and artillery support. Apparently no one was willing to take chances this time. In a letter to his son Henry, Governor-General Monck remarked that "the Fenians have been threatening a good deal lately and I thought it safest to be prepared for the worst."[19]

While Canadians waited for something to happen, the Fenian Brotherhood assembled in Troy, in upstate New York, for another of its boisterous conventions. Four to five hundred delegates, including some from the Stephens camp, opened the session on 4 September in Harmony Hall.[20] But brotherly love and unity of thought and action were once more noticeably absent. President Roberts and Secretary of War Sweeny now accused each other of mishandling the Niagara and St. Albans invasions, and the few Stephens delegates present kept clamoring for abandonment of the Canadian invasion scheme. There was only one major point of agreement: the assembled body of Fenians overwhelmingly endorsed a resolution thanking "General John O'Neill and the officers and men of his command, who at Limestone Ridge and Fort Erie so gallantly upheld the honour of our flag and vindicated the traditional heroism of our race."[21]

When the convention concluded on 8 September, a considerable internal shakeup had been effected. Henceforth the Brotherhood's plans would be formulated in greater secrecy to prevent vital information from falling into British hands long before the event was to take place. Thomas Sweeny was induced to resign from office, and rumors were spread that the well-known Union General Phil Sheridan would be asked to take over his command. William Roberts, in spite of his initial reluctance, was persuaded to retain the presidency of the organization, and John O'Neill was appointed inspector-general of the Fenian Army. The Canadian party of the Brotherhood was obviously still in command within the movement.

Canadians took a great interest in these proceedings. First, the unexpected escape of Michael Murphy and five companions from the confines of an old jail in Cornwall during the early hours of 2 September had given renewed publicity to the Fenian danger.[22] Now these "despicable wretches," as the *Globe* called the Fenians, were apparently preparing to carry out another raid on Canadian territory. On 14 September the *Globe* cited an editorial from the pro-Fenian *New York World*, which stated that "We are revealing no secret when we say that the recent meeting of the Fenian Congress at Troy will be followed, sooner or later, by another invasion of Canada. The programme has been arranged, the leaders appointed, and the money raised to initiate the war." And the *Toronto Irish Canadian* (7 September) remarked, perhaps a little maliciously: "It is quite probable that there is a little excitement in store for the people of Canada."

As usual, the *Toronto Leader* sought to minimize the danger of another invasion and was supported by the *Stratford Beacon*, which strongly deplored the *Globe's* constant "appeal to arms."[23] But many Canadians were apparently aroused to renewed anger. The *Sarnia Observer* (14 September), a frontier weekly generally not given to strong anti-Fenian outbursts, declared itself "positively tired" of the constant threats of another raid. "Our country," wrote the paper, "is becoming a camp. Investment is checked, business languishes, and a feeling of insecurity prevails." John A. Macdonald, still keeping himself well informed about the Fenian activities through Gilbert McMicken, was also somewhat concerned about the continuous state of alarm that the invasion rumors produced. "It is really astonishing," he wrote to Angus Morrison, a fellow politician from Toronto, "to witness the panic of the people on the Frontier."[24]

John A. Macdonald would have been even more concerned if he had read the *Rochester Union* in late September when that sensation-mongering upstate New York newspaper printed this information:

> There is a reign of terror in Canada in view of the anticipated raid of the Fenians. Attorney-General Macdonald has issued a circular directing the seizure of arms in the possession of suspected parties and the arrest of all persons, travellers or residents, who may be believed to have any connection with the Fenian order. ... With such a state of things existing in Canada, it is not safe for Americans to visit the province. ... The situation in Canada as we gather from the press and conversation with Canadians is frightful. All branches of business are prostrated. ... Taxes are swelling to enormous proportions. ... Under all this, there is growing a widespread desire for annexation to the United States as the only means of checking the Fenians and obtaining a road to stable government and prosperity.[25]

In spite of continued rumors, and even reported shipments of arms and ammunition to the frontier, the Roberts faction failed to carry out its threats. The Canadian-American border remained undisturbed and no attempts were made by members of the Brotherhood to launch another raid. The rather dilapidated state of the Brotherhood's finances and a growing apathy and disenchantment among its members and supporters simply made another Canadian venture unfeasible. And in any case, the constant vigilance of the Canadian authorities would have rendered such an enterprise futile. Perhaps it was a fitting climax when the *Globe* somewhat sarcastically reported in its 1 October issue that a group of Fenians were apparently preparing to head south "to liberate Mexico from the French."

During the last two weeks of September, Stephens's headquarters in New York City experienced a brief flurry of activity. A successful picnic sponsored by the Fenian Sisterhood and a small influx of private donations had encouraged the Chief Organizer to announce at a rally in Jones' Wood that before the end of the year he would leave for Ireland and raise once more the standard of revolt against Britain, "even though I should be taken and hanged."[26] Yet Stephens continued to ask for additional funds and arms. More picnics were organized and the Fenian Sisterhood inaugurated its First Annual Ball in order to raise more money. It seemed only too true, as Finley Peter Dunne's "Mister Dooley" would later observe: "If Ireland cud be freed be a picnic, it'd not on'y be free today, but an impire."[27]

The Roberts party, too, remained active and sought to keep alive its Canadian scheme while awaiting more money and arms. The Roberts followers held their own fund-raising picnics and were able to entice the former Mexican dictator and victor at the Alamo, General Antonio López de Santa Anna, to speak to one of their rallies on Staten Island on behalf of the revolutionary cause.[28] In mid-October their fortunes received a tremendous boost when the United States government decided to return all Fenian arms captured during the June raids. Furthermore, the Roberts wing hoped that the opening of the trials of several Fenian prisoners in Toronto in late October would provide the Brotherhood with another golden opportunity to fan the flames of anti-British sentiment in the United States.

Yet even as their fortunes seemed to take a turn for the better, a small but steady current of dissatisfaction with the policies of the leadership gradually spread throughout the ranks of the Roberts supporters. Many individuals finally began to question the sincerity of their leaders, and soon the small but steady stream of financial contributions began to dry up. The Roberts party gained some support in late November when it declared its intention of invading Canada to free the prisoners held in Canadian jails. But, as usual, it was all talk and no action.[29]

Then in late November the rumor was spread that James Stephens was ready to fight. The various New York City newspapers could no longer account for his presence in the city, and the assumption was made that he had sailed for Ireland to make good his promise "to fight by New Year's dawn."[30] The talk of revolution in Ireland now increased, and on 27 November, the pro-Fenian *New York World* created enormous excitement with a report claiming Ireland was in revolt.[31] Thousands of Irish-Americans rejoiced when they heard or read this sensational news. But reliable information provided by the trans-Atlantic telegraph quickly shattered another Fenian pipedream.

New Year's Day came in Ireland and no insurrection took place. In fact, James Stephens was still in New York City, hiding out at 11 West Eleventh Street. He had recently been denounced by his long-time associate Thomas J. Kelly, who accused him of cowardice, and now apparently wanted to replace him as chief organizer of the I.R.B.

Nevertheless, James Stephens continued to perpetuate the myth that an Irish uprising was imminent. He boasted that "we have plenty of men (and) sufficient war material," even though he knew that the I.R.B. in Ireland had no more than 2000 rifles, several thousand old shotguns, a few hundred revolvers, and a large number of pikes.[32]

Stephens finally prepared to embark for home on Saturday, 12 January 1867, but he missed his boat because it sailed two hours earlier than he thought it would. He did leave America at the end of the month but did not return to Ireland. The "Fenian Chief" landed in France on 8 February 1867, and eventually headed for Paris, where he would spend the next few years.[33]

The Fenian movement in the New World and in Ireland was now resting on very shaky foundations. Its heyday seemed to have passed, for battle after battle had been lost. Yet the Fenian war against Britain was not over. The "Fenian snake" would continue to rear its head for years to come before its last remains would be forever interred.

James Stephens, Head Centre of the I.R.B.
Courtesy of The Library of Congress.

John O'Mahony, American Fenian Leader.
Courtesy of The Library of Congress.

William Randall Roberts,
American Fenian Leader.
Courtesy of The Library of Congress.

Thomas Sweeny, Commander in Chief of the Fenian Army, 1865-66.
From J. Denieffe, *A Personal Narrative of the Irish Revolutionary Brotherhood.*

Sir John A. Macdonald, first Prime Minister of the Dominion of Canada.
Courtesy of the Public Archives of Canada.

General John O'Neill, the hero of Ridgeway.
From *Canadian Illustrated News* (Montreal, 10 September 1870); courtesy of the Public Archives of Canada.

THE UNITED STATES STEAMER "MICHIGAN" WITH CAPTURED FENIANS ON A SCOW-BOAT.—[SKETCHED BY J. P. HOFFMAN.]

The U.S.S. Michigan.
From *Harper's Weekly* (1866); courtesy of the Metropolitan Toronto Library Board.

(a—g) A Canadian cartoonist's view of the Fenian raids of 1866.
From D. Gauust, *History of the Fenian Invasion of Canada;* courtesy
of the Metropolitan Toronto Library Board.

(a) Council of War.

(b) *Scene at the Battle of Ridgeway.*

(c) *Ancient Fenian Chivalry.*

(d) *Sic semper tyrannis.*

(e) *"Reinforcements" arrive.*

(f) Col. O'Neill addressing his troops.

(g) Capture of Colors of Queen's Own.

THE YANKEE FIREMAN KEEPS HIS WORD.

Yankee. "YOU SEE I'M READY WHEN WANTED, MISS CANADA."

A complimentary view of the United States government's intervention in the affairs of the Fenian Brotherhood.
From *Punch* (1866); courtesy of the Metropolitan Toronto Library Board.

Thomas D'Arcy McGee, anti-Fenian politician.
Courtesy of the Public Archives of Canada.

11

THE FENIAN PRISONERS

AND THE IRISH VOTE

As the summer months of 1866 passed by, the lingering effects of the recent Fenian raids were more widely felt than was perhaps expected, in both Canada and the United States. First, there was the problem of the large number of Fenian prisoners who had been captured by the Canadians in June and who were now awaiting trial in a Toronto jail. These "Fenian trials" had been postponed for several months because Canadian authorities felt that full justice could not be done if the prisoners were tried in the highly emotional aftermath of the invasion. But now, in the early autumn of 1866, the time had come to deal with this matter. The American government had, of course, dealt with its Fenian prisoners very swiftly and easily—it simply released them all either on bail or their own recognizance, and then decided never to bring the cases to trial. Canadians, however, had no intention of letting the Fenian raiders go unpunished. Yet the final verdicts in the upcoming trials would undoubtedly affect the subsequent political and diplomatic relations of Canada, Britain, and the United States.

Moreover, 1866 was apparently becoming a critical year in American politics. In late autumn the American people would vote in the congressional election, and the campaign between the various contending factions—Democrats, Radical Republicans, and the supporters of Andrew Johnson—was developing into an unusually bitter contest for votes. The group of "radicals" within the Republican Party, which had slowly gained strength after Lincoln's death, was now determined to impose its own reconstruction policies on the defeated Confederacy. To implement their program of "Black Republican" ascendancy, they needed a decisive victory at the polls. Therefore no efforts were spared to win votes. And the "Irish vote" was one of the most formidable voting blocks in the United States.

The Irish element in American society had become a substantial force by the 1860s. The Great famine and the Revolt of '48 had increased dramatically the number of Irish in the United States. The census of 1860 listed 4,138,697 foreign-born in the United States, of whom 1,611,304 were of Irish birth.[1] These Irish immigrants quickly began to make a definite impact on American politics. Yet, even in a new country, their attachment to their homeland remained strong as ever. Thus the "Irish fact"—or perhaps more accurately the Irish vote—became a force to be reckoned with by all who wished to become involved in public life.[2]

The forthcoming congressional election and the importance of the Irish vote forced many American politicians to perform a difficult tightrope act. And the existence of the Fenian prisoners forced the Johnson administration, as well as other politicians, to make a number of decisions based more on political expediency and short-term opportunism than on sincere personal conviction.

The captured Fenian raiders now awaiting trials in Canadian prison cells could scarcely expect leniency. The temper of the Canadian people in the immediate aftermath of the raid had been violent. As early as 5 June, the *Toronto Leader* had demanded a quick trial and the death penalty for the prisoners "as a warning and an example" to others who "may be disposed to follow [their] example." The *Globe* reemphasized these points two days later in its own editorial comment: "These men must be tried and punished for their crimes, and punished in such a way as to prevent similar outrages in the future, no matter where we may arouse morbid sympathy." Even the *New York Times* (4 June), which had suggested after the June raids that "every ruffian that crossed the frontier might be . . . hung," was calling on the Canadian government by 23 June not "to demand [its] Pound of Flesh." The *Times* now suggested that "a sanguinary policy, in dealing with the Fenian prisoners, will work a fatal change in the popular mind. . . . It will furnish a provocation for renewing the conflict, and with a united determination on the part of the countrymen of these prisoners, to avenge their execution."

But anti-Fenian sentiment continued to run high in Canada, not only among the general population but also in some official quarters. For example, Chief Justice Draper of the province, while addressing the Yorkville

Volunteers at a dinner meeting on 29 June, expressed his opinion that these prisoners "should simply be dealt with as a party of robbers, whose fate ought to be the gallows."[3]

The Canadian government was sensible enough not to hold the trials during this state of public excitement. Canadian authorities correctly judged that fairness and objectivity could not be provided until a later date. Hence the only action taken during June was the removal of the prisoners from various frontier jails to a larger prison in Toronto. The trials were postponed until autumn. Yet at least one observer did not get carried away with his emotions; he made an excellent point when he suggested to a friend that Canadians should not vent their wrath upon "those poor ignorant and sadly misled wretches [in Canadian jails], while the prime movers and leaders of the affair are safe within the arms of Uncle Sam."[4] And the British authorities, already concerned about the possibility of a deterioration in Anglo-American relations over the issue of the Fenian prisoners, expressed the first signs of possible clemency, when Sir Frederick Bruce suggested to Governor-General Monck that "these misguided men may be dealt with leniently" for the sake of "the future tranquility of Canada and her relations with the United States."[5]

In the months preceding the fall elections, both major American parties actively courted the Irish vote. The Democrats, traditionally the beneficiaries of Irish electoral support, sought to retain it in order to strengthen their congressional representation during the expected reconstruction debate. The Republicans were equally determined to win the votes of the Irish to implement their own reconstruction schemes. Consequently, the Fenian Brotherhood, despite its notorious character, was permitted to continue its illegal preparations within the borders of the United States. No astute politician aspiring for public office in areas heavily populated with Irish was willing to alienate this potential voting block during the summer and autumn of 1866, for "to provoke the antagonism of the Irish electorate in Municipal or State contests [was] to court defeat, and in some instances disaster."[6]

Several Radical Republicans, in their anxiety to win Irish favor, introduced federal legislation that would enable the Brotherhood to operate more freely within United States territory. As early as 11 June, a resolution was introduced in the House of Representatives by Sydenham E. Ancona of Pennsylvania urging "that the House Committee on Foreign Affairs be . . . instructed to report a bill repealing an act approved April 20, 1818, entitled 'An act in addition to an act for the punishment of certain crimes against the United States,' and to repeal the act therein mentioned, it being the neutrality law, under the terms of which the President's proclamation against the Fenians was issued."[7] His colleague Representative Robert C. Schenck of

Ohio then presented his own resolution asking the president of the United States to "reconsider the policy which has been adopted by him as between the British Government and that portion of the Irish people who, under the name of Fenians, are struggling for their independent nationality."[8]

Both resolutions were overwhelmingly defeated, but their sponsors had established themselves as Fenian sympathizers and were hoping to reap the benefits of their political opportunism in the fall elections. In fact, other members of the House soon jumped on the bandwagon. Several weeks later, Representative Reader W. Clarke of Ohio submitted a resolution asking the president "to urge upon the Canadian authorities and also the British Government the release of the Fenian prisoners recently captured in Canada." On the same day his colleague Rufus P. Spalding (Ohio) made the suggestion that "the prosecution instituted in the United States courts against the Fenians . . . be discontinued, if compatible with the public interest."[9]

Although these grandstand plays in Congress produced no legislative changes, they had their desired effects upon the American Irish. The feelings of the Fenian leadership, recently ruffled by the government's rigid enforcement of the nation's neutrality laws, were soothed considerably. In fact, some Fenian leaders even took to the campaign trail for the Republican party. And if any Irishmen doubted the sincerity of these politicians, the Banks Bill of early July was meant to dispel all remaining skepticism.

This curious bill, introduced in the House on 2 July 1866 by Nathaniel P. Banks, chairman of the House Foreign Affairs Committee, provided for the admission of Nova Scotia, New Brunswick, and the two Canadas into the American Union.[10] It was favorably received in many Northern states. The *New York Herald* hailed the measure as the ideal solution for the problems of British North America; the Banks Bill, if acted upon, would "keep off the Fenian chills, the Confederation cramps . . . the Reciprocity itch . . . and all other political distempers which have afflicted feeble little Canada."[11] In the Midwest, the *St. Paul Press* saw it as "an able and comprehensive measure," and even the *Detroit Free Press*, generally quite sympathetic to Canadians, called it an intelligent plan showing a great deal of foresight, since "nature itself had decreed that the provinces and Northern and Western States of the United States must be governed by the same laws and controlled by the same powers."[12]

The Banks Bill, despite the powerful position of its sponsor, disappeared at the committee stage. Even if it somehow had managed to survive the House of Representatives, it would most certainly have been killed by Senator Sumner, the chairman of the Senate Foreign Relations Committee.[13] Charles Sumner was not against the expansion of American territory into British North America, but he favored a "peaceful" approach, preferring to await Britain's ultimate withdrawal of her forces from North America. Banks's sponsorship of the measure, however, boosted his electoral strength in his Boston district and he easily won re-election in November that year.

The bill appealed to some Americans, but it found little support in British North America. The *Toronto Globe* denounced it as "so silly a bit of impudence" that it should be laughed off (5 July). Then its editor took aim at the man who was responsible for drafting the measure, James W. Taylor, and suggested that "Mr. Taylor might try his hand on a plan for the annexation of the moon" (7 July). In the New Brunswick legislature, Charles Skinner facetiously proposed that a bill be passed granting Massachusetts, Maine, New York, and other states admission into the Confederation.[14]

Thus the Radical Republicans lost no opportunities to court the Irish vote, and throughout the subsequent campaign the Irish were repeatedly told that their only hope for the future rested with the Republican party's radical wing. As early as July, John O'Neill had told a group of Irishmen in Nashville that his own policy would be "to adhere to that party which is in favor of Irish independence."[15]

As the election drew nearer, the Fenian leadership, well aware how eagerly the Irish vote was sought by all parties, tried to apply a little political blackmail. A delegation of Fenians met with President Johnson in mid-September and demanded that the American government secure the release of all the Fenian prisoners still in Canada, the return of the captured arms and supplies from the June raids, and the removal from office of certain unpopular high government officials, including Secretary of War Edwin Stanton. In return, the delegates promised Johnson the Irish vote[16]—a promise that undoubtedly could be more easily given than fulfilled.

President Johnson was confronted with a difficult situation. His abortive attempt to rally moderate support from around the nation at a National Union Convention in Philadelphia in mid-August and the disastrous failure of his subsequent Western speaking tour had placed him in an extremely precarious position. The fall elections were only weeks away and he not only faced a resurgent Democratic party but also was locked in a suicidal struggle with the radical wing of his own party, which accused him of being a "copperhead" and excessively lenient toward the Confederate states. At this point it did not make much political sense to antagonize the Irish vote any further. Johnson, after all, had been the man who issued the Neutrality Proclamation several months earlier, an act which Fenian leaders had found difficult to forgive or forget. Johnson therefore decided to listen to the Fenian arguments and asked for more time to think things over.

But in spite of trying to accommodate the Fenian organization to secure the Irish vote, Johnson appeared to be heading toward his own destruction.

The first election results foreshadowed what was to follow. In the first week of October, the states of Maine and Vermont went to the polls, and the Andrew Johnson moderates were badly beaten. Fearing that the New England Fenians had been very instrumental in this defeat, the Johnson administration now announced that *all* prosecutions against Fenians in the United States would cease immediately.[17] But when Pennsylvania, Ohio, Indiana, and Iowa went to the polls on 9 October, the results were no more comforting for President Johnson. The Republican party retained forty-eight of the sixty seats in these four states, but the vote in the larger cities, where most Irish lived, had gone overwhelmingly to the Democrats. Furthermore, the vast majority of the victorious Republicans were members of the radical wing of the party.[18] Johnson was in serious trouble; he had become a president without a party.

In sheer desperation, Johnson now ordered the release of all the Fenian weapons seized during the June raids. He also removed from his post Attorney-General William Dart, whom the Fenians loathed for his rigid enforcement of the neutrality laws in June. Finally Johnson asked his secretary of state to intercede on behalf of the Fenian prisoners in Canada. With these measures, the beleaguered president hoped to win the crucial New York election on 6 November.

Bitter denunciations and harsh invective made up the final weeks of the campaign. The Radicals had succeeded in making loyalty to the Union the central issue, and Johnson was accused of aiding and abetting Southern truculence and defiance with his excessively liberal reconstruction scheme. Of course, the real issue at stake in this most crucial election was one of political supremacy in postbellum America. The Radicals knew that once they had entrenched themselves in Congress and implemented their own particular reconstruction plans, Northern political supremacy would be assured for years to come. Only then, according to the Radical program, would the Southern states be allowed to seek readmission to the Union.

When the remaining Northern states went to the polls on 6 November the outcome, already indicated several weeks earlier, was confirmed. The Radical Republicans swept the country. They won the important state of New York by a 20–11 congressional majority. The final majority in the House of Representatives was 143–49, and in the Senate the margin was an overwhelming 42–11.[19] Yet despite its overall majority, the Republican party lost votes in the larger urban centers. Some Radical candidates were, in fact, defeated in districts where the Irish vote usually meant victory or defeat.[20] The *Cleveland Leader* (9 November 1866) was therefore led to remark:

> The results of the fall elections demonstrate two things; first, that the Union party cannot get low enough in the dirt to obtain the Irish vote. . . . In this city a special effort was made to obtain the Fenian vote . . . [but] the Irish wards of the city . . . gave heavier majorities for the Democrats

than before. . . . On the other hand the Union party, with the Irish vote as usual solidly against it, has carried every northern state and retained a two thirds majority in Congress. If it cannot obtain the Irish vote, it can at least do without it.[21]

No amount of persuasion by the Fenian leaders had enabled them to "deliver" the Irish vote to the Radical Republicans. Whether it was the past conduct of the Republican party or merely traditional loyalty to the Democrats, the American Irish chose to cast their votes and fortunes with the Democratic party.

After the congressional elections, interest in Irish affairs dwindled rapidly. Newspapers which had been sympathetic to the Fenian cause suddenly found other interests to pursue and other causes to support. Even the Fenian trials in Canada, which had aroused numerous angry editorial comments in the American press before the fall elections, were soon relegated to the back pages of American newspapers.

While their American neighbors were involved in one of the most decisive congressional elections in their history, Canadians went about the business of trying those Fenians still held in jails in Toronto and Sweetsburg.

At a preliminary hearing during the summer, a substantial number of the captured Fenians had been released by the Canadian authorities for lack of sufficient evidence and had been quickly deported across the border.[22] Finally, fifty-six prisoners were held for trial, as the Crown attorney's office was convinced enough evidence had been collected to indict them.

When the Canadian government announced that the trials would commence in early October, the Toronto papers, particularly the *Globe* and the *Leader*, immediately demanded a stern application of the law to all prisoners. The press as a whole, with the sole exception of the *Toronto Irish Canadian*, gave the distinct impression in its editorials that the prisoners were automatically guilty and that their trials would be merely a legal formality. This hostile sentiment was quickly felt by many pro-Fenian newspapers in the United States, and one of the most vociferous of these, the *Rochester* (New York) *Union*, made this bold prediction: "The execution of the first man now under arrest in Canada for Fenianism will be the signal for a movement here that will wrest Canada from the men who now control it, and make it part of the American Union."[23]

On Monday morning, 8 October, the long-awaited trials of the Fenian prisoners finally began. The small Toronto courtroom was completely filled when Mr. Justice John Wilson opened the proceedings. Mr. Justice Wilson briefly reviewed the history of the Fenian movement and deplored the Fenian activities and the American government's dubious conduct in the affair. Then he turned to the twelve jurors before him and remarked:

The accused are said to be chiefly of that young, reckless, unthinking class, but in part of an older and more depraved one, which are seen in the principal cities of the United States, and probably most of them joined this nefarious enterprise with the approbation of those to whom they naturally looked up, as a cause worthy of true manhood, the prosecution of which would yield, at least, excitement, and its consummation applause and renown. These considerations and others which they suggest will, I hope, tone down your minds to judicial calmness in the investigations now to come before you. Remember, the law presumes these men innocent, and your duty is to consider them so until, by legal evidence, their guilt appears.[24]

Mr. Justice Wilson then proceeded with the formal indictment, and turning to the prisoners he charged them "with having feloniously entered Upper Canada on the first and second days of June last and with the intent to levy war against Her Majesty, and with being found in arms against Her Majesty here." He now explained to the prisoners the legal implications of the charges, informing them that their conduct during the June invasion had made them liable to a court martial and probably death. Instead, they were now being given every opportunity to save their lives in a civilian court.

All the above charges referred to the prisoners who were not British subjects. Mr. Justice Wilson then explained that British subjects on trial would not only be charged with all previous indictments but also with treason. Thus the question of citizenship became an additional complicating factor in the trials of the Fenian prisoners. Finally, Mr. Justice Wilson again reminded the jury that the prisoners were to be considered innocent until proven guilty by due process of law, and that they should not show any bias in their deliberations. "Let the feeling of resentment find no place in your minds," were his concluding remarks to the jurors, not one of whom, incidentally, was a Roman Catholic.

The *Globe* (27 October) considered Wilson's charge "perfectly impartial," and even the *Irish Canadian* (12 October) called it "a most impartial document, conceived in a proper spirit, and delivered with a view to correct and tone down any prejudices that may have arisen in the community." Yet defense lawyer Matthew C. Cameron was quoted—in the *Globe*— complaining about the obvious partiality of the judge's charge to the jury.

On 24 October 1866, the first major trial began, with Mr. Justice John Wilson again presiding. The Crown had brought in the best prosecuting attorneys, including Solicitor-General James Cockburn and John Hillyard Cameron, Member of Parliament and Grand-Master of the Orange Lodge, while the defense had lined up its own top-flight talent, James Doyle, Richard Martin, and Matthew Crooks Cameron. The American consul in Toronto attended all sessions involving American citizens, while the United States government engaged two Toronto lawyers, and later another counselor from Detroit, to represent the interests of those imprisoned Fenians holding American citizenship.

The first man to be tried was Robert B. Lynch. J.H. Cameron opened the case for the Crown. He too talked at length about the history of the Fenian movement and condemned its attitude and conduct toward Canadians. Then he called upon several witnesses who identified the prisoner in the dock as one "Colonel Lynch," who had been in command of a group of Fenians at Fort Erie during the June invasion. Defense attorney Richard Martin conceded the point that his client had been present among the Fenian raiders at Fort Erie. But he argued that Lynch had not been a fighting Fenian; rather, he had only acted as a reporter. Several fellow prisoners then testified to support this contention. Martin also discredited one of the prosecution's star witnesses when he managed to have that man's own mother testify unfavorably about her son's honesty and reputation. Finally, the defense counsel brought up the possibility of an actual case of mistaken identity, since Colonel Hoey of New York apparently greatly resembled the accused prisoner. As a matter of fact, Martin argued, Robert Lynch was legally still a British subject, having been born in Ireland, and should therefore not have been charged as an alien.

The province's solicitor-general, the Honorable James Cockburn, presented the summation for the Crown. He emphasized the point that by his own admission Lynch was an American citizen and therefore quite properly charged. Furthermore, he insisted that enough evidence of Lynch's conduct had been presented, and that the story about "being a reporter" was a mere fabrication to save his life.

The jury, comprised of farmers and working men, deliberated only one and a half hours before returning with the verdict. Mr. Justice Wilson, ignoring the prisoner's pleas of innocence, then delivered a harsh verbal attack against Fenianism before sentencing Robert Lynch to hang on 13 December 1866. He did, however, allow the condemned man the right to appeal the verdict. The *Globe's* terse and smug commentary on 26 October was: "A more righteous sentence was never recorded."

John McMahon was the next prisoner in the dock. Again the prosecution insisted that the prisoner's mere presence at Fort Erie implied full complicity and therefore automatic guilt. Crown Attorney Robert A. Harrison produced several witnesses who testified that the accused man had not only been part of the marauders but had actually borne arms and given orders. The defense, surprisingly enough, called no witnesses of its own, but did cross-examine one of the Crown's witnesses, forcing him to admit that at the time in question he had been totally drunk, a state he seemed to maintain during the cross-examination.

Then Richard Martin explained that his client, who was a priest in Indiana, had actually been on his way to Montreal to look after a small legacy left by his brother when the Fenians captured him at Fort Erie and forced him to act as their chaplain. On their arrival in the village the Canadian militia had arrested him and accused him of being a member of the Brotherhood. There was no positive proof, argued Martin, that McMahon had ever been armed; in fact, he had apparently administered religious rites to soldiers on both sides. J.H. Cameron replied for the prosecution and insisted that the jury rely on the credibility of his witnesses, which included several officers and enlisted men of the Canadian militia. He questioned McMahon's "story" and asked the jury to return the only verdict possible, given the evidence.

Mr. Justice Wilson again charged the jury to perform its appointed duty. He also reminded them that a priest was no different from any other participant in the raid, and even if he had borne no arms himself, the mere fact of giving the enemy moral support was sufficient evidence of his guilt. The defense counsel immediately objected to the judge's last remarks. To everyone's surprise the objection was sustained and Mr. Justice Wilson did withdraw these particular directions to the jury. But surely the desired impact had already been made.

Within the hour the jury had brought in another verdict of guilty as charged. McMahon was also sentenced to hang on 13 December. The defendant took the verdict calmly but did remark: "If I was guilty, I would submit, but if you execute me, my blood will cry to heaven for vengeance upon those who are the cause of my death innocently."[25]

The first two trials and their guilty verdicts produced a strong reaction in the United States. The *Buffalo Courier* warned that if the Canadian government "spills a drop of Irish blood . . . a hundred Fenians will arise in place of one to avenge the execution of their comrade."[26] A mass rally of Fenians and all other "friends of liberty" was hurriedly called for Sunday evening, 28 October, in St. James Hall in Buffalo. Irishmen everywhere were asked to attend in order to see what could be done for the "Irish patriots [who] are about to be sacrificed on the altar of English despotism."[27] Meanwhile the *New York Daily News* resorted to its own unique brand of melodrama:

> Every drop of blood in the veins of the condemned man will breed a Fenian soldier. His martyrdom . . . will be worth armies to the cause of Ireland's independence. . . . Even as the sacrifice of Lucretia wrought the overthrow of the Kings of Rome, so may the immolation of that single Fenian bring war and desolation to the soil of Canada.[28]

The United States government now decided to intervene in the legal proceedings in Toronto. On 27 October Secretary of State William H. Seward, having been pressured from within the Republican party,[29] wrote a long dispatch addressed to Sir Frederick Bruce, hoping that the British government would intercede on behalf of the Fenian prisoners. After reviewing briefly the cases of Lynch and McMahon, and informing Bruce that the American government had asked its consul in Toronto to attend the trials, Seward made these comments: "It is the opinion of this Gov't [*sic*] that sound policy coincides with the best impulses of a benevolent nature in recommending tenderness, amnesty and forgiveness in such cases.[30] He concluded his comments by asking that "a policy of clemency and forgiveness in the case of the parties concerned" would surely be most appropriate.

However, not all Americans shared the same sentiments about the prisoners. The *Detroit Tribune*, for example, maintained that the prisoners had forfeited their lives by their own actions and deplored "the cowardly defences" put forward by the accused men. The *Chicago Tribune*, too, was convinced of the prisoners' guilt; however, it did suggest "a judicious exercise of clemency" at the present moment.[31]

Public reaction to Seward's remarkable diplomatic intervention was swift and generally harsh throughout British North America. Not only the Toronto press but also many newspapers in other provinces editorialized in no uncertain language. The editor of *Le Journal de Québec* (30 October 1866) praised the authorites in Canada West for the fairness and impartiality shown in the trials to date and concluded

> Nous espérons que le gouvernement de Sa Majesté se montrera dans les circonstances à la hauteur de ses droits, de sa dignité et de son honneur, et que quelles que soient les suites, s'il se laisse fléchir par la prière, il ne cédera jamais devant la menace.

Meanwhile Montreal's *La Minerve* (27 October 1866), having already stated that "ceux qui seront condamnés recevront le châtiment que mérite leur barbare conduite," mocked the "violentes protestations de nos voisins contre la condamnation à mort des prisonniers féniens," and publicly asked "si notre gouvernement va fléchir et prêter l'oreille aux conseils de la clémence?" (31 October). The *Halifax Morning Chronicle* (1 November 1866) observed that "this is an hour ... in which justice should be done though the heavens should fall," and then concluded:

> Should the Canadian authorities yield to external pressure, and allow their prisoners to go free, they will deserve the contempt of every honest man. . . . We believe in the present case not only the dignity of the British Empire, but the protection of its Colonies requires justice to be done.

And the *St. John Morning Telegraph* (3 November 1866) stated its position in these terms:

> It is to be hoped that Canadian Courts will deal with the convicts without reference either to England or the States. . . . We hope the sentence of the Courts will be firmly carried out, notwithstanding the rage of the American Fenians and the diplomacy of Mr. Seward.

Not all the newspapers demanded that Canadian justice be swift and always exact the supreme penalty. In fact, as early as 26 October the *Toronto Leader* had remarked that "we cannot hang all that may be found guilty; the prisoners are too numerous for that." About two weeks later the same paper suggested that "perhaps an admixture of royal clemency" might be handed out along with "punishment proportioned to their [Fenians'] crime."[32] Meanwhile the *Quebec Gazette* (2 November 1866) argued that "the public mind has considerably softened towards the poor misguided men . . . and few persons will desire a large holocaust of victims." And while the *Montreal Gazette* (5 November 1866) still pressed the government to do its duty and prevent further "harrying raids, such as those of last summer" by insisting that the letter of the law be carried out, the *Quebec Morning Chronicle* (29 October 1866) had already correctly predicted future events when it editorialized on Seward's diplomatic intervention:

> His appeal for the merciful treatment of the offenders will also, we have no doubt, be favourably considered, as he will be assured that on grounds of policy as well as humanity, it has long been the established practice of the British Government to treat convicted persons, whose offences are at all of a political character, with utmost clemency.

The thought of making the Fenian prisoners political martyrs, whose deaths would only serve to publicize and enhance the Fenian cause, weighed particularly heavy on the mind of the Canadian government. Governor-General Monck conveyed his own feelings and those of his ministers in the government to the Earl of Carnarvon in these words: "It is the unanimous opinion of my Council that the sentences of death in these cases [i.e., Lynch and McMahon] should not be carried into effect, and with that view I entirely concur."[33] Thomas D'Arcy McGee, long known for his strong anti-Fenian sentiment, was fully convinced of the guilt of the convicted prisoners, but he publicly expressed the hope that their punishment might be tempered with mercy. "These men deserve death," he told a large Irish audience at a concert in Montreal on 14 November, but then slowly added—just as the hissing in the audience subsided—that "the spirit of our times is opposed to capital punishment."[34]

The *Irish Canadian* (2 November 1866), however, complained that justice had hardly been done in the cases of Lynch and McMahon. The paper now accused Mr. Justice Wilson of lacking proper impartiality and taking "advantage of his position to heap coals of fire upon the heads of those whom he was so soon to condemn to death." Furthermore, it was again pointed out that not a single Roman Catholic had been selected for jury duty, and that the accused men had not been able to avail themselves of such crucial witnesses as Colonel O'Neill and Colonel Starr because these Fenian leaders would be arrested upon stepping on Canadian soil.

In the meantime the trials of the Fenian prisoners had continued in Toronto. One of the accused men, the Reverend David Lumsden, formerly of Trinity Church in Syracuse, New York, was acquitted when his brilliant defense lawyer, Matthew Cameron, was able to prove by way of reliable witnesses that Lumsden had actually tried to induce the citizens of Fort Erie to resist the Fenian raiders even though he acted as the chaplain of the Fenian force. Perhaps the fact that his wife made a personal plea for mercy in the courtroom and that Lumsden was a "Protestant" may well have influenced the Canadian jurors.[35]

Other prisoners did not regain their freedom so easily, and when the court began its Christmas recess, seven men had been sentenced to hang on 13 December 1866: Robert Lynch, John McMahon, William Slavin, William Hayden, Daniel Whalen, John Quinn, and Thomas School.[36] The punishment seemed harsh, but when John A. Macdonald, the attorney general of the province, was asked by Bishop Lynch of Toronto to re-examine the evidence, he replied: "I do not think I have any right to interfere." To another correspondent, Macdonald wrote that the fate of the Fenian prisoners "is now concerning Imperial as well as Colonial interests and will be dealt with, I have no doubt, properly by the higher powers.[37] He then prepared to sail for England to participate in the London Conference scheduled to begin in early December.

The matter of punishment of the convicted prisoners had indeed become a matter of concern for the British government by this time. As early as 12 November the colonial secretary had telegraphed Governor-General Monck and asked him to "spare the lives of the convicts in question, but do not settle commutation of their sentences till you hear again."[38] Less than two weeks later, Monck received these final instructions from the Earl of Carnarvon:

I have therefore thought it my duty to recommend to Her Majesty to extend Her prerogative of mercy to the Prisoners Lynch and McMahon now lying under sentence of Death, and to commute the sentence to twenty years of Penal servitude or imprisonment as the Law of Canada may warrant you in assigning.[39]

It seems quite clear that Britain was not willing to risk any complications in her own sensitive relations with the United States at this time, and since the American government had spoken out on behalf of the Fenian prisoners, a policy of clemency was adopted. Without doubt, international diplomacy had much to do with saving the lives of the convicted Fenians.

The prisoners, however, were not yet officially informed of the commutations. Governor-General Monck at first merely granted the condemned men a respite till 13 March 1867, and although the seven men awaiting death in the Toronto jail must have experienced a moment of immeasurable relief, their leaders in the United States, who had already heard of the British policy of clemency, did not entirely welcome the commutations. Fenian leaders like William Roberts had in fact been quite prepared to see one or more of their followers hanged by the Canadian authorities, for they were convinced that such executions would provide the fading Fenian cause with instant martyrs who, in the words of one observer, would "give them [Fenians] further material for agitation."[40] When William Roberts informed Robert Lynch by letter that clemency would probably be shown for all the condemned men, he revealed this "remarkable" Fenian logic:

> I regret to tell you that you are not going to be hanged. So great a crime upon a non-combatant like yourself would make every Irishman in America a Fenian, and furnish our exchequer with the necessary means to clear Canada of English authority in short order. . . . Therefore I say I regret that you will not be hanged.[41]

The American government did make public its efforts on behalf of the Fenian prisoners when President Johnson, in his Annual Message to Congress on 3 December, revealed that his administration had made representations to the British government on behalf of the convicted men. Johnson then expressed the hope that "an enlightened and humane judgment, will . . . induce in their cases an exercise of clemency and a judicious amnesty to all who were engaged in the movement."[42] This appeal was probably made more for public consumption than anything else, for the Canadian and British authorities had already made their final decisions.

A much less publicized trial of Fenian prisoners had taken place in Sweetsburg, Canada East, at about the same time.[43] In the prisoner's dock were sixteen Fenians who had been captured during the raids along the Missisquoi frontier. The trial lasted throughout most of the month of December, until Mr. Justice G.G. Johnson sentenced three men—Thomas Madden, Thomas Smith, and Michael Crowley—to hang on 15 February 1867.[44] This small number of convictions so angered the *Toronto Globe* that on 5 January 1867 it called for a special parliamentary investigation.

However, on the last day of 1866 the Canadian government officially commuted all death penalties of the ten convicted Fenians,[45] and on 3 January 1867 they were all sentenced to twenty years hard labor in the Provincial Penitentiary at Kingston. Lieutenant-General Sir John Michel, who was the acting head of government while Governor-General Monck was attending the London Conference, informed the Earl of Carnarvon on 4 January about the final arrangements, and he promised "to make special provision for the safe keeping of the prisoners in the Penitentiary at Kingston by stationing there some Volunteer Militia in addition to the ordinary garrison of regular troops."[46]

On 12 January the trials of the remaining Fenian prisoners in Toronto commenced. By the end of the month, another fourteen Fenians had been sentenced to death: Patrick Norton, Timothy Kiley, John Rogan, John O'Connor, Patrick O'Neill, Daniel Quinn, Peter Ledwith, Michael Purtell, Barney Dunn, John Gallagher, Owen Kennedy, Thomas Cooney, Thomas Maxwell, and James Burke.[47] But not surprisingly the sentences of these men too were commuted to twenty years hard labor. One prisoner still had his case pending. On some technical grounds an appeal was made by Patrick Magrath to the court of the Queen's Bench. Yet the delay did not save Magrath and he also was sentenced to hang; he, too, however, was saved from the gallows and on 7 June 1867 he joined his comrades in Kingston to begin serving a twenty year sentence.[48]

The Fenian trials were finally over. It had cost the country nearly $37,000 to carry out justice and convict a total of twenty-five accused Fenians. Yet not one of these men completed his twenty-year term in Kingston. All but one man were eventually pardoned and returned home to the United States. Thomas Maxwell died in prison on 24 September 1869, while still in his early twenties.[49]

The first recipient of a government pardon was John O'Connor, who was released on 4 April 1867, just a little more than a month after his arrival in Kingston. The next man to leave his prison cell was John McMahon, who won his freedom on 22 July 1869, largely as a result of some active representations made by several prominent persons, including Archbishop Thomas Connolly of Halifax. Prime Minister Sir John A. Macdonald explained his action in a letter to the archbishop, printed in the *Montreal Gazette* on 24 July 1869. Macdonald noted that the Canadian government owed "a debt of gratitude" to the Catholic clergy, who had "spared no pains to prevent the spread of the Fenian organization through the Provinces." Therefore the Canadian government, fully appreciative of these actions and aware of Connolly's sentiments about McMahon, "has the honour to recommend that the remainder of the sentence of the prisoner be remitted, and that he be discharged."

John McMahon's pardon prompted Archbishop Joseph Lynch of Toronto to write the prime minister about the release of all the other remaining prisoners in Kingston.[50] Macdonald did not react immediately, but on 30 May 1870 William Slavin received his pardon. The first Fenian to be convicted, Robert B. Lynch, was released next, on 6 April 1871. The last prisoner to walk out of his Kingston cell was Daniel Whalen, who was freed on 26 July 1872.[51]

In concluding this account of the Fenian prisoners, it is perhaps interesting to remark how well several of them felt they had been treated while in the Kingston Penitentiary. Warden John Creighton was apparently most kind and understanding toward his unique crew of political prisoners. Robert Lynch wrote Creighton after he had returned home to Chicago in April 1871, expressing his "deepest felt gratitude to you—which I shall always remember."[52] And Peter Ledwith expressed a similar admiration and respect for Warden Creighton in a letter written from Louisville, Kentucky, dated 15 March 1872, less than two months after his release from jail:

> There is going to be great doings and sayings on St. Patrick's Day here. I am to be presented with a complimentary ticket to the Banquet that night. It is expected I will say something about my confinement while in Prison. I know they would like to raise some excitement for speculation, but I am going to disappoint them very much. I reckon there will be enough of spouters besides your humble servant. In fact Frank if I did say anything about Prison Rules and Prison treatment—especially since that noble Warden Mr. Creighton took his place there, I could not say anything but what was gentlemanly towards him, for I give you my word of honor I love and esteem him the same as if he was my own Father or Brother.[53]

Not every pardoned Fenian prisoner had such kind words to say about Kingston Penitentiary and its warden. John McMahon, for example, who had been released before John Creighton became warden of the penitentiary, lost little time in appearing publicly in several American cities while "reciting the story of his persecutions in Canada."[54]

Canadian justice, in spite of popular demands for violent revenge from a small segment of the Canadian community, had declined to exact its "pound of flesh." A policy of calculated leniency toward the convicted Fenian prisoners prevented them from becoming the political martyrs, which the sagging fortunes of the Fenian movement so badly needed. The wisdom of this policy probably did much to ensure the early demise of the Fenian Brotherhood.

12

CONFEDERATION

AND THE RENEWAL

OF FENIAN ACTIVITIES

During the final months of 1866, the Confederation scheme had taken on a renewed sense of urgency. The British government was at last ready to deal with the proposed union of its four British North American colonies, and Canadians were now far more concerned with events at Westminster than with the activities of Fenians south of the border.

On 4 December, the initial session of the London Conference was held. The Canadian delegation, led by John A. Macdonald, George E. Cartier, Alexander T. Galt, Charles Tupper, and Samuel L. Tilley, opened the discussions by presenting the Quebec Resolutions to the British authorities. It was already Christmas Eve when the first draft of the British North America Act was finally prepared by the imperial law officers, and further discussions were required during late January 1867. Several more revisions were made before the British North America Act was given its first reading in the House of Lords on 12 February 1867.

The second reading of the Act followed exactly one week later, and it was then that Lord Carnarvon tried to impress upon his peers that the bill in question was "one of the largest and most important measures which for many years it has been the duty of any Colonial Minister in this country to submit to Parliament."[1] He argued that the few existing disadvantages of the scheme were far outweighed by the advantages it provided, most notably in such matters as defense, trade, and commerce. Lord Carnarvon rejected the pleas of the Canadian anti-Confederation movement for delay of the measure by suggesting that the union of the provinces was urgently needed, because these British provinces "stand to each other almost in the relation of foreign States."[2]

The bill passed the House of Lords without any serious opposition, and on 26 February it was read for the first time in the House of Commons. Here it was managed by the under-secretary for the colonies, C.B. Adderley, who expressed his belief that a British North American Union would not only be materially beneficial but would also enable the colonies "to keep the peace, and . . . remove every temptation to aggression."[3] Despite some half-hearted opposition from John Bright and a few others, the bill passed all three readings successfully and on 29 March it received the royal assent. The Dominion of Canada had finally been born.

Yet it was hardly a joyous event for the Canadian delegates watching in the parliamentary galleries. England had fulfilled her obligation and passed the constitutional measure creating the new Dominion, but her enthusiasm and interest left much to be desired. Canadians experienced a definite feeling of being unwanted. As early as 14 January, A.T. Galt had raised this point in a letter to his wife: "I am more than ever disappointed at the tone of feeling here as to the Colonies. . . . I cannot shut my eyes to the fact that they want to get rid of us."[4] John A. Macdonald himself could not help but remark that "the Union was treated by them much as if the British North America Act was a private Bill uniting two or three English parishes."[5] Even Joseph Howe, still unconvinced of the merits of the "Botheration Scheme," as he called it, correctly analyzed the motives for Britain's eagerness to create the new Dominion. "The fact is," wrote Howe, "they think only of themselves, and having made up their minds that the Provinces are a source of peril and expense to them—the prevailing idea is to set them adrift . . . and to leave them to defend themselves if they can."[6]

These exact sentiments were soon expressed by the *Times* (London, 1 March 1867) in an editorial about Canadian confederation:

> We look to Confederation as the means of relieving this country from much expense and much embarrassment. . . . We appreciate the goodwill of the Canadians and their desire to maintain their relations with the British Crown. But a people of four millions ought to be able to keep their own defences.

The high cost of defending the colonies was indeed one of the major reasons for Britain's continuous attempts to withdraw from North America. In the spring of 1867 there were over 15,000 British troops in North America, and the military expenditures of the previous year had amounted to the staggering sum of £622,000.[7] Such outlays of men and money appeared increasingly anomalous to many Englishmen. The Canadian desire to form a new nation seemed an ideal means for British statesmen to relieve the English taxpayers of what they felt was an unnecessary expense. Once united, British North America surely would be able to defend itself.[8]

During the spring of 1867 the people of British North America were so preoccupied with the progress of confederation that the affairs of the Fenian Brotherhood were pushed to the background. Periodic reports of Fenian activities in the United States continued to be printed in Canadian newspapers, but the urgency of past Fenian threats was now missing. Canadians gave less and less consideration to the Brotherhood.

But Fenianism had not disappeared entirely from the scene. Another abortive rising took place in Ireland on 5 March 1867, and the remnants of the O'Mahony wing of the American Fenian movement, now led by John Savage, made a belated attempt to assist in the revolt. In mid-April, a vessel loaded with five thousand guns, three small artillery pieces, and a great deal of ammunition set sail for Ireland, its cargo well hidden in piano cases, sewing machines, and wine barrels. The consignment labels had been addressed to a Cuban port in order to clear customs, and several dozen Fenian soldiers boarded the vessel, rechristened the *Erin's Hope*, after she cleared New York harbor. But the expedition turned into a fruitless venture, for the March uprising in Ireland had been quickly suppressed by British authorities. When the *Erin's Hope* reached Ireland on 23 May, she could not land her men and materials, and consequently returned to America. Meanwhile, the Roberts wing of the American Fenians was not prepared to abandon its struggle against the British foe, and in May 1867, another Fenian congress met in Troy. Immediately Canadians expected another invasion, and soon the familiar rumors circulated that battle plans were being drawn up by the Brotherhood, and that another raid was in the making.[9] But no raids materialized. In fact, President Roberts decided to spend the next few months in Europe before calling another congress for September in Cleveland. It had become apparent that the Brotherhood needed money if it was to do anything. William Roberts was painfully aware of his organization's financial plight, for less than $20,000 was currently in the Fenian treasury[10] and without additional funds, future raids were completely out of the question. But Roberts's hopes for more cash were never fulfilled and he expressed his wish to resign. He was obviously convinced that the Fenian movement would never again be able to attempt another massive invasion of Canada. The hero of Ridgeway, John O'Neill, was elected to succeed Roberts as the president of the Fenian Brotherhood as of 1 January 1868.

O'Neill encountered the same problems experienced by his predecessor. The constant lack of funds hampered the activities of the organization at every turn. An attempt to reunite with the old O'Mahony wing of the Brotherhood failed, and a third Fenian faction, led by Michael Scanlan, had appeared as well to further divide the weakened Fenian movement.

Nevertheless, the government of Canada continued to keep a watchful eye on all Fenian activities. Not only their own detectives, but a number of planted spies and Fenian traitors provided the Canadian authorities with a constant flow of information.[11] The newly knighted Sir John A. Macdonald, now the Dominion's first prime minister, did not ignore the possibility of another raid. In early February 1868 he wrote Colonel Edward Ermatinger: "The United States are now convulsed with the presidential election contest, and excitement will continue until next December. Both Republicans and Democrats will fish for the Irish vote and therefore will wink as much as possible at any action of the Fenian body."[12] And several weeks later, Sir Edward Thornton, the British minister in Washington, was instructed by his government to call the attention of the United States government to the continuing Fenian activities within its borders,[13] which might well endanger the fragile relations between Britain and the United States.

In June 1868, Canadians were aroused from their preoccupation with domestic affairs when the *Toronto Globe* (10 and 27 June 1868) reported that another Fenian invasion was about to take place and called upon the authorities to be "semper paratus." But this alarm, like so many others, proved to be false.

President O'Neill sought to rally his followers during the seventh Fenian congress in Philadelphia from 24 to 29 November 1868. One month earlier, the British vice-consul in New York, J. P. Edwards, had remarked in a dispatch to Governor-General Monck: "O'Neill appears to be thoroughly earnest in his intentions to undertake a hostile movement in the Spring on as large a scale as may be practicable."[14] Just before the Philadelphia congress met, O'Neill had sent out an earnest plea to all Irish-Americans, urging them to redouble their efforts on behalf of their homeland now that "the sacred work" seemed to be on "the eve of consummation." The circular concluded:

> Any sacrifice is not too great that will help to achieve the liberation of one's native land; the proud satisfaction of having co-operated in breaking the shackles from her limbs is an abundant recompense for all labors undergone, all hardships encountered. Besides brothers, the sky of our future seems bright with hope, as the clouds of opposition are disappearing, one after the other, from its horizon.[15]

Considering the past failures and misfortunes experienced by the Fenian Brotherhood, it is hard to accuse its leaders of a lack of enthusiasm. Yet time was running out for them.

Whereas the Brotherhood's optimism may have been unlimited, its financial assets were extremely limited. In fact, a grand total of only $4746.36 was in the organization's treasury at the end of 1868.[16] Thus it is chiefly due to the absence of sufficient funds that no Fenian raid took place during this period. Whatever money was contributed tended to disappear in the seemingly bottomless pit of the Fenian headquarters in New York.

During the summer of 1869 Consul Archibald reported renewed Fenian activity. At another convention held in Pittsburgh from 29 June to 2 July, President O'Neill and his senate agreed to launch another raid into Canada. On 12 July Archibald wrote John A. Macdonald: "I am now enabled to say that a movement on Canada has been positively decided on."[17] And before long, President O'Neill was reported to be traveling about trying to secure financial support. A special $10 levy on all members of the Brotherhood was called for by the Brotherhood's executive. And in early September, O'Neill set the invasion date "on or about the first of October; provided the requisite means are forthcoming."[18] Not surprisingly, the necessary funds were never collected, and another invasion plan had to be discarded. The total amount in the Fenian treasury at the end of November 1869 was only $1129.58.[19] This was hardly enough to pay the salaries of the headquarters staff for the following month.

The repeated failures to raise sufficient funds for another raid on Canada greatly diminished the militancy of the Fenian senate. In fact, the senators now began to oppose the idea of another attack upon Canada; in light of the chronic lack of men and money any future effort appeared utterly useless. John O'Neill, however, refused to accept their decision, and soon began to quarrel with the senate's leaders, P.J. Meehan and James Gibbons, over the movement's future policies. By late February 1870, the conflict between president and senate began to reach the crisis stage. On 8 February, President O'Neill had issued another "call-to-arms" from his headquarters at 10 West Fourth Street in New York City. He appealed "To the Officers and Members of Circles now in bad standing on the books of these Headquarters" to return to the fold and "to go earnestly and zealously to work" for the cause of Irish liberty. O'Neill had urged them to join in a final "practical endeavor to solve the problem of Irish Independence."[20] The senate, now furious, renewed its attempts to weaken O'Neill's influence.

O'Neill in return sought to oust some uncooperative senators from their positions. But one of his followers, Secretary for Civil Affairs Patrick Keenan, shot and wounded Senator Meehan during an argument, and O'Neill had no choice but to deplore Keenan's stupid act.[21] The repercussions of the incident were totally unfavorable to O'Neill. There was talk of his impeachment, and he was forced to consent to the senate's immediate demand for another Fenian convention in Chicago on 11 April, to decide once and for all the merits of another Canadian venture.

Yet as the immediate shock of the Meehan shooting wore off, O'Neill resumed his private war with the senate. First he transferred the locale of the planned Fenian convention from Chicago to New York City, where he originally had sought to hold the congress. He justified his decision by arguing that New York was much more accessible to most members of the Brotherhood than Chicago. Then he lashed out against the senate in another circular:

> For a long time now I have been convinced that the Senate as a body, did not mean to fight. I have felt that it was the purpose of its members to have the organization live on indefinitely, so that they might profit politically through their prominent connection with it, and to prolong its *inactive* life, the scheme of holding the Congress in Chicago or some other point far West was hit upon. Those interested knowing full well that the people could not be represented at said Congress, and that consequently they, holding the power, could make speedy fight impracticable.[22]

Thus on 19 April, O'Neill held his own convention in New York City and his followers gave him a carte blanche to prepare for another invasion.

Yet O'Neill's triumph was a hollow victory, for the supporters of the senate had met separately in Chicago on 11 April to confirm their earlier opposition to further raids into Canada. Not since the O'Mahony-Roberts split in early 1866 had the Fenian Brotherhood experienced such bitter dissension.

The Fenian organization now seemed indeed to rest on shaky foundations not only in Ireland but also in the United States. The movement had suffered one setback after another in the last few years. Its only moment of good fortune had been the death of Thomas D'Arcy McGee, the man whose bitter attacks on Fenianism had earned him the Brotherhood's undying enmity. McGee was murdered in the early morning hours of 7 April 1868, as he returned from a late night session of the Canadian House of Commons to his lodgings at Mrs. Trotter's boarding house in Ottawa.[23]

The alleged assassin was an Irishman named Patrick Whelan, and when the police searched his room they found pictures of several Fenian leaders as well as other evidence of pro-Fenian sympathies. Much of the evidence, although circumstantial, pointed to Whelan as the murderer. Particularly incriminating was the fact that during his arrest Whelan was carrying a recently fired revolver alleged to be of the same caliber as the one that had inflicted the lethal wound in McGee's neck. Patrick Whelan was found guilty by the jury and executed—all the while protesting his innocence.

It is doubtful that the Fenian Brotherhood had actually conspired to murder McGee, even though he was Fenianism's most vocal enemy in Canada. Although there apparently had been a price placed on McGee's head as early as the spring of 1866,[24] the deed itself appears to have been the result of an individual's personal vendetta rather than a movement's organized conspiracy. The Canadian government was never able to prove a direct connection between Whelan and the Fenian Brotherhood. A recent study of Whelan's trial concludes that "there was no conclusive evidence that James Whelan was the assassin."[25]

John O'Neill now decided to go ahead with his own Canadian invasion scheme and began to mobilize his forces on 28 April 1870. Orders were issued to all circles to be ready to move at a moment's notice to various points along the Canadian-American frontier. Queen Victoria's birthday, 24 May, was designated as the day of O'Neill's second invasion of Canadian territory. By mid-May, formal marching orders were issued, and Fenian soldiers were asked to leave their home bases immediately and assemble at either Malone, New York, or St. Albans, Vermont.

Interestingly enough, O'Neill ordered all his followers to leave for their border destinations simultaneously, regardless of whether they came from such nearby places as Boston and Buffalo or from more distant points like St. Louis and New Orleans. This maneuver, O'Neill felt, would camouflage the imminent invasion, and the tardy arrival of some Fenian troops at the border would not seriously affect the overall success of the undertaking. O'Neill was convinced that the Fenians from New England alone could hold their own until everyone had arrived on the scene.[26]

The Canadian government had prepared itself for this raid since the early days of April. It had expected O'Neill to launch his second attack upon Canada even before the Fenians met at their New York convention, for information had been received from various sources during late March and early April that the Fenians were once more on the move. Governor-General Sir John Young, expecting the attack on 15 April, had even ordered the minister of militia and defense to call out several volunteer units on 9 April. Young then had contacted Sir Edward Thornton and informed him of the defensive actions the Canadian government had taken.

Meanwhile the American government once again took an equivocating position vis-à-vis this renewal of Fenian activities. Although General Meade personally recommended the immediate seizure of all Fenian arms and ammunition stored along various frontier points, President Ulysses S. Grant saw no need to hurry and bluntly remarked that "the British did not seize or stop the Alabama."[27] Hamilton Fish, secretary of state in the Grant administration, explained that while his department was well aware of the Fenian activities and had, in fact, communicated all pertinent information to Sir Edward Thornton, "no law authorizes their seizure ... without evidence of intent to use the arms improperly."[28]

The invasion expected by Canadians on 15 April of course did not occur. O'Neill still had too many problems, not the least of which was an inadequate supply of men and money. The Fenian president felt he required at least 10,000 men and $50,000 before a successful campaign could be waged against Canada.[29]

Consequently the people and authorities of Canada once again relaxed and considered the latest Fenian scare as merely another rumor without firm basis. The incessant talking and planning of the Fenians seemed once more to have fizzled out. Therefore by the end of April, most of the militia forces on frontier duty had been ordered to return home.

During early May, rumors again circulated that O'Neill was actively organizing in northern New York and Vermont. But few people seemed to notice or care very much. After all, this kind of activity had been continuing for a long time, and one did not get overly excited by such rumors. But the Fenians were at last ready for action and their constant talk of invasion again became a reality for Canadians; for the second time in four years Canada was to be invaded. On Sunday, 22 May, Gilbert McMicken sent a memorandum to Sir George Etienne Cartier, the minister of militia and defense: "From three distinct sources of information I am positively assured that an attack by the Fenians will be made on our Frontier on Wednesday night next or Thursday at farthest. . . . The main attack will be East of Lake Champlain. . . . The other attack is to be by way of Malone advancing on the line bearing upon Huntingdon."[30] Cartier and his colleagues, Lieutenant-General Sir James Lindsay, who commanded all Her Majesty's forces in Canada, and the commissioner of the dominion police, J.C. Coursol, reacted swiftly to McMicken's information. All commanding officers in the areas affected by the imminent Fenian invasion were immediately informed of these developments and put on the alert.

Meanwhile the scheduled festivities to honor the queen's birthday got under way in Montreal on Tuesday, 24 May. Most of the officers and men of the various militia regiments assembled in the city were not aware that their parade would turn into something much more serious. Cartier had followed Gilbert McMicken's advice and decided to remain silent about the actual day of the expected invasion until Victoria Day, hoping that his secrecy would inflict a more decisive defeat upon the Fenian invaders.

Early morning showers forced the cancellation of the military parade, but to everyone's surprise, the volunteers were ordered to remain armed and ready while further orders were awaited from Ottawa. Something was obviously happening and every soldier knew it. As rumors spread that the Fenians were about to attack in the Missisquoi and Huntingdon frontier districts the city began to buzz with excitement and anticipation. Yet many citizens also wondered whether this was the real thing or merely another Fenian scare.

In the early afternoon the wild rumors were finally confirmed as the volunteer force was informed by Lieutenant-Colonel Osborne Smith that the Fenians had indeed appeared, and that several companies would be required for immediate frontier duty. The volunteers were ordered to return quickly to their homes to get adequate food and supplies before returning to the Champ de Mars by 4 P.M.

The six companies selected by Lieutenant-Colonel Smith began to march to the railroad station to the music of two military bands. Hundreds of citizens lined the streets and thronged the railway station as the volunteers prepared to board a train for St. Jean, where they would be sent off to various strategic frontier positions.

In the meantime, the Toronto press was expressing its concern about the danger that might ensue if the Fenians were to join with the rebellious Métis, a French Canadian-Indian minority fighting to retain a unique way of life in the Red River colony.[31] These reports did have some factual basis, for John O'Neill's master plan did call for Fenians from the western United States to give assistance to Louis Riel, the Métis leader, if he chose to fight.[32]

13

THE FINAL RAIDS

As early as 10 February 1870, Governor-General Young echoed the sentiments of many Canadians when he expressed the hope that the Fenians would finally launch another attack on Canada. Canadians were becoming annoyed at the periodic bursts of Fenian activity that never materialized into actual raids. They were getting tired of the constant rumors of raids which forced them to make unwanted expenditures to keep the volunteer units in readiness for the anticipated attack. The government and people of the new Dominion were prepared "to give the raiders a lesson which will not easily be forgotten."[1] If only the Fenians would appear!

The Dominion of Canada was much better prepared to deal with any Fenian raid in 1870 than the old Province of Canada had been four years earlier. The reforms contained in the Militia Act of October 1868 (as well as those carried out in the aftermath of the '66 raids) had created an "active militia" of 40,000 men, all adequately armed and equipped, well drilled, and under a unified command. Together with the remnant of British regulars, this force of defenders would prove formidable to any Fenian raiders.

Furthermore, the Canadian authorities were still amazingly well informed about the latest activities of the Fenian Brotherhood. The espionage system created by Gilbert McMicken in the mid-1860s worked in a superb manner, and when the McMicken "detectives" were unable to ferret out some important details, the British minister, Sir Edward Thornton, had his own "sources" from which he could draw crucial information. In fact, the Fenian movement continued to be weakened by traitors and spies. Rudolph Fitzpatrick was still a most reliable source of information for Consul Archibald in New York City, and Gilbert McMicken received detailed reports of all the latest Fenian activities from Henri Le Caron, a man who became John O'Neill's trusted aide and friend while acting as a British spy from June 1868.[2]

Thus being better defended and always aware of the latest plans of the Fenian leadership, the Canadian government could await any Fenian venture with complete confidence. Yet in spite of this situation, the attack on 25 May did create a minor panic among government officials and the citizens of the frontier regions of Canada.

John O'Neill's campaign strategy was much simpler than the elaborate scheme devised by Thomas Sweeny in 1865–66. O'Neill's immediate military objective was to gain a firm foothold on Canadian soil. This, he felt, was the crucial point. If successful, the action would cement many Fenian sympathizers in the United States and Canada to the Fenian cause.

To accomplish his goal, O'Neill planned to capture the towns of St. Jean and Richmond, south of the St. Lawrence down river from Montreal. Possession of these key points would give the Fenians full control over the railroad lines running through them toward the frontier. The Fenian forces were then to converge upon this occupied area from various directions, some from Malone in the west, some from Rouses Point, New York, in the south, and others from Franklin, Vermont, in the east. Diversionary raids were planned in the Lake Erie region and the Red River colony. But O'Neill's invasion plan was never really implemented.[3] While sufficient arms and ammunition were available this time, the anticipated number of Fenian soldiers again failed to appear. For example, O'Neill expected over 1000 men from the state of Massachusetts, but when he met the morning train from Boston at the St. Albans railroad station, less than 50 men stepped down. Similarly, the contingent from Vermont and northeastern New York amounted to fewer than 100 men, less than one-sixth of the expected number.

Therefore the Fenian leader was forced to alter his campaign strategy. He abandoned the attempt to occupy St. Jean and Richmond, for his lack of manpower made this portion of the scheme completely unfeasible. Instead, O'Neill, still counting on at least 1500 Fenians to appear from various eastern states, decided to concentrate all his available manpower at Franklin. From here he would cross the border and establish a firm foothold on Canadian territory. The original plan called for the Fenians to enter Canada during the night of 24 May or early the following morning, then to occupy Eccles Hill, from which they could defend their position with relative ease. However, the Fenian Army was still in Franklin in the early morning hours of Wednesday, 25 May, because O'Neill had postponed the invasion to await the arrival of 200 New York Fenians who had appeared in St. Albans late Tuesday night. This short delay would soon prove disastrous to O'Neill's expedition.

The Fenians were not only troubled by a shortage of manpower during the critical hours of 24–25 May, but they were also being confronted again by the American authorities. President Grant issued a neutrality proclamation and warned "all good citizens of the United States and all persons within the territory and jurisdiction of the United States against aiding, countenancing, abetting, or taking part in such unlawful proceedings"[4] as were presently being undertaken along the Canadian frontier. Furthermore, federal marshals in the troubled areas were ordered to arrest all persons breaking America's neutrality laws. In fact, U.S. Marshal George Foster and a deputy actually appeared in the Fenian camp at Franklin and read Grant's proclamation to the astonished Fenian soldiers, who quickly formed a wall to protect O'Neill, fearing that he might be arrested on the spot. General John Donnelly then told the marshal that he had already seen the document and Foster quickly left the camp, after requesting that the main road not be blocked by the Fenian force.

Shortly before noon, O'Neill decided he could delay no longer, and with a force of less than 200 men he moved toward the border. As his small army reached the Canadian frontier, it once again encountered George Foster. The marshal had been on the Canadian side, and he now told the Fenians that Canadian defenders were already deployed on Eccles Hill and that they would open fire on the Fenians as soon as they cleared the next hill. His advice was acknowledged but not heeded. The Fenians now discarded their baggage and heavy overcoats and quickly prepared to do battle.

Meanwhile the Canadian militia had established a commanding position on Eccles Hill. Although Lieutenant-Colonel Brown Chamberlin had less than 100 men at his disposal at this moment, most of them were excellent riflemen and they were well hidden and protected. Marshal Foster had warned Chamberlin of the Fenians' approach, and knowing that ample reserves would soon appear, the Canadians calmly awaited the enemy.

Then the Fenians came. But as the first skirmishers sent out by O'Neill reached the small creek that ran below Eccles Hill and sought to cross the wooden bridge that spanned it, the Canadians opened fire. One Fenian was immediately killed and another badly wounded, and within minutes the Fenian vanguard was retreating toward O'Neill's field headquarters, located several hundred yards to the rear. O'Neill frantically tried to order his men back into battle, but the rifle fire from the hill continued to harass the Fenians.

One more soldier was killed and two others wounded while the disorganized raiders hastened for cover in a wooded area below the Canadian position. The Fenians began firing wildly into the rocks and trees that hid the Canadians, but before long they realized that their position had become untenable.[5]

John O'Neill desperately sought to calm his men, but his pleas and orders were now falling on deaf ears. Reluctantly he ordered his terrified followers to fall back far enough to be out of range of the Canadian riflemen. Then, according to his own account, he lashed into his motley crew of soldiers: "Men of Ireland, I am ashamed of you. You have acted disgracefully today; but you will have another chance of showing whether you are cravens or not. Comrades, we must not, we dare not go back with the stain of cowardice on us."[6] John O'Neill was not yet ready to admit defeat. He still hoped for the arrival of the large contingent of New York Fenians. He was convinced that these reinforcements, which consisted of many old veterans, would steady his young followers while increasing his total strength and firepower.

When no reinforcements appeared, O'Neill finally decided to look for his missing soldiers in person; however, he managed to find only one of his men lying, badly wounded, in a farmhouse. Shortly after he emerged from this house, he was once again confronted by Marshal Foster and his deputy Thomas Failey, who had been patiently observing the fighting at Eccles Hill and had followed O'Neill to the farmhouse. The two officials now seized the opportunity to arrest the Fenian leader, who, for the second time in four years, had openly violated the neutrality laws of the United States.

The arrest itself had overtones of a comic opera. Foster confronted O'Neill as he emerged from the house and shook hands with the Fenian president before ordering him into a waiting carriage and warning the prisoner not to shout for help if they passed any Fenians on the road. Then the driver whipped the horses into motion and the carriage headed away from the border. Marshal Foster kept a sharp eye on O'Neill and threatened to seize him by the throat if the Fenian leader called out for help. Suddenly, as the horses and carriage sped toward the jail in Burlington, Vermont, the tardy Fenian contingent from New York appeared on the road. O'Neill, however, kept silent and remained unrecognized by his fellow Fenians, who merely stared in amazement at the wild coach and driver that enshrouded them in a cloud of dust. When news of O'Neill's arrest reached his soldiers, they knew it was all over. And after a short council meeting, most of the Fenians decided to give up the battle. Some of the braver souls talked about heading to Malone, but most only wanted to go home.

By mid-afternoon the Canadian defenders had grown in numbers. Lieutenant-Colonel Osborne Smith, who had headed for Stanbridge before noon, hurried back to Eccles Hill and was soon joined by the Montreal cavalry unit, the Victoria Rifles, and a detachment of Missisquoi volunteers. Early in the evening, the Canadian forces emerged from their cover and marched toward the enemy lines. Several Fenian stragglers were flushed from their hiding places and taken prisoner. Some Canadians were so elated by their easy victory that they were talking of crossing the border to chase the Fenians. Lieutenant-Colonel Smith, however, prevented this, thereby avoiding potential friction with the American authorities who, after all, had been most helpful on that particular day.

Thus by the evening of 25 May, the "Battle of Eccles Hill" was over. The Canadians were jubilant. They had won a decisive victory over the Fenians and had suffered not a single casualty. The Fenians, however, had been badly beaten. Four or five of their men had been killed and fifteen others had been wounded.[7] Unlike the Ridgeway campaign in 1866, the fight at Eccles Hill had proved to be a glorious experience for the Canadian volunteers and a humiliating defeat for the Fenians.

While most of the disillusioned Fenians in the St. Albans area now started for home, the more boisterous decided to take the train for Malone where a group of battle-scarred veterans was said to be ready for action. Meanwhile John O'Neill was already languishing in a Burlington jail cell because he could not raise the $20,000 bail imposed by a local judge.

But like their comrades at Eccles Hill, the Fenians at Malone were unsuccessful. About 450 men crossed the border by 26 May and set up camp.[8] They captured a telegraph office, cut the wires, and gave every appearance that their main objective was the town of Huntingdon, located about ten miles from the border. Here Lieutenant-Colonel Archibald McEachern had 240 men under his command, and as he began to hear reports of increasing Fenian strength in the area, he thought of retreating to Lake St. Francis, which offered a better defensive position. But before he could move, he received word that Lieutenant-General James Lindsay was sending Colonel Bagot with a force of 500 regulars to reinforce his command. Together with the recently arrived but unarmed men of the Montreal Garrison Artillery, McEachern now had over 1000 men for the defense of Huntingdon, and the plan to retreat was quickly discarded. Shortly thereafter Colonel Bagot's regulars marched into town.

On the morning of Friday, 27 May, Colonel Bagot, who had taken over the command of all forces, roused his men from sleep at 3:30. Breakfast was served a half hour later, and within the hour the entire force of 1000 men was marching toward the Fenian enemy now entrenched at Trout River. The two enemy forces finally met about 8:30 in the morning and soon a familiar picture began to emerge. After firing several volleys at the approaching Canadians, the Fenians decided it was impossible to defend their hastily formed barricades and once again headed for the forest or the border.

As soon as the Canadians realized that the Fenians were trying to escape instead of fight, they whooped it up and eagerly tried to pursue the retreating enemy, firing wildly at everything that moved. Not until Colonel Bagot had a bugler sound the cease-fire did the excited Canadians stop their pursuit. Colonel Bagot was astonished at the easy victory, but an explanation was soon provided. Apparently the defenses thrown up by the Fenians had been manned on that particular morning by only a portion of the Fenian force, for many Fenians had openly refused to fight until reinforcements arrived. Thus a force of little more than 200 men had met Bagot's troops at the barricades. Once more, as at Eccles Hill, the Canadians had sustained no casualties. The Fenian raiders had again been routed and sent scurrying back to the safety of the American border, leaving behind one dead and several wounded "brothers."

The members of the Fenian Army in the 1870 campaign against Canada were now completely disillusioned. Their leaders had been arrested and put in jail by federal authorities and most of their supplies were being confiscated. In the Malone area alone, twenty-five wagonloads of Fenian stores had already been seized by United States officials. Thus the disappointed Fenian soldiers in various frontier towns decided to return to their homes and families. Those who had some money took the first available train, but others had to wait for private funds—some coming from highly placed New York State politicians[9]—to enable them to leave the scene of their dismal failure. Certainly the treasury of the Brotherhood was unable to give financial aid, for its till was so empty that the headquarters in New York City could not pay for a telegram from the front on 31 May. A small sum had to be borrowed to cover this embarrassing situation.[10]

On the whole, however, the raids of 1870 had been better organized and more practically planned than those of 1866. The arms and supplies were ample and carefully distributed among key border towns. But what hurt the Fenians most in May of 1870 was the fact that again only a small percentage of the expected fighting force actually appeared at their appointed locations. John O'Neill later summed up the problem:

> The people so often deceived and disappointed in the past could not believe that we were in earnest, and thousands of good men who were anxious to be with us kept indulging their doubts and fears until it was too late to be of service. As a general thing the best men did not leave their homes until after the movement had commenced.[11]

In addition, the Fenian raiders faced a much more formidable and better prepared opponent in 1870 than in 1866, and the American government again caused the Brotherhood much trouble by enforcing the neutrality laws.

Furthermore, men like Lieutenant-Colonel Smith and Colonel Bagot were much better soldiers than Booker and Peacocke, and Marshal Foster showed a zeal that no American official demonstrated in 1866.

The Canadians were justifiably proud of their successful defense of their country. Particularly gratifying was the way the militia had conducted itself during the various skirmishes. Indeed, congratulatory telegrams soon poured in from all sides. The British government had warm praise for the Canadian defenders, and several officers, including Smith, Chamberlin, and McEachern, were made "Companions of the Order of St. Michael and St. George." The commander-in-chief of Her Majesty's Forces in Canada, Lieutenant-General James Lindsay, fully recognized the splendid performance of the Canadian volunteers in this official dispatch from his Montreal Headquarters on 4 June 1870:

> Canada has once more been invaded by a body of Fenians, who are citizens of the United States, and who have again taken advantage of the institutions of that country to move without disguise large numbers of men and warlike stores to the Missisquoi and Huntingdon frontiers, for the purpose of levying war upon a peaceful community.
>
> From both these points the invading forces have been instantly driven with loss and in confusion, throwing away their arms, ammunition and clothing, and seeking shelter within the United States. Acting with a scrupulous regard for the inviolability of a neighboring territory, the troops were ordered to the halt, even though in pursuit, upon the border.
>
> The result of the whole affair is mainly due to the promptitude with which the militia responded to the call to arms, and to the rapidity with which their movements to the front were carried out, and the self-reliance and steadiness shown by this force, as well as by the armed inhabitants on the frontier. The regular troops were kept in support, except on the Huntingdon frontier, where one company took part in the skirmish.
>
> The proclamation of the President, and the arrival of the Federal troops at St. Albans and Malone, were too late to prevent the collection and transport of warlike stores, or an inroad into Canada.
>
> The reproach of invaded British territory, and the dread of insult and robbery, have thus been removed by a handful of Canadians, and the Lieutenant-General does not doubt that such services will receive the recognition of the Imperial Government.
>
> The Lieutenant-General congratulates the militia upon this exhibition of their promptness, discipline and training, and in dismissing the men to their homes, he bids them carry with them the assurance that their manly spirit is a guarantee for the defence of Canada.[12]

The Fenian raids of 1870 were over, and once again Canada had managed to escape becoming an unwilling pawn in the struggle for Irish independence. The presence of the Fenians did, of course, produce some initial panic among the Canadians in border towns, and valuable belongings were hidden while livestock was driven into the woods or further to the rear. But no looting took place and in no way did the Fenian soldiers behave in a lawless manner. Although some farmers of Irish ancestry did show friendliness toward the Fenians by providing them with some freshly baked bread and pies, most Irish-Canadians remained totally resentful of the Fenians' presence because it tended to create chaos and unrest, particularly for those engaged in business affairs.[13]

The Fenian leaders arrested by the United States government were soon tried before the courts for breaking the American neutrality laws. However, unlike 1866, the American courts did prosecute and sentence the most important Fenians held in their jails. John O'Neill, despite an eloquent plea on his own behalf and a firm promise to desist from any further encroachments on the neutrality laws, was sentenced by Judge Woodruff to a prison term of two years. Woodruff made it clear to O'Neill that this was his second offense, and that he felt "constrained to make an example" of the Fenian leader.[14] Other Fenians, including Owen Starr and John Donnelly, received similar prison terms.

But while the law inflicted its required penalties upon the Fenian leaders, the desire of the United States to reach a rapprochement with Britain continued to work heavily in favor of the imprisoned Fenians. As early as October 1870, the Grant administration suggested to the British government that all Fenian prisoners on both sides of the Canadian-American border immediately be pardoned. Britain, eager to improve Anglo-American relations, was most agreeable to the proposal but could not persuade the Macdonald government in Canada to agree with the scheme. Thus President Grant decided to act on his own. He granted a full pardon to the eight Fenian leaders still in American prisons. John O'Neill was free again. Would he now keep his word, given during his trial, that he would no longer entertain any thoughts of another Canadian invasion?

The Fenian raids in May 1870 aroused another wave of indignation and resentment in Canada. But whereas most citizens fulminated over the American government's permissive attitude toward Fenian preparations, some individuals raised their voices in anger not only against the United States but also against Britain for allowing "such outrages on its loyal subjects without making a demand for adequate preparation."[15] One angry Canadian, Judge John O'Connor of Ontario, wrote a series of letters to Governor-General Young in which he discussed the problem of Fenianism and its effect on the Canadian scene during the last six years, concluding: "The time has come when the British Government, in justice to Canada and in vindication of its honour, should interfere diplomatically, determinedly, and unconditionally."[16]

When the United States and Britain finally agreed during the early months of 1871 to seek a solution to their remaining differences in North America, it was the sincere hope of most Canadians that some positive action against the Fenian Brotherhood would be demanded by the British delegation. After all, was not their own prime minister, Sir John A. Macdonald, one of the five British representatives at the Washington Conference? At the least, Canadians hoped they might receive some financial compensation for the losses and expenses sustained during the Fenian raids of 1866 and 1870. They recalled that they had paid for the damage done during the St. Albans raid within less than six months. Surely the American government could not ignore forever the numerous *bona fide* bills presented to it as a result of damages caused by the Fenian raids.

Although the difficulties over the *Alabama* claims, the rights of American fishermen to Canadian waters, and the San Juan boundary dispute were eventually either settled or passed on to a mutually agreeable arbiter, the "Fenian claims" were not even placed on the agenda of the Joint High Commission. What Macdonald had feared at the outset of the discussions came true. Canadian interests were sacrificed on the altar of better Anglo-American relations. Earl de Grey, the head of the British delegation, was much more concerned with the interests of the Empire than the claims of the Canadian government.[17] When the Canadian minister affixed his signature to the Treaty of Washington on 8 May 1871, he knew he had been outmaneuvered and he found it difficult to conceal his bitterness.[18] The Fenian Brotherhood, without setting a foot upon Canadian soil, was still a thorn in the side of Canadians.

But the final chapter of the Fenian story—at least as far as Canada is concerned—was soon to be written. On 5 October 1871, John O'Neill, forgetting his promise to Judge Woodruff, crossed the Manitoba border in the hope of striking a final blow against British power in North America.

The Manitoba raid of 1871 was not really organized by the Fenian Brotherhood. Rather it was the result of the personal ambitions of William O'Donoghue, a former member of Louis Riel's provisional government, who hoped to win either independent status for the Red River Colony or annexation to the United States. O'Donoghue made several futile attempts to win support for his scheme from the American government and finally turned to the Fenian organization in New York City for assistance.[19] But the Brotherhood's zeal for any further "raids" had gone forever and the Fenian council rejected O'Donoghue's pleas for support. One member of the council, however, was willing to listen—none other than John O'Neill, who had recently been released from jail and had just been elected a member of the New York Fenian Council.

When the Brotherhood refused to back O'Donoghue's wild scheme, O'Neill saw it as a final opportunity to cause trouble for Great Britain. He quickly resigned from the Fenian Council and soon boasted that he could manage the whole affair without any formal assistance, if only his Fenian colleagues "would not denounce or oppose the movement." The Fenian council agreed to this small request but demanded, in return, that O'Neill not disturb any of the Fenian circles with his project. The Council did, however, give its former leader a supply of 400 breechloaders from its meager arsenal. But the man who actually issued the rifles to O'Neill was none other than Henri Le Caron, who now accompanied his "old friend" to the places where the arms were hidden. Then Le Caron performed the service for which he had been engaged by McMicken, and informed the Canadian and British authorities of the imminent raid.[20] In the meantime, William O'Donoghue and John O'Neill discussed the possibility of arousing the Métis of Manitoba to join their cause, which, at this point, had absolutely nothing to do with Irish independence.

Lieutenant-Governor Adams Archibald of Manitoba became aware of O'Neill's presence in the St. Paul area of Minnesota by early September. He did not give too much credence to rumors that a raid was being planned. But on Monday, 2 October, reports were received in Fort Garry (now Winnipeg) that a raiding party was gathering south of the border. Archibald now hurriedly issued a proclamation calling on all British subjects, regardless of nationality or religion, to unite in the defense of their country. As far as Archibald was concerned, another "Fenian" raid was imminent.

The response in Fort Garry was overwhelming. Over 1000 volunteers stepped forward and declared themselves ready to meet the enemy. But most of the Métis remained aloof; only a handful offered their services as mounted scouts. The reluctant attitude of the Métis greatly worried Archibald. Would these people, who had their own suspicions and resentments toward the Canadian government, decide to cast their support with these so-called Fenians?

But the anxiety of the lieutenant-governor was short-lived. O'Donoghue and O'Neill, followed by about three dozen adventurers from all walks of life, crossed the border during the early morning hours of 5 October.[21] They captured a Hudson's Bay Company trading post at North Pembina and made its proprietor their first prisoner. By 9 A.M. the raiders had taken twenty prisoners, for they arrested everyone they could lay their hands on. Only one man, an American citizen, protested strongly and was quickly released. This individual, however, was so annoyed by his experience that he hurried immediately to the nearby U.S. Army post at Fort Pembina and told his tale about the marauding Americans north of the border.

Soon Captain Lloyd Wheaton was on his way with thirty troopers, determined to arrest the American lawbreakers. He passed through the town of Pembina about 11 A.M., and within the hour he saw the occupied buildings before him. About half a mile from the Hudson's Bay post, the troops jumped from the wagon that had carried them and approached the buildings in full skirmishing order, for the post was surrounded by a stockade about eight to ten feet high. The occupants of the trading post, however, had already decided that the time had come to vacate the premises. Suddenly the doors burst open before the startled United States soldiers, and several dozen men ran in all directions in great confusion. Wheaton's troopers stormed after them, and soon they had captured John O'Neill, and ten other men. By 3 P.M., Captain Wheaton, with his prisoners in tow, was passing once more through Pembina on his way back to the fort. In the meantime, William O'Donoghue had been captured by a group of Métis as he frantically tried to flee across the Red River in a canoe, and the former college professor was soon able to join his friends in the stockade of Fort Pembina.

On 6 October the prisoners were charged with violating section six of the 1818 Neutrality Laws which made it a criminal act "to retain another person to go beyond the limits of the United States with the intention to be enlisted into the service of either belligerent." But the prosecution of the prisoners, although taking up two full days of the local court commissioner's time, resulted in the discharge of all the prisoners on the basis of some legal technicalities which the defense lawyers, Enos Stutsman and George F. Potter, fully exploited. John O'Neill lost no time upon hearing the verdict, and he left quickly for St. Paul. Here he was once more arrested but soon released because of "insufficient evidence" against him.

Thus ended the last Fenian-inspired attempt to capture Canadian territory. The Brotherhood in the United States was unmistakably moribund. Although the organization did hold a convention as late as 1885, gone were the days when men and money flocked to the Fenian standard. It is true, of course, that the Irish vote continued to be courted by American politicians, particularly in the crowded urban centers of the East. But most had long ago realized that the Fenian Brotherhood, despite its repeated claims, did not speak for or represent the views of the majority of Irish-Americans. So the once popular and influential Fenian movement faded slowly away. Meetings continued to be held and policy statements were occasionally issued until the mid-1880s, but the Brotherhood's period of political influence had waned long ago.

One by one the old Fenian faces disappeared from the scene. John O'Mahony was persuaded to come from retirement in 1872 to head the movement once again. But the days of action were gone forever. If Ireland was to win its independence, it would have to be done on the Emerald Isle itself; the New World could no longer offer massive assistance. O'Mahony died on 6 February 1877, in a small, unheated room in a New York tenement. His last years had been years of poverty, disease, and even hunger. A lung disease finally killed him and his body was sent back to Ireland for burial in Dublin's Glasnevin Cemetery. One of his old Irish colleagues later remarked: "No Irishman had better claim to the name of patriot," and another felt that while O'Mahony "was not, indeed, an ideal leader, he was an ideal Irishman."[22] William Randall Roberts, the man who conceived the Canadian scheme and thus divided the American Fenians, fared much better in life. He had retired from the Brotherhood after the failure of his venture and lived off his substantial income from successful business and real estate investments. In late 1870 he was elected to represent his Brooklyn, New York, district in the House of Representatives and he served as a Democratic congressman until 1875. He served as American minister to Chile from 1885 to 1889. He died in a hospital in New York City on 9 August 1897.[23] Thomas William Sweeny, after resigning from the Fenian Brotherhood during the Troy congress in September 1866, was reinstated in the U.S. Army and retired from the service in 1870 as a brigadier-general. His remaining years were spent in the pleasant surroundings of his Long Island home, Astoria. He died there on 10 April 1892, at the age of seventy-two.[24] James Stephens, the founder of the Irish Revolutionary Brotherhood, had gone to live in France after he was deposed as leader of the I.R.B. in 1867. He did come to the United States again for a short period of time as the New York City agent for a Bordeaux wine house, but he decided to spend most of his remaining years in Switzerland until the British government permitted him to return home to Ireland in September 1891. He lived another decade before joining several of his old colleagues of '48 and the Fenian movement in the "Patriot's Plot" in Glasnevin Cemetery.[25] John O'Neill, the Brotherhood's only "fighting general," decided to settle in the American west after the Manitoba fiasco. There he hoped to find fame and fortune in land speculation in the state of Nebraska. But a streak of bad luck and apparently too much alcohol ruined his marriage and probably hastened his death at the age of forty-four. He died in Omaha on 7 January 1878. However, the name of the hero of Ridgeway is forever enshrined by the existence of a small town in Nebraska bearing the name of O'Neill.[26]

Yet there is one final tale to be told about the Fenian Brotherhood. It appears that while the organization was dying a slow death in the 1870s, at least one member of the Brotherhood remained determined not to give up the struggle. Young John Phillip Holland, a parochial school teacher in Paterson, New Jersey, was convinced he had found a way to defeat the British navy. His plan was to build an underwater torpedo boat.[27] His fellow Fenians, although perhaps somewhat skeptical about this "dream project" of John Holland's, financed the scheme, and a model submarine was finally built and eventually tested on the nearby Passaic River. To everyone's surprise, the vessel proved operational. Quickly another $23,000 was put into the project and a larger model, the *Fenian Ram*, was constructed. This primitive boat apparently had many of the key features of the modern submarine.

But the Fenians never managed to make effective use of their secret weapon, for Holland now turned his eyes toward the U.S. Navy in the hope of seeing his work recognized and further developed. The navy, however, had its own ideas, and the inventive Holland soon became frustrated and proceeded to build his own vessel, which he proudly named after himself. Holland died in 1914, never able to witness the effective use the German Navy would make of his invention against the British Empire, the very enemy he had in mind.

Thus ends the almost fantastic story of the Fenian Brotherhood and its repeated attempts to win the liberty of the beloved Irish homeland. The movement ultimately failed, as perhaps it was destined to from the outset, because its schemes were usually too grandiose to be completed. Yet the Fenians did not fail for the lack of trying. They had simply undertaken a task that even a better organized and better equipped organization would have found difficult.

14

FENIANISM:
ITS IMPACT AND LEGACY

Fenianism appeared and briefly flourished because of the long-standing and deeply rooted enmity which permeated centuries of Anglo-Irish history. British rule in Ireland had produced a legacy of bitterness and resentment that made a *modus vivendi* between the people of the two nations virtually impossible. The Famine and the Revolution during the 1840s further exacerbated Anglo-Irish relations, and the frustrations of Irish nationalists found temporary relief in the Fenian movement.

When the American Civil War broke out in 1861, many Irish-Americans regarded the conflict as a fortuitous event in the struggle for Irish independence. The war not only provided thousands of young Irishmen with valuable military experience, but it also strained Anglo-American relations sufficiently so that the American Fenians could build their military strength relatively unmolested by the American authorities. The most optimistic Fenian leaders even talked of an imminent war between Britain and the United States. Such a conflict—if it were to develop—would certainly have facilitated any attempts to carry out a successful revolution in Ireland.

One thing was certain. When the Civil War was over, large numbers of unemployed war veterans roamed the cities and the countryside of the United States, and the Fenian leadership enticed many of these men to enlist in the ranks of the rapidly growing "Fenian Army" with generous promises of immediate fortune and glory.

It seems indeed unlikely that the Fenian Brotherhood would ever have risen to any sort of public prominence in the United States had federal and municipal authorities not condoned, at least initially, the organization's illegal activities. But the need for a vast reservoir of manpower for the Northern war effort and later the importance of the Irish vote were factors that could not be ignored easily by American politicians.

The Fenian movement in North America failed for a number of reasons. In fact, the Fenians had little chance of success from the outset. Perhaps the most glaring weakness of the Brotherhood was its inability to secure not only a sufficiently large but also a loyal following; only a small percentage of Irish Americans ever actively joined the ranks of the organization. Furthermore, the bitter internal dissension and open jealousy among Fenian leaders, their repeated vacillations at crucial moments, their diverging aims and unrealistic expectations, the constant lack of sufficient money, and the continuously firm opposition of the Roman Catholic hierarchy all proved to be fatal obstacles to the movement. And there existed the common but utterly mistaken belief that the Irish-born population of British North America would eagerly espouse the Fenian cause and rise enthusiastically in rebellion against the British authorities once the first Fenian soldiers crossed the Canadian border. Moreover, many Irish-Canadians were Ulster Protestants who were openly hostile to the aims of Fenianism. And most of the Irish Catholics in Canada remained unequivocally loyal to the British connection during the Fenian invasions. Finally, the American government, although thoroughly disenchanted with Britain's conduct during the Civil War, had no desire to become involved in another costly conflict, in spite of the militant speeches of some prominent politicians. Consequently there was no real chance of an Anglo-American war from which Fenian strategists might profit.

The various Fenian schemes to liberate Ireland, especially the invasion of Canada, were certainly novel in their conception. However, the problem of execution remained unsolved.[1] The leaders of the Brotherhood developed plans that looked good on paper but were utterly dependent on legions of non-existent Fenian troops. O'Mahony's plan for an insurrection in Ireland as well as Sweeny's Canadian scheme were based on this false assumption. Furthermore, both men failed to give full consideration to such vital military information as the enemy's current manpower, his great mobility, and his vast reserves. For example, it is almost incredible to read that General Sweeny fully expected a number of Fenian privateers to engage the powerful British navy and merchant marine in actual warfare. Finally, Fenianism's success or failure depended chiefly on the American government's continuously favorable disposition toward the Fenian cause. But whereas the United States government was willing to overlook many of the illegal activities of the Fenian Brotherhood for the sake of the Irish vote, it would never let itself become involved in a military confrontation with Britain for the sake of Ireland's struggle for independence.

If the Fenian Brotherhood ever hoped to win any military success which it could use as a bargaining point with the British government in negotiations for Ireland's future, its attacks should never have been directed at the well-fortified defenses of Britain's eastern North American possessions; rather, a massive attempt should have been made to capture the British North West, either at the Minnesota-Manitoba border or in the Crown colony of British Columbia. Only in the West *might* the Fenians have gained a firm foothold on Canadian territory and used it as a bargaining point with Britain.[2]

The Fenians did not secure the liberation of their Irish homeland, but they did not fail through any lack of effort. The task was simply too difficult for the limited strength of the Brotherhood, and the obstacles were far too numerous.

Nevertheless, the activities of the Fenian Brotherhood were not without some direct and lasting consequences. Although the alertness of the British authorities in Ireland had almost eliminated the Irish Revolutionary Brotherhood as a political force in late 1865, its spirit lingered on in such organizations as Michael Davitt's Land League and Charles Stewart Parnell's Home Rule movement during the late 1870s and 1880s. The Fenians had stirred nationalistic feelings in the breasts of many Irishmen and their activities had left "an indelible impress on the national consciousness of Ireland."[3] The appearance of the Brotherhood prevented the cause of Irish nationalism from fading into oblivion. James Stephens explained it this way: "If Fenianism had not aroused the Irish race from its torpor, a generation would have passed away without any uprising against English supremacy; and the succeeding generation might possibly bury the hatchet for ever, and accept accomplished facts."[4]

Yet it was in British North America that "these assiduous but inept practitioners of the arts of revolution," as Professor C.P. Stacey called them,[5] made their most significant contributions, although none of these contributions had been anticipated by the Fenians, even in their wildest dreams. For the irritating and troublesome presence of the Brotherhood south of the border undoubtedly helped expedite and confirm the confederation scheme in Canada. In fact, the Fenians had now become the "invaluable, though involuntary benefactors"[6] of the confederation movement. In New Brunswick, for example, the rash raid of O'Mahony's followers had been directly responsible for swinging public support behind the Confederation party of Samuel Tilley. And in the Province of Canada, the violence of the June raids of 1866 convinced many a reluctant Canadian that a union of the various British North American provinces was highly desirable.

The only group, other than the Fenians themselves, which suffered directly from the actions of the Brotherhood was the Roman Catholic Irish population in Canada. The conduct of the American Fenians did much to discredit the Irish character for years to come. It was already difficult to be an Irish Catholic in a country where "the Battle of the Boyne" was vividly remembered. The hard feelings created by Fenian activities did not improve the situation.

Moreover, the hostile activities of the Fenians throughout much of the 1860s were partly responsible for the disappearance of most pro-American sentiment that lingered in British North America. A marked anti-American feeling arose in Canada and the Maritimes as a direct consequence of the American government's handling of the illegal Fenian preparations for war.[7]

The machinations of the Fenian Brotherhood also effected major changes in the defense system of British North America. The entire militia system was reorganized and strengthened, and new equipment was provided for Canada's armed forces.[8]

But perhaps the most important result of Fenianism was the impetus it gave to the development of Canadian nationalism.[9] The various Fenian raids had a catalyzing effect on confederation and they aroused a new wave of patriotic sentiment among the inhabitants of British North America. "The growth of Canadian national feeling," wrote W.S. Wallace several decades ago, "might reasonably be regarded as the central fact in Canadian history."[10] In British North America, nationalism was at its highwater mark in the mid-1860s, and much of this was the result of the Fenian menace. The confederation concept could only benefit from this new sense of nationalism.

Confederation was, of course, not a simple process. Various factors are responsible for its inception: political deadlock, British policy, big business, westward expansion, defense, fear of annexation, and nationalism were the most important ingredients. But the hostile actions of the Fenian Brotherhood gave a sense of urgency to the problem of national defense. "The desire to unite," writes Professor D.G. Creighton, "grew out of the will to survive,"[11] and survival vis-à-vis the American Republic meant union of the various provinces and a common defense policy. The Fenian raids convinced many Canadians that safety lay in unity. The *Niagara* (Ontario) *Mail* (27 June 1866) writing from the center of the Fenian operations in 1866, noted quite accurately:

> The Fenian invasion has had the effect of not only rallying all classes of the Canadian people to the defence of the country, but it had the additional effect of Uniting [*sic*] the North American Colonies, as one, for the defence of the whole.

And the *Toronto Daily Telegraph* on 11 June 1866, while mourning the death of the heroes of Ridgeway, remarked that the recent event had finally united Canadians as a people, and suggested that the blood of the fallen heroes had sealed "the covenant of our nationality." Thus there can be little doubt that the Fenian invasions generated a distinct "rise of national feeling"[12] in British North America, a sentiment which made confederation possible as early as 1867.

Confederation of some sort would have occurred in any case. After all, the Province of Canada had accepted the Quebec Resolutions as early as 11 March 1865, and British influence and economic pressures would probably eventually have converted the Maritime Provinces. But Fenianism created a sense of immediacy which made quick action an absolute necessity. Procrastination might have meant a more severe penalty, for many Canadians still believed that the American government might someday turn its attentions once more to the isolated British colonies in North America, in the hope of fulfilling its recurrent dream of "manifest destiny."

The rise and fall of the Fenian Brotherhood should be regarded as significant to Canadian history, for the movement's prominence during the mid-1860s exerted a strong influence upon political developments in North America at this time. Canadians, on the whole, profited considerably from the Fenian experience. In the spring of 1870, the *Weekly Globe* summed up the Fenian contribution in these words:

> Canadians have gained more in national character during the last six years than in any previous twenty; and . . . the outrageous proceedings of Fenians and their abettors [in the United States] have been among the chief agencies.[13]

Thus the affairs of the Fenian Brotherhood in the 1860s, particularly its troublesome raids into British territory, should not be treated as a mere footnote in Canadian history but rather as an important factor in creating a new nation north of the forty-ninth parallel.

NOTES

ABBREVIATIONS

AP	*Archibald Papers*
CHAR	*Canadian Historical Association Report*
CHR	*Canadian Historical Review*
CM	*Canadian Magazine*
CP	*Clarke Papers*
FP	*Ford Papers* (Ontario Archives)
Hansard	*Hansard's Parliamentary Debates*
KPPR	*Kingston Penitentiary Prison Records*
ML	*Macdonald Letterbooks*
MP	*Macdonald Papers*
OH	*Ontario History*
SP	*Sessional Papers*
WCHSPR	*Welland County Historical Society Papers and Reports*

CHAPTER 1

1. C. Woodham-Smith, *The Great Hunger* (New York, 1962), p. 409.
2. Ibid., p. 243.
3. E.R. Green, "The Fenians," *History Today* 8 (1958): 698.
4. D. Ryan, *The Fenian Chief: A Biography of James Stephens* (Dublin and Sidney, 1967), pp. 6–7, 22–34, 35–42 offers fuller details of this story.
5. According to one participant of these tumultous events in Ireland, Fenianism was "the direct and . . . inevitable outcome of '48. . . . And the immediate origin of the movement is undoubtedly to be found among the '48 refugees in America." See J. O'Leary, *Recollections of Fenians and Feniansim,* 2 vols. (London, 1896), 1:79.
6. About 1.5 million Irish came to the United States between 1846 and 1861. See *The Statistical History of the United States* (Stamford, 1965), p. 57.
7. W. D'Arcy, *The Fenian Movement in the United States: 1858-1886* (Washington, D.C., 1947), pp. 7–8.
8. O'Leary, 1:82 ff, and Ryan, pp. 85–96.
9. Ryan, p. 43.
10. The general outline of the character sketch is drawn from O'Leary, 1:135, and John Devoy, *Recollections of an Irish Rebel* (Shannon, 1969), pp. 272–79.
11. Devoy, p. 160.
12. Ryan, p. 91.
13. Ibid., p. 92.
14. Ibid., pp. 92–93.
15. Ibid., p. 327.
16. Ibid., p. 321.
17. Ibid., p. 224, and W. O'Brien, "Was Fenianism Ever Formidable?," *Contemporary Review,* 71 (1897): 681–83.
18. Ryan, p. 158.
19. D. Malone, ed., *Dictionary of American Biography* (New York, 1928–37), 7:2:35–36.
20. The character description is from O'Leary, 1:134–35.
21. Cited in Ryan, p. 158, and J. Rutherford, *The Secret History of the Fenian Conspiracy: Its Origins, Objects and Ramifications,* 2 vols. (London, 1877), 1:206–7.
22. Ryan, p. 149. In fact only about £1500 was contributed by the American Fenians in the first five years, according to O'Leary (1:135–36).
23. J. Savage, *Fenian Heroes and Martyrs* (Boston, 1868), pp. 109–18.
24. D'Arcy, pp. 28, 47. Some representatives came from as far away as Florida, Louisiana, and even California.

CHAPTER 2

1. O'Leary, 1:150.
2. See Ryan, pp. 175–77, for a detailed account of the funeral procession.
3. J. Denieffe, *A Personal Narrative of the Irish Revolutionary Brotherhood* (New York, 1906), pp. 166–67.
4. See the *Toronto Globe,* 10 December 1861, and F. Landon, ed., *The Diary of Mrs. Amelia Harris* (*London* [Ontario] *Free Press* 1922), the entry marked 17 December 1861.

5. O'Leary, 1:232, and P.H. Bagenal, *The American Irish and their Influence on Irish Politics* (London, 1882), pp. 136–48.

6. J.G. Coyle, "General Michael Corcoran," *Journal of the American Irish Historical Society* 13 (1910): 123–24.

7. O'Leary, 1:99, suggests that T.F. Meagher's unit was "a brigade which was Fenian to a man."

8. Rutherford, 1:231, writes that one circle from the yate of Connecticut enlisted to a man and soon thereafter other circles followed from various states in the Union.

9. Bagenal, p. 138; see also P. Higgins and F. Connolly, *The Irish in America* (London, 1909), p. 54, and B.I. Wiley, "Johnny Reb and Billy Yank," *American History Illustrated* (April 1968): 4.

10. Rutherford, 1:234–35 and G.T. Denison, *History of the Fenian Raid on Fort Erie . . .* (Toronto, 1866), p. 12.

11. Bagenal, pp. 139–41.

12. The phrase is O'Mahony's and is quoted in a letter from O'Mahony to Charles Kickham, a fellow Fenian in Ireland, dated 17 October 1863; cited in D'Arcy, p. 33.

13. O'Leary, 1:135–36. He also suggests that these amounts were collected over the next few years: £1500 between 1858 and 1864; £28,500 between 1864 and 1866; and another £2500 in 1866. James Stephens acknowledged the sum of £30,000 from America during all the years of activity, see [Anon.], *Life of James Stephens and Fenianism* (New York, 1866), p. 115.

14. Denieffe, p. 66–67.

15. O'Leary, 1:217.

16. D'Arcy, pp. 32–36.

17. Ibid., pp. 37–38.

18. Resolution I in *Proceedings of the First National Convention of the Fenian Brotherhood held in Chicago, Illinois, Nov. 1863* (Philadelphia, 1863).

19. Cited by C.L. King, "The Fenian Movement," *University of Colorado Studies* 6 (1909): 193.

20. O'Leary, 1:256.

21. J.A. Cooper, "The Fenian Raid of 1866," *Canadian Magazine* 10 (1897): 41, and L.B. Shippee, *Canadian-American Relations: 1849-1874* (New Haven, 1939), p. 214.

22. J.A. Macdonald, *Troublous Times in Canada: A History of the Fenian Raids of 1866 and 1870* (Toronto, 1910), p. 98.

23. M. Crawford and K. Armstrong, *The Fenians* (Toronto, 1970), p. 1.

24. O'Leary, 2:9.

25. Ryan, p. 200.

26. Rutherford, 2:12.

27. O'Leary, 2:24–25; see also Denieffe, pp. 183–86, for two letters from Stephens to O'Mahony about the recent visit to America. These letters mention where Stephens had gone and how he assessed the visit.

28. Ryan, pp. 200, 204–5.

29. D'Arcy, pp. 46–47.

CHAPTER 3

1. Cited by Shippee, p. 185.

2. McGee gave this speech before the Irish Protestant Society in Quebec City on 10 May 1862 (T. D'Arcy McGee, *Speeches and Addresses* [London, 1865], p. 34).

3. *The Times* (London), 6 June 1862.

4. The Militia Bill in the Province of Canada was defeated by a vote of 61–54 on 20 May 1862. It had proposed an annual military expenditure of $500,000 and sought to create a militia force of 30,000 men; see C.P. Stacey, *Canada and the British Army, 1846–1871* (Toronto, 1963), p. 133.

5. J.M. Hitsman, *Safeguarding Canada, 1763–1871* (Toronto, 1968), pp. 231–32.

6. Newcastle to Monck, 21 August 1862; cited in W.H. Russell, *Canada: Its Defences, Conditions, and Resources* (Boston, 1865), pp. 209–10.

7. For further details see Hitsman, pp. 185–86, and C.P. Stacey, "The Fenian Troubles and Canadian Military Development, 1865–1871," *CHAR*, 1935, pp. 22, 24.

8. Russell, p. 76.

9. An excellent short account of the St. Albans raid is found in a pamphlet issued by the Franklin County Bank of St. Albans (E.H. Royce, "St. Albans Raid, October 19, 1864" [1968]).

10. *Chicago Tribune*, 14 December 1864; cited in J.P. Smith, *The Republican Expansionists of the Early Reconstruction Era* (Chicago, 1933), p. 12.

11. These warnings and proposals were presented in a "Message to Congress," 17 December 1864 (J.D. Richardson, ed., *Messages and Papers of the Presidents, 1789–1897* [Washington, 1901], 6:243, 246).

12. *Sessional Papers of the Province of Canada*, No. 16 (1865), p. 20.

13. *Sessional Papers of the Dominion of Canada*, No. 75 (1869), p. 64.

14. Landon, *Diary of Mrs. Amelia Harris* (16 December 1864).

15. F. Monck, *My Canadian Leaves: An Account of a Visit to Canada in 1864–5* (London, 1891), p. 103.

16. A union of the various British North American provinces had been proposed by many men on several earlier occasions. The attorney-general of Nova Scotia, R.J. Uniacke, advanced such a scheme in 1826, and the British North American League argued for a union in 1849. Alexander Tilloch Galt, who played a leading role in bringing about confederation in 1867, had written as early as 22 November 1858 to Lord Lytton: "The question is simply one of Confederation with each other or of ultimate absorption in the United States." (Cited in O.D. Skelton, *The Life and Times of Sir Alexander Tilloch Galt* [Toronto, 1920], p. 252.)

17. Ibid., p. 220.

18. *Parliamentary Debates on the Subject of the Confederation of the British North American Provinces* (Quebec, 1865), p. 55 (7 February 1865).

19. Ibid., p. 967 (13 March 1865).

20. Ibid., p. 131 (9 February 1865).

21. W.H. Seward to C.F. Adams, 10 March 1865; cited in D.F. Warner, *The Idea of Continental Union* (Louisville, 1960), p. 50.

22. *Hansard*, 3d series, vol. 178, p. 171 (23 March 1865).

23. N.F. Morrison, *Garden Gateway to Canada* (Toronto, 1954), p. 53.

24. Cited in the *Toronto Leader*, 19 April 1865.

25. *Detroit Free Press*, 17 July 1865, gave full coverage to this gathering of delegates.

26. See Smith, p. 54.

27. Cited by Warner, p. 47, as well as E.W. Watkin, *Canada and the States: Recollections, 1851–1886* (London and New York, 1887), p. 422.

28. Smith, pp. 32–33.

29. W.L. Morton, *The Critical Years: The Union of British North America, 1857–1873* (Toronto, 1964), p. 184.

CHAPTER 4

1. E.M. Archibald to Sir F. Bruce, 13 and 18 May 1865. *AP.*
2. Cited in the *Toronto Globe,* 8 May 1865.
3. Stacey, *Canada and the British Army,* p. 188, notes that already 640,000 men of the 1 million in arms had been discharged from the army.
4. *Toronto Globe,* 7 November 1864.
5. Letter from a citizen of Ridgetown to Gilbert McMicken, 28 December 1864. *MP,* 234:100, 831.
6. Cited by A. Brady, *Thomas D'Arcy McGee* (Toronto, 1925), p. 127. The speech had been made in March 1861.
7. McGee, *Speeches and Addresses,* p. 144.
8. Mrs. Sidney Jones to Beverly Jones, 7 June 1865. *FP.*
9. Edward Mortimer Archibald was the British consul in New York City for many years and watched the Fenian activities with great care. His correspondence is preserved in the Public Archives of Canada, and his daughter, Edith, wrote a rather adoring account of her father's career in her *Life and Letters of Sir Edward Mortimer Archibald* (Toronto, 1924).
10. Ibid., p. 166; see also Ryan, pp. 202–4.
11. Archibald to Lord Monck, 16 September 1865. *AP.*
12. John A. Macdonald to G. McMicken, 22 September 1865. *ML,* 8:259–60.
13. Macdonald to Monck, 18 September 1865. Ibid., pp. 221–22.
14. Information on this uprising and its aftermath from Ryan, pp. 206–7, 216–17, 222–23, 232–33, 321.
15. Ibid., p. 232.
16. Further details of this important Fenian convention are described in D'Arcy, pp. 79–81.
17. Devoy, p. 268, and *Dictionary of American Biography,* 8:1:19–20.
18. O'Leary, 2:213.
19. The information about Thomas William Sweeny comes from W. Sweeny, "Brigadier-General Thomas W. Sweeny, United States Army," *Journal of the American Irish Historical Society* 27 (1928): 257–72.
20. An edited version of Sweeny's plan is found in Macdonald, pp. 15–16; also see T.W. Sweeny, "Official Report of General Thomas W. Sweeny . . . ," *Journal of the American Irish Historical Society* 23 (1924): 194–203 (also Denieffe, pp. 255–62).
21. Sir F. Bruce to Lord Russell, 31 October 1865, cited by Shippee, p. 216.
22. G. van Deusen, *William Henry Seward* (New York, 1967), pp. 501–3, offers more information about Seward and the American Irish.
23. The Fenian Brotherhood of the State of Illinois to W.H. Seward, 21 September 1865. *Seward Papers.*
24. Ibid.
25. Seward to B. Killian, 20 November 1865. *Seward Papers.*
26. Ibid.
27. Lord Clarendon to Sir F. Bruce, 16 November 1865, cited by Shippee, p. 217.
28. Sir F. Bruce to W.H. Seward, 26 December 1865. *Seward Papers.*
29. Archibald to Sir John Michel, 1 November 1865. *AP.*
30. Morrison, pp. 54–55.
31. *SP,* No. 4 (1866), p. 65.
32. Four new military training schools had just been opened in Montreal, Kingston, Hamilton, and London; see the *Report on the State of the Militia in the Province of Canada* (Ottawa, 1866), pp. 15–21.
33. Further information is found in the following letters: Archibald to Sir John Michel, 27 November 1865. *AP;* Archibald to Michel, 30 November 1865. *MP,* 56:22489–90; Archibald to Macdonald, 21 December 1865. *MP,* 56:22542–43.

34. Only a Fenian official called "The Financial Agent of the Irish Republic" could validate the bonds with his personal signature. A dispute had arisen between O'Mahony and the Senate over the candidate for the important position, and as a result a delay developed. O'Mahony therefore decided to act independently and signed the new bond issue himself. The Senators were, of course, furious.
35. Denieffe, pp. 207-8.
36. Cited in the *Toronto Globe*, 3 January 1866.
37. E.R. Cameron, *Memoirs of Ralph Vansittart* (Toronto, 1924), p. 219.
38. Sweeny, "Official Report," pp. 194-95.
39. Macdonald, *Troublous Times*, p. 15.
40. Cited in the *Toronto Globe*, 29 January 1866.
41. Cited by Macdonald, p. 15.

CHAPTER 5

1. *Hansard*, vol. 181, p. 724 (17 February 1866); p. 1042 (23 February 1866).
2. *Toronto Globe*, 2 March 1866.
2. *Toronto Globe*, 2 March 1866.
3. *New York Tribune*, 3 March 1866.
4. *New York Tribune*, 5 March 1866. The news report not only quotes Archbishop McCloskey's speech and O'Mahony's comments but also notes how the platform, filled with speakers and special guests, collapsed under all that weight causing great confusion and minor bruises.
5. McMicken to Macdonald, 12 March 1866. *MP*, 237:103,338.
6. Lord Monck to Edward Cardwell, 9 March 1866. *SP*, No. 75 (1869), pp. 139-40.
7. *SP*, No. 4 (1866), p. 6.
8. One Canadian returned home from as far away as South Carolina, and others came from all over the United States (*SP*, No. 4 [1866], p. 7, and the *Toronto Globe*, 22 March 1866).
9. *SP*, No. 4 (1866), pp. 6, 9.
10. Ibid., p. 69.
11. Reported in the *Niagara Mail*, 14 and 21 March 1866.
12. Landon, *Diary of Mrs. Amelia Harris*, 8 March 1866.
13. The frontier town of Sarnia was one of the few places bypassed by the excitement. Its volunteers had been called out, but the citizens of the town showed no "signs of trepidation or uneasiness" (*Sarnia Observer*, 16 March 1866).
14. Reported in the *Toronto Globe*, 10 March 1866.
15. Reported in the *Hamilton Spectator*, 12 March 1866.
16. Cited in the *Toronto Globe*, 19 March 1866.
17. A. McLeod to Macdonald, 12 March 1866. *MP*, 57:22,725-28.
18. Quoted by T.P. Slattery, *The Assassination of D'Arcy McGee* (Toronto and New York, 1968), p. 300.
19. See, for example, the reports in the *New York Times*, 18 March 1866, and *Detroit Free Press*, 18 March 1866.
20. Archibald to D. Godley, 17 March 1866. *MP*, 57:22,789.
21. In Canada West there were 3573 volunteers on frontier duty and Canada East had 1717 men watching the frontier. *SP*, No. 4 (1866), pp. 69-70.
22. D'Arcy, p. 108.
23. See the *Toronto Globe*, 14 December 1864.
24. See letter from P. Nolan to G. McMicken, 31 December 1865. *MP*, 236:103, 111-13.

25. Reported in the *Toronto Globe,* 18 March 1864.

26. P. Nolan to McMicken, 31 December 1865. *MP,* 236:103,112–13.

27. Ibid., p. 103,111.

28. *Montreal Gazette,* 20 August 1867; see also McGee, *Speeches and Addresses,* 11 January 1865, p. 144.

29. D.C. Lyne, "The Irish in the Province of Canada. . . . " M.A. dissertation, McGill University, 1962, pp. 55, 57, 63.

30. J.M.S. Careless, *Brown of the Globe,* 2 vols. (Toronto, 1959, 1963), 2:222.

31. For a detailed discussion of the Irish immigration to British North America, see G. Tucker, "The Famine Immigration to Canada, 1847," *American Historical Review* 36 (1931): 533, 547.

32. D'Arcy, pp. 108–9.

33. See the *Toronto Leader,* 12 February 1866.

34. See the full story of Murphy in C.P. Stacey, "A Fenian Interlude: The Story of Michael Murphy," *CHR* 15 (1934): 133–54.

CHAPTER 6

1. Rutherford, 2:232.

2. Rutherford, 2:242.

3. O.R. Gowan to Macdonald, 19 March 1866. *MP,* 57:22,806–7.

4. Cardwell to Gordon, 11 November 1865, and Bruce to Gordon, 2 December 1865, both cited in H.A. Davis, "The Fenian Raid on New Brunswick," *CHR* 36 (1955): 318. Davis's account is by far the best of the Campobello raid.

5. Archbishop Connolly to Gordon, January 1866; quoted in Morton, *Critical Years,* p. 191.

6. See the letter from Lieutenant-Governor Gordon to Cardwell, 25 March 1866, cited by Davis, p. 322.

7. Davis, p. 322.

8. Cited in the *Toronto Globe,* 6 and 7 April 1866.

9. Macdonald to Mitchell, 10 April 1866. *ML,* 9:159.

10. *St. Croix Courier,* 14 April 1866, cited by Davis, p. 323.

11. D'Arcy, p. 137.

12. The following paragraphs make extensive use of Davis and M. Vesey, "When New Brunswick Suffered Invasion," *Dalhousie Review* 19 (1939–40): 197–204.

13. Cited by Shippee, p. 223.

14. H.K. Beale, ed., *Diary of Gideon Welles, 1861–1869,* 3 vols. (New York, 1960), 2:486 (17 April 1866).

15. *Eastport Sentinel,* 25 April 1866, cited by Davis, p. 327.

16. G. Meade, ed., *The Life and Letters of George Gordon Meade,* 2 vols., (New York, 1915), 2:285 ff.

17. *Eastport Sentinel,* 25 April 1866, cited by Davis, p. 327.

18. Ibid., pp. 329–30.

19. Vesey, pp. 199–200.

20. Quoted in the *Toronto Globe,* 28 April 1866.

21. Rutherford, 2:169.

22. Cited by Davis, p. 334.

23. From a letter to the *Halifax Morning Chronicle,* 12 April 1866, cited by P. Waite, *The Life and Times of Confederation, 1864–1867* (Toronto, 1962), p. 268.

24. Compare the election results on the two maps in D.G. Creighton, *The Road to Confederation* (Toronto, 1965), pp. 261 and 387.

25. *New Brunswick Debates of the House of Assembly for 1867*, pp. 124–25, cited by Davis, p. 333.

26. *New York Tribune*, 12 May 1866.

27. Lord Monck to Henry Monck, 19 April 1866. W.L. Morton, *Monck Letters and Journals, 1863-1868* (Toronto, 1970), p. 293.

CHAPTER 7

1. See Stacey, "Fenian Interlude," pp. 133–54, for the details.

2. Macdonald to McMicken, 21 May 1866. *ML*, 9:244.

3. *New York Times*, 11 May 1866.

4. Cited in the *Globe*, 1 May 1866.

5. Information on Sweeny's invasion scheme from Sweeny, "Official Reports," pp. 195–96, 199–201.

6. McMicken to Macdonald, 17 May 1866. *MP*, 237:103,745.

7. Quoted in the *New York Times*, 30 May 1866.

8. A. Lawe to R. Cartwright, 5 April 1866. *Cartwright Papers*.

9. McMicken to Macdonald, 17 May 1866. *MP*, 237:103,745–47; also H. Hemans to McMicken, 26 May 1866. *MP*, 237:103,799–801.

10. Colonel George T. Denison asked permission to take his unit, the Governor-General's Horse Guards, on frontier duty, but his request was refused by his superiors who felt there was no imminent threat. See G.T. Denison, *Soldiering in Canada: Recollections and Experiences* (Toronto, 1901), pp. 86–87.

11. Quoted in the *Toronto Globe* and the *Toronto Leader*, 30 May 1866. Both papers also printed this curious dispatch; it came from Cleveland, Ohio, and stated that "300 or 400 Fenians . . . passed here last night and today, going *east*. They were orderly and quiet and claimed to be marching to *California* to work on the railroad."

12. *Buffalo Courier*, 30 May 1866; cited in the *Toronto Leader*, 31 May 1866.

CHAPTER 8

1. H. Le Caron, *Twenty-five Years in the Secret Service* (London, 1892), pp. 38–40. Henri Le Caron, whose real name was Thomas Beech, was a spy in pay of the British government. He became a close friend of John O'Neill and was completely trusted by the Fenian leader in all affairs of the Brotherhood. Le Caron used his position effectively and informed the British and Canadian authorities of every Fenian move south of the border. In his book, he does greatly exaggerate his own importance and is on many occasions quite in error about facts.

2. J. O'Neill, *Official Report of Gen. John O'Neill . . .* (New York, 1870), pp. 37–38, provides much information from the viewpoint of the Fenian commander. It must, of course, be used with caution.

3. *SP*, No. 4 (1866), p. 22, and C.F. Hamilton, "The Canadian Militia: The Fenian Raids," *Canadian Defence Quarterly* 45 (1929): 347.

4. *Toronto Globe*, 6 June 1866. A John Ford and fifty-six fellow Canadians had come all the

way from Chicago, Illinois, to help in the defense of Canada. They crossed the border at Windsor on 4 June, too late for any action.

5.   W. Ellis, "The Adventures of a Prisoner of War," *The Canadian Magazine* 13 (1899): 199. Corporal Ellis participated in the battle at Ridgeway and was captured by the Fenians. Later in life he became a professor at the School of Practical Science at the University of Toronto.

6.   Ellis, p. 199, and W.T. Barnard, *The Queen's Own Rifles of Canada, 1860-1960* (Don Mills, 1960), p. 17.

7.   *Toronto Leader*, 2 June 1866.

8.   Ellis, p. 199, and A. Somerville, *Narrative of the Fenian Invasion of Canada* (Hamilton, 1866), p. 46.

9.   This song is recalled by a contemporary of the times (M.G. Sherk, "My Recollections of the Fenian Raid," *WCHSPR* 2 [1926]: 64).

10.   G. Wells, "The Fenian Raid in Willoughby," *WCHSPR* 2 (1926): 57–59.

11.   Denison, *Fenian Raid*, p. 19.

12.   Cited in Macdonald, p. 30.

13.   O'Neill, *Official Report. . .* , p. 39. Colonel O'Neill hoped "to get between the two columns, and, if possible, defeat one of them before the other could come to its assistance."

14.   Colonel Booker was the senior officer in the area and commanded these volunteer units: the Thirteenth Battalion from Hamilton, the York and Caledonia Volunteers, and the Queen's Own Rifles from Toronto (Ellis, p. 199).

15.   E.A. Cruikshank, "The Fenian Raid of 1866," *WCHSPR* 2 (1926): 31.

16.   The total strength of Canadian defenders in the Niagara area at this moment was about 2400 men. Colonel Peacocke commanded about 1500 men and Colonel Booker's force numbered about 900. See F.M. Quealy, "The Fenian Invasion of Canada West," *Ontario History* 53 (1961): 50.

17.   Cruikshank, pp. 32–33. According to the 1865 Militia Report (*SP*, No. 16 [1865], p. 23), each soldier was to be supplied with these rations: one pound of bread and meat; two pounds of potatoes; two ounces of butter, rice and sugar; one pint of milk; and a small amount of coffee and tea. These were daily rations.

18.   Ellis, pp. 199–201. Ellis was soon released by his captors for he had won their sympathy when he had helped a wounded Fenian. Ellis even recalled that John O'Neill bought him a glass of beer at a roadside tavern (pp. 201–3).

19.   Cited by Slattery, p. 326.

20.   Information from Cruikshank (see pp. 34–37 of that book for more details). For Booker's critical order to "Form Square," see Denison, *Fenian Raid*, pp. 44–45.

21.   J.S. Brusher, "The Fenian Invasions of Canada," Ph.D. dissertation, St. Louis University, 1943, p. 76.

22.   J.F. Dunn, "Recollections of the Battle of Ridgeway," *WCHSPR* 2 (1926): 52, claims that O'Neill himself acknowledged the importance of the fatal command: "Up to the time when they made the fatal mistake of forming the square, they had driven in all my skirmishers and were advancing on my main position. . . . We were just on the point of retiring to the woods nearby, when the enemy, seeing a few of my men who had horses they had picked up, formed a square to prepare for cavalry."

23.   *Proceedings and Report of the Court of Inquiry on the Late Engagement at Lime Ridge,* in Macdonald, pp. 241–42; the *Toronto Globe,* 1 August 1866, also has a complete summary of the inquiry.

24.   "Official Report of Lt. L. McCallum," in the appendix of Denison, *Fenian Raid,* p. 92.

25.   O'Neill, *Official Report,* p. 40.

26.   H. Hemans to Monck, 3 June 1866. *SP,* No. 75 (1869), p. 142.

27.   The instructions are reprinted in the *New York Tribune,* 4 June 1866.

28.   Cited by Macdonald, p. 92.

29. Richardson, 6:433.

30. Beale, *Diary of Gideon Welles,* 2:519–21, notes the open reluctance of Seward and Secretary of War Stanton to act against the Fenians between 2 and 4 June. Welles noted in his diary: "Seward was in a fog. Did not want to issue a proclamation . . . Stanton wanted to keep clear of the question." In the end, President Johnson was forced to act and on 5 June he ordered Attorney-General James Speed "to cause the arrest of all prominent, leading, or conspicuous persons called 'Fenians' who . . . have been or may be guilty of violations of the neutrality laws of the United States." See Richardson, 6:447.

31. Macdonald, p. 118.

32. Ibid., p. 93.

33. Quoted in the *Toronto Globe,* 9 July 1866.

34. Most of the arrested Fenians were soon free. The rank and file merely had to promise to appear if a trial became necessary, and the leaders posted a $500 bond in order to stay out of jail. The *Daily Telegraph* in Toronto could not restrain its sarcasm when it publicly asked on 6 June 1866 whether or not the bail could be paid in Fenian bonds.

35. Cited in King, p. 206.

36. *St. Paul Pioneer,* 5 June 1866, cited in A.C. Gluek, *Minnesota and the Manifest Destiny of the Canadian Northwest* (Toronto, 1965), pp. 205–6.

37. A monument was built to commemorate the Fenian raid and it still stands in Queen's Park in Toronto today. There also is a plaque inside the doors of the Ontario Legislature and a stained glass window in Toronto's University College to recall the events of June 1866. In 1899, General Service Medals were issued to all living survivors of the Fenian raids.

38. O'Neill, *Official Report,* p. 42, maintains that eight of his men were killed and fifteen others wounded. Canadian sources place the figures somewhat higher. See the letter written by one Robert Denby to his brother Frederick, dated 3 June 1866, informing him of the death of their cousin Albert John during the fighting at the front. The angry letter writer refers to "those damning Fenians. May the Lord curse the lot." Letter is in the possession of the *Toronto Historical Board: Fort York.*

39. On 8 June 1866, the *Toronto Leader* reported that several irresponsible American newspapers were apparently printing stories telling of Fenian prisoners in Canada being summarily shot and even scalped.

40. Macdonald, p. 56.

41. B. Cumberland, "The Fenian Raid of 1866 and Events on the Frontier," *Proceedings and Transactions of the Royal Society of Canada,* 3rd series, 4 (1910): 96–97.

42. G. Wells, "A Romance of the Raid," *WCHSPR* 2 (1926): 80–81.

43. Cited by M.F. Campbell, *Niagara: Hinge of the Golden Arc* (Toronto, 1958), pp. 224–25.

44. Printed in the *Toronto Globe,* 2 June 1866, for C. Potter, 20 King St. East, Toronto.

45. Cumberland, p. 99.

46. This point is supported by Ellis, pp. 201–2, Denison, *Fenian Raid,* p. 69, and N. Brewster, "Recollections of the Fenian Raid," *WCHSPR* 2 (1926): 76.

47. C.P. Stacey, "Fenianism and the Rise of National Feeling in Canada at the Time of Confederation," *CHR* 12 (1931): 242.

CHAPTER 9

1. See the reports in the *Toronto Leader* and the *Toronto Globe,* 4-7 June 1866.

2. Quoted in the *New York Tribune,* 5 June 1866.

3. *Quebec Morning Chronicle,* 7 June 1866; cited by Waite, p. 279.

4. *Toronto Leader,* 8 June 1866, cited two American papers (*Buffalo Dispatch* and *New York Commercial Advertiser*).

5. The American revenue cutter the *S.P. Chase* patrolled the American side of the St. Lawrence River in the Ogdensburg area; see J.W. Dafoe, "The Fenian Invasion of Quebec, 1866," *CM* 10 (1898): 347.

6. Denieffe, p. 251; S. Spear to T. Sweeny, 7 June 1866.

7. Ibid., pp. 251–52.

8. Ibid., pp. 252–53; S. Spear to T. Mechan, 8 June 1866.

9. Dafoe, p. 345.

10. Major Nixon commanded a force composed of these units: the Granby and Waterloo Volunteers, a detachment of men from the Royal Artillery with two twelve-pound guns, two rifle brigade companies, three companies of the Twenty-Fifth Regiment, and a cavalry unit—the Royal Guides—under Captain Macdougall; see Dafoe, p. 345.

11. The interview between Dafoe and the Canadian cavalryman is printed in Dafoe, p. 346.

12. Cited in Macdonald, p. 120.

13. Cited in R. McGee, *The Fenian Raids on the Huntingdon Frontier, 1866 and 1870* (Huntingdon, 1967), p. 13. The Source is Private S. Shorey of the Victoria Rifles.

14. Dafoe, p. 347.

15. Cited by Macdonald, p. 119.

16. *SP,* No. 75 (1869), p. 144, estimates that the total Fenian strength in the Malone area never exceeded 3000 men and in the St. Albans region never more than 2000. These numbers probably overestimate the strength of the Fenians.

17. Monck to Cardwell, 8 June 1866 (ibid., p. 142) and Monck to Cardwell, 14 June 1866 (ibid., p. 144).

18. The song is printed in the *Toronto Irish Canadian,* 14 September 1866.

19. *The Times* (London), 22 June 1866. Less than a half dozen references are made about the Fenian raids in this paper during the period from late June to early August.

20. *Statutes of the Province of Canada, 1866,* pp. 3–5; under the terms of the bill the government could detain even suspects "without bail" for the next twelve months.

21. Cited in the *Toronto Globe,* 16 June 1866.

22. Cited in the *Toronto Globe,* 18 June 1866.

23. *Toronto Globe,* 2 June 1866.

24. *Irish Canadian,* 6 June 1866.

25. The *Toronto Daily Telegraph,* (11 June 1866) reported several arrests had been made in the city as well as in the Port Credit area.

26. J.A. Macdonald to R. Macdonald, 29 September 1866. *ML,* 10:189.

27. *SP,* No. 75 (1869), p. 146.

28. Sweeny, "Official Report," p. 203.

29. For an interesting account of the Fenian uprising in Canada West that never materialized, see W.S. Neidhardt, "The Abortive Fenian Uprising in Canada West," *Ontario History* 61 (1969): 74–76.

CHAPTER 10

1. *Toronto Globe,* 19 June, 25 June, 9 July 1866. The monument in question was of course erected and the medals were struck some years later. See ch. 8, note 37.

2. Defense appropriations for the period from 1 July 1865 to 30 June 1866 had been $589,265, but an additional $500,000 was voted on 10 April 1866 and another $300,000 was added on 4 June, during the excitement of the June raids (*SP,* No. 20 [1866], pp. 2–6).

3. *Parliamentary Debates of the Parliament of the Province of Canada*, 22 June 1866. (microfilm)

4. The *Globe* expressed these sentiments on 16, 27, and 30 August 1866 and similar feelings had been expressed in the *Niagara Mail*, 4 July 1866.

5. See *SP*, No. 35 (1867–1868), p. 105.

6. From a letter printed in the *Stratford Beacon*, 24 August 1866.

7. By 12 July the city of Toronto alone had collected $27,901.45 and had disbursed $14,133.33 (*Toronto Globe*, 4 August 1866).

8. George Sheppard to Charles Clarke, 30 July 1866. *CP*.

9. Quoted in the *New York Times*, 4 July 1866.

10. Quoted in the *Toronto Globe*, 27 June 1866.

11. *Toronto Leader*, 28 July 1866.

12. The alleged Fenians were apparently a group of tough-looking Americans who had come across the border to witness a prizefight at Point Abino, a small village on the north shore of Lake Erie (*Toronto Leader*, 30 July 1866).

13. Cited in the *Toronto Globe*, 1 August 1866.

14. See stories in the following newspapers: *Toronto Globe*, 1 August 1866; *London* (Ontario) *Free Press*, 14 August 1866; *Grand River Sachem*, 8 August 1866; *St. Catharines Constitutional*, 2 August 1866.

15. During the excitement of the June days, Berlin had remained aloof and almost disinterested. The town did not even call out its volunteers; see the *Berliner Journal*, 16 August 1866.

16. See the reports in the *Toronto Globe*, 18 August 1866, and the *New York Times*, 19 August 1866.

17. *Statutes of the Province of Canada, 1866*, p. 8.

18. Macdonald to McMicken, 25 August 1866. *ML*, 10:60.

19. Lord Monck to Henry Monck, 6 September 1866. Morton, *Monck Letters*, p. 308.

20. The *Toronto Globe* (6 September 1866) provided a detailed account of the proceedings in Troy.

21. Brusher, "Fenian Invasions," p. 142.

22. Stacey, "A Fenian Interlude," pp. 151–53, and the *Hamilton Spectator*, 3–4 September 1866.

23. *Toronto Leader*, 12 September 1866, and *Stratford Beacon*, 14 September 1866.

24. Macdonald to A. Morrison, 29 September 1866. *ML*, 10:185.

25. Cited by the *London* (Ontario) *Free Press*, 29 September 1866.

26. *New York Tribune*, 29 October 1866.

27. Cited in Stacey, "Fenianism and the Rise of National Feeling," p. 238.

28. Reported in the *Toronto Globe*, 11 October 1866.

29. See the reports in the *New York Times*, 12 November 1866, and the *Toronto Globe*, 29 November 1866.

30. Ryan, p. 249.

31. Quoted in the *Toronto Globe*, 29 November 1866.

32. Ryan, pp. 251–52.

33. Ibid., pp. 252–53.

CHAPTER 11

1. *Statistical History of the United States*, p. 66.

2. Thomas D'Arcy McGee estimated the number of Irish votes in the United States to be close to one million; see I. Skelton, *The Life and Times of Thomas D'Arcy McGee* (Gardenvale, Quebec, 1925), p. 442.

3. Quoted in the *Toronto Irish Canadian,* 6 July 1866.

4. J.D. Anderson to C. Clarke, 24 June 1866. *CP.*

5. *Governor General's Office, Numbered Files;* R.G. 7, G 21, vol. 403, File No. 7792; F. Bruce to Monck, 30 June 1866.

6. Higgins and Connolly, *Irish in America,* p. 58.

7. *Congressional Globe,* 39th Congress, 1st session, 11 June 1866, p. 3085.

8. Ibid., pp. 3085-86.

9. Ibid., 23 July 1866, pp. 4047–48.

10. Ibid., 2 July 1866, p. 3549.

11. *New York Herald,* 12 July 1866; quoted by Waite, p. 280.

12. *St. Paul Press,* 7 July 1866, and *Detroit Free Press,* n.d.; quoted by Gluek, *Minnesota,* pp. 208-9.

13. See B. Jenkins, *Fenians and Anglo-American Relations during Reconstruction* (Ithaca, N.Y., 1969), p. 184.

14. Cited by Waite, pp. 280–81.

15. Quoted in M. Walker, *The Fenian Movement* (Colorado Springs, 1969), p. 116.

16. Reported in the *Toronto Globe,* 21 September 1866.

17. Jenkins, p. 200; the *New York Tribune,* 21 August 1866, had printed the first story which suggested that the American government would not prosecute the Fenians.

18. See the reports in the *Toronto Globe,* 12 and 17 October 1866.

19. *Statistical History of the United States,* p. 691.

20. The *Toronto Globe* (9 November 1866) reported that the pro-Fenian editors of both the *New York Tribune* and the *Buffalo Express* were defeated in their attempts to win a seat in the House of Representatives.

21. Cited in Walker, p. 120.

22. Proper and accurate identification of the numerous prisoners apparently became quite a serious problem (A. Reavley, "Personal Experiences in the Fenian Raid," *WCHSPR* 2 [1926]: 73).

23. Reported in the *Toronto Globe,* 10 October 1866.

24. Material dealing with the trials comes from G. Gregg and E. Roden, *Trials of the Fenian Prisoners at Toronto* (Toronto, 1867).

25. Ibid., p. 135.

26. Cited by the *Toronto Globe,* 31 October 1866.

27. From a poster in the collection of the Toronto Historical Board Collection at Fort York; also a copy in the *Kirby Papers* (Ontario Archives).

28. Cited by the *Toronto Globe,* 31 October 1866.

29. Jenkins, p. 205.

30. W.H. Seward to F. Bruce, 27 October 1866. *Colonial Office: Original Correspondence,* vol. 98. (microfilm; reel B-813)

31. Cited in the *Toronto Globe,* 31 October 1866.

32. *Toronto Leader,* 8 November 1866.

33. Monck to Carnarvon, 3 November 1866. *Governor General's Office, Numbered Files,* No. 7792.

34. Slattery, p. 349.

35. Gregg and Roden (pp. 139–85), offer full details of the Lumsden trial and acquittal.

36. *KPPR,* R.G. 13, B 12, vol. 53.

37. J.A. Macdonald to Bishop Lynch, 6 November 1866. *ML,* 10:434; J.A. Macdonald to G. Creighton, 7 November 1866. *ML,* 10:446–47.

38. Jenkins, p. 207.

39. Carnarvon to Monck, 24 November 1866. *Governor General's Office, Numbered Files,* No. 7792; Dispatch No. 108.

40. Alexander Lawe to Richard Cartwright, 10 November 1866. *Cartwright Papers.*

41. This unique letter was written 30 November and printed in the *Toronto Globe,* 17 December 1866.

42. Richardson, 6:475.

43. The *Toronto Globe* gave extensive coverage to the Sweetsburg trials; see the issues of 5, 7, 11–14, and 19–29 December.

44. *KPPR.*

45. *MP,* 62:25,550.

46. Sir John Michel to Carnarvon, 4 January 1867. *Governor General's Office;* File No. 7792.

47. *KPPR.*

48. Full details about the Patrick Magrath case can be found in the files of the *Provincial Secretary's Office, Canada West.*

49. *KPPR.*

50. Lynch to J.A. Macdonald, 4 October 1869. *MP,* 60:24,505–6.

51. *KPPR.*

52. R.B. Lynch to Warden Creighton, 21 April 1871; typed transcript of this letter, and the subsequent items below, are in the possession of the author thanks to the kindness of J. Alex Edmison.

53. P. Ledwith to Francis Clifford, 15 March 1872.

54. Quoted in the *Canadian Illustrated News,* 20 November 1869.

CHAPTER 12

1. *Hansard,* vol. 185, p. 557 (19 February 1867).

2. Ibid., p. 574.

3. Ibid., p. 1172 (28 February 1867).

4. Skelton, *Sir Alexander Tilloch Galt,* p. 410.

5. Cited by Slattery, p. 364.

6. Ibid., p. 364.

7. Stacey, *Canada and the British Army,* pp. 193, 202.

8. However, as late as 1869 Britain still had 12,000 regulars on Canadian soil. It was not until 11 November 1871 that the British Army left Canada forever, except for two naval bases. See C.P. Stacey, "Britain's Withdrawal from North America, 1864–1871," *CHR* 36 (1955): 185–98.

9. See Denis Godley to Macdonald, 31 May 1867. *MP,* 56:23,812–13.

10. E.M. Archibald to D. Godley, 3 September 1867. *MP,* 56:23,862–68.

11. See Consul Archibald's dispatches to John A. Macdonald on 20 April 1867, 3 September 1867, and 4 February 1868 (*MP,* 59).

12. Macdonald to E. Ermatinger, 4 February 1868. *ML,* 11:482.

13. *SP,* No. 26 (1872), p. 9.

14. J.P. Edwards to Monck, 21 October 1868. *MP,* 59:24,387.

15. A Fenian circular dated 17 November 1868. *MP,* 59:24,400.

16. *MP,* 60:24,426.

17. Archibald to Macdonald, 12 July 1869. *MP,* 60:24,453.

18. Archibald to Macdonald, 3 September 1869. *MP,* 60:24,478–79.

19. Archibald to Macdonald, 15 September 1869. *MP,* 60:24,589.

20. Fenian Circular from the collection of the Missouri Historical Society.

21. Detective W.M. McMichael to McMicken, 22 February 1870 (*MP*, 60:24,646–49) and 2 March 1870 (*MP*, 60:24,672–75).

22. Brusher, p. 159.

23. See the two books by T. Slattery for the death of D'Arcy McGee and the trial of Patrick Whelan.

24. On 12 March 1866, Detective McLeod had informed Macdonald that McGee's life was in danger. *MP*, 57:22,725–28.

25. T. Slattery, *They Got To Find Mee Guilty Yet* (Toronto, 1972), p. 353.

26. O'Neill, p. 14.

27. A. Nevins, *Hamilton Fish: The Inner History of the Grant Administration* (New York, 1936), p. 392; see the entry in the Fish Diary dated 15 April 1870.

28. Ibid., p. 392.

29. Ibid., pp. 392–93; entry of 28 April 1870.

30. McMicken to G.E. Cartier, 22 May 1870. *MP*, 245:109,885.

31. See the *Toronto Globe*, 24, 25, and 30 May 1870.

32. O'Neill, p. 15.

CHAPTER 13

1. Governor-General Young to Earl Granville, 10 February 1870, G Series (P.A.C.), p. 575; cited by Brusher, p. 165.

2. The full story of Le Caron is found in his book, *Twenty-five Years in the Secret Service.*

3. O'Neill's *Official Report* offers much information about this 1870 raid.

4. Richardson, 7:85.

5. O'Neill, pp. 20–21.

6. Ibid., p. 21.

7. From the report of Lieutenant-Colonel Osborne Smith; cited by Brusher, p. 182.

8. Most of the information about the events in the Huntingdon area is taken from McGee, *Fenian Raids.*

9. O'Neill (p. 54) says that much of the money came from Boss William Tweed in New York City.

10. Nevins, p. 394.

11. O'Neill, p. 27.

12. Printed in Macdonald, p. 184.

13. H. Donovan, "Fenian Memories in Northern New York," *Journal of the American Irish Historical Society* 28 (1929–30): 149–50.

14. O'Neill (pp. 57–62) gives an account of the trial.

15. See "The Report of a Committee of the Canadian Privy Council" in *SP*, No. 26 (1872), pp. 1–3.

16. D.B. Read, *Lives of the Judges of Upper Canada and Ontario* (Toronto, 1888), p. 474.

17. The British government promised to compensate Canadians for the financial and property losses incurred during the various Fenian raids; see *SP*, No. 26 (1872), p. 11.

18. D.G. Creighton, *John A. Macdonald*, 2 vols. (Toronto 1952, 1955), 2:101–2.

19. Information on this raid from J.P. Pritchett, "The Origins of the so-called Fenian Raid on Manitoba," *CHR* 10 (1929): 38 ff.

20. Le Caron, p. 98.

21. An interesting personal memoir of these events is R.P. Johnson, "The Fenian Invasion of 1871," *Historical and Scientific Society of Manitoba,* series III, no. 7 (1952): 35–39.

22. Devoy, p. 271; O'Leary, 2:213.

23. Roberts had suffered a stroke while serving in Chile, and never fully recovered his health; see *Dictionary of American Biography,* 8:1:20.

24. Sweeny, "Brigadier-General Thomas W. Sweeny," pp. 267–68.

25. Ryan, p. 316.

26. *Dictionary of American Biography,* 7:2:45; Johnson, pp. 32–34; Dunn, p. 99.

27. The story is related in J.C. Furnas, *The Americans: A Social History of the United States, 1587-1914* (New York, 1969), pp. 702–3.

CHAPTER 14

1. Before relegating the Fenian strategists completely to the realm of the absurd, Canadians might well consider the fact that as late as 12 April 1921, Colonel J.S. Brown, the Dominion's "Director of Military Operations and Intelligence," formulated his famous DEFENCE SCHEME NO. I. For nearly a decade this remarkable document was part of the defensive strategy of the Dominion of Canada. Colonel "Buster" Brown believed that the major external threat to Canadian security came from none other than the United States of America, and among the 200 pages of detailed information and plans are precise instructions for an immediate offensive campaign into such strategic American areas as Seattle, Portland, Fargo, Minneapolis, and St. Paul. Read this intriguing story in J. Eayrs, *In Defence of Canada* (Toronto, 1964), 1:71–78; 323–28.

2. Gluek (p. 276) cites an editorial from the *St. Paul Press* (30 April 1870) which makes this precise point: "If the Fenians really desire to strike an effective blow against British power on this continent, the place, and the only place to strike is Western British America."

3. Devoy, p. 279.

4. Ryan, p. 326.

5. Stacey, "Fenianism and the Rise of National Feeling," p. 261.

6. *SP,* No. 4 (1866), p. 7. The Fenian invasions of Canada in 1866 were also responsible for the only Victoria Cross ever won on Canadian soil. On 9 June 1866, Private Timothy O'Hea of the Montreal Rifle Brigade successfully extinguished a fire in a railroad boxcar full of ammunition. His bravery saved the lives of many comrades and citizens of Danville, Quebec, and he was awarded the Victoria Cross. See W.S. Neidhardt, "A Victoria Cross won far from the presence of the enemy," Canadian Forces *Sentinel* 6, no. 4 (1970): 44–45.

7. See R. Cartwright, *Reminiscences* (Toronto, 1912), p. 61.

8. See G.F. Stanley, *Canada's Soldiers, 1604-1954* (Toronto, 196), p. 231; C.P. Stacey, "The Fenian Troubles," pp. 26–35; and Hamilton, "The Canadian Militia," pp. 350–52.

9. Not since their successful defense of Upper and Lower Canada against the American invaders during the War of 1812 had Canadians displayed such a strong spirit of patriotism and national pride. See M. Zaslow, ed., *The Defended Border* (Toronto, 1964).

10. W.S. Wallace, "The Growth of Canadian National Feeling," *CHR* 1 (1920): 136.

11. Creighton, p. 385.

12. Stacey, "Fenianism and the Rise of National Feeling," p. 261.

13. Ibid., p. 261.

SOURCES

A NOTE ABOUT THE SOURCES

This book is based on a variety of materials, including manuscript and printed sources, newspapers, memoirs, pamphlets, historical monographs, articles, and unpublished dissertations.

By far the most important single source of information is the *John A. Macdonald* collection in the Public Archives of Canada (P.A.C.). This rich storehouse of primary material yields abundant information about the affairs of the Fenian Brotherhood, particularly in volumes 56 to 62 of the collection. The *Macdonald Letterbooks* (P.A.C.), volumes 8 to 10, also offer many personal letters which reflect the public and private thoughts held by many prominent Canadians about the Fenian movement. The *Archibald Papers* (P.A.C.) and the *Colonial Office: Original Correspondence* (P.A.C.) also contain much information about the Fenian Brotherhood, as does File Number 7792 in the *Governor General's Office: Numbered Files* (P.A.C.) In the Archives of the Province of Ontario, the *Cartwright Papers* and the *Clarke Papers* provide some additional personal references to Fenianism. The *Seward Papers* at the University of Rochester are valuable for an examination of the Fenian Brotherhood's relationship with the American government. Some excellent printed primary material is found in the *Sessional Papers* of both the Province of Canada and the Dominion of Canada during the years from 1864 to 1872. The *Confederation Debates* (Canada) and the *Congressional Globe* (United States) remain, of course, indispensable sources of information with regard to what the politicians said "for the record."

Another valuable source of printed information is the Canadian and American press of the period. A general survey of some of the large urban newspapers and numerous provincial dailies and weeklies produces a wealth of data about public reaction to the activities of the Fenians in Canada and the United States.

Most of the material consulted in writing this book came from the following archives and libraries: the Public Archives of Canada, the Public Archives of Ontario, the Toronto Public Library, the John P. Robarts Library in Toronto, the Detroit Public Library, the Buffalo and Erie County Public Library, the Rush-Rhees Library at the University of Rochester, the Missouri State Historical Society, and the libraries of the U iversity of Toronto and the University of Western Ontario. Some important information about the fate of the Fenian prisoners was generously provided by Professor J. Alex Edmison, Q.C., of the Department of Criminology, University of Ottawa, who made the *Kingston Penitentiary Prisoners Record* (P.A.C.) available to me.

PRIMARY SOURCES

Manuscripts

Ottawa. Public Archives of Canada: John A. Macdonald Papers; Edward Mortimer Archibald
  Papers; Governor General's Office, Numbered Files (number 7792, R.G. 7, G 21, vol.
  403); *Colonial Office: Original Correspondence* (C.O. 537, vol. 98, microfilm reel B-813);
  Kingston Penitentiary Prisoners Record (R.G. 13, B 12, vol. 53); *Records of the
  Provincial Secretary's Office, Canada West* (R.G. 5, C 1, vols. 863 and 869).
Toronto. Public Archives of Ontario: *Richard J. Cartwright Papers; Charles Clarke Papers.*
Rochester. Rush Rhees Library, University of Rochester: *William H. Seward Papers.*

Printed Sources: Province of Canada

Parliamentary Debates, 1866-1867 (excerpts published in the contemporary newspapers have
  been microfilmed by the Canadian Library Association).
*Parliamentary Debates on the Subject of the Confederation of the British North American
  Provinces*, 3d sess., Eighth Provincial Parliament of Canada, Quebec, 1865.
Sessional Papers, 1864-1868, vols. 23-27.
Statutes of the Province of Canada, 1866, Quebec, 1866.

Printed Sources: Dominion of Canada

Parliamentary Debates, 1867-1873.
Sessional Papers, 1867-1872, vols. 1-5.

Printed Sources: Great Britain

Hansard's Parliamentary Debates, 3d ser., vols. 177, 178, 181, 184, 185, 1866-1867.

Printed Sources: United States

Congressional Globe, 39th Cong., 1st and 2nd sess., 1865-1866. (microfilm).
*Proceedings of the First National Convention of the Fenian Brotherhood held in Chicago,
  Illinois, Nov. 1863*, Philadelphia, 1863.
Richardson, J. D. (ed.), *Messages and Papers of the Presidents, 1789-1897*, vols. 6 and 7
  (Washington, 1901).
The Statistical History of the United States from Colonial Times to the Present (U.S. Bureau of
  the Census and the Social Research Council: Stamford, 1965).

Newspapers: Great Britain

The Times (London)

Newspapers: United States

The Buffalo Courier; The Buffalo Express; The Chicago Tribune; The Cincinnati Commercial; The Cleveland Leader; The Detroit Free Press; The Eastport (Maine) *Sentinel; The New York Herald; The New York Times; The New York Tribune; The Providence* (Rhode Island) *Daily Journal; The Rochester* (New York) *Union; The St. Paul Pioneer; The St. Paul Press*

Newspapers: Canada

The Berliner Journal (Kitchener, Ontario); *The Canadian Illustrated News; The Grand River* (Ontario) *Sachem; The Halifax* (Nova Scotia) *Morning Chronicle; The Hamilton* (Ontario) *Spectator; The Huntington* (Quebec) *Canadian Gleaner; La Minerve* (Montreal); *Le Journal de Québec; The London* (Ontario) *Free Press; The Montreal Gazette; The Niagara* (Ontario) *Mail; The Quebec Gazette; The Quebec Morning Chronicle; The Saint John* (New Brunswick) *Morning Telegraph; The Sarnia* (Ontario) *Observer; The St. Catharines* (Ontario) *Constitutional; The St. Croix* (New Brunswick) *Courier; The Stratford* (Ontario) *Beacon; The Toronto Daily Telegraph; The Toronto Globe; The Toronto Irish Canadian; The Toronto Leader.*

Contemporary Accounts, Pamphlets, Diaries, Memoirs, and Speeches

A Brief Account of the Fenian Raids on the Missisquoi Frontier: 1866 and 1870. Montreal, 1871.

Archibald, E. J. *Life and Letters of Sir Edward Mortimer Archibald.* Toronto, 1924.

Bagenal, P.H. *The American Irish and their Influence on Irish Politics.* London, 1882.

Beale, H. K., ed. *Diary of Gideon Welles, 1861–1869.* 3 vols. New York, 1960.

Cameron, E. R. *Memoirs of Ralph Vansittart.* Toronto, 1924.

Cartwright, R. J. *Reminiscences.* Toronto, 1912.

Denieffe, J. *A Personal Narrative of the Irish Revolutionary Brotherhood.* New York, 1906. (In its lengthy appendix are numerous letters from important Fenian leaders including Sweeny, Stephens, and O'Mahony.)

Denison, G. T. *History of the Fenian Raid on Fort Erie: With an Account of the Battle of Ridgeway.* Toronto, 1866. (The appendix contains the "Official Reports" of such participants as Peacocke, Booker, Dennis, and Akers.)

———. *Soldiering in Canada: Recollections and Experiences.* Toronto, 1901.

Devoy, J. *Recollections of an Irish Rebel.* Reprint. Shannon, 1969.

Gauust, D. *History of the Fenian Invasion of Canada.* Hamilton, Ontario, n.d.

Gregg, G. R., and Roden, E. P. *Trials of the Fenian Prisoners at Toronto who were captured at Fort Erie, C. W. in June, 1866.* Toronto, 1867.

Landon, F., ed. *The Diary of Mrs. Amelia Harris. London* (Ontario) *Free Press,* July–November 1922.

Le Caron, H. *Twenty-Five Years in the Secret Service.* London, 1892.

Life of James Stephens and Fenianism. New York, 1866.

Macdonald, J. A. *Troublous Times in Canada: A History of the Fenian Raids of 1866 and 1870.* Toronto, 1910. (The appendix includes Booker's "Court of Inquiry.")

McGee, T. D'Arcy. *Speeches and Addresses.* London, 1865.

———. *The Irish Position in British and Republican North America.* Montreal, 1866.

McMicken, G. *The Abortive Fenian Raid on Manitoba.* Winnipeg, 1888.

Meade, G., ed. *The Life and Letters of George Gordon Meade.* 2 vols. New York, 1915.

Monck, F. E. O. *My Canadian Leaves: An Account of a Visit to Canada in 1864-5.* London, 1891.

Morton, W. L., ed. *Monck Letters and Journals, 1863-1868.* Toronto, 1970.

O'Leary, J. *Recollections of Fenians and Fenianism.* 2 vols. London, 1896.

O'Neill, J. *Official Report of Gen. John O'Neill,* President of the Fenian Brotherhood . . . New York, 1870.

Pope, J., ed. *Correspondence of Sir John Macdonald: 1840-1891.* Toronto, 1921.

———. *Memoirs of the Right Honourable Sir John Alexander Macdonald.* 2 vols. Toronto, 1930.

Russell, W. H. *Canada: Its Defences, Conditions, and Resources.* Boston, 1865.

Rutherford, J. *The Secret History of the Fenian Conspiracy: Its Origins, Objects and Ramifications.* 2 vols. London, 1877.

Savage, J. *Fenian Heroes and Martyrs.* Boston, 1868.

Somerville, A. *Narrative of the Fenian Invasion of Canada.* Hamilton, 1866.

Sweeny, T. W. *Official Report of General Thomas W. Sweeny, Secretary of War, Fenian Brotherhood, and Commander-in-Chief of the Irish Republican Army. Journal of the American Irish Historical Society,* 23 (1924), 194-203.

Watkin, E. W. *Canada and the States: Recollections, 1851-1886.* London and New York, 1887.

SECONDARY MATERIAL

Books

Barnard, W. T. *The Queen's Own Rifles of Canada, 1860-1960: One Hundred Years of Canada.* Don Mills, Ontario, 1960.

Beale, H. K. *The Critical Year: A Study of Andrew Johnson and Reconstruction.* New York, 1958.

Brady, A. *Thomas D'Arcy McGee.* Toronto, 1925.

Brebner., J. B. *North Atlantic Triangle: The Interplay of Canada, the United States and Great Britain.* New Haven, 1945.

Brown, T. N. *Irish-American Nationalism, 1870-1890.* Philadelphia and New York, 1966.

Callahan, J. M. *American Foreign Policy in Canadian Relations.* New York, 1937.

Campbell, F. W. *The Fenian Invasions of Canada of 1866 and 1870.* Montreal, 1904.

Campbell, M. F. *Niagara: Hinge of the Golden Arc.* Toronto, 1958.

Careless, J. M. S. *Brown of the Globe.* 2 vols. Toronto, 1959, 1963.

Crawford, M., and K. Armstrong. *The Fenians.* Toronto, 1970.

Creighton, D. G. *John A. Macdonald.* 2 vols. Toronto, 1952, 1955.

———. *The Road to Confederation.* Toronto, 1965.

Curtis, E. *A History of Ireland.* London, 1957.

D'Arcy, W. M. *The Fenian Movement in the United States: 1858-1886.* Washington, D. C., 1947.

Dent, J. C. *The Last Forty Years: Canada since the Union of 1841.* Toronto, 1881.

Gluek, A. C. *Minnesota and the Manifest Destiny of the Canadian Northwest: A study in Canadian-American Relations.* Toronto: University of Toronto Press, 1965.

Hassard, A. R. *Famous Canadian Trials.* Toronto, 1924.

Harmon, M. *Fenians and Fenianism.* Dublin, 1968.

Higgins, P., and Connolly, F. *The Irish in America.* London, 1909.

Hitsman, J. M. *Safeguarding Canada, 1763-1871.* Toronto, 1968.

Jenkins, B. *Fenians and Anglo-American Relations during Reconstruction.* Ithaca, N.Y. and London, 1969.

Keenleyside, H. L. *Canada and the United States: Some Aspects of the History of the Republic and the Dominion.* New York, 1929.

Landon, F. *Western Ontario and the American Frontier.* Toronto, 1941.

Lower, A. R. M. *Canadians in the Making.* Toronto, 1958.

Macdonald, H. G. *Canadian Public Opinion on the American Civil War.* New York, 1926.

McGee, R. *The Fenian Raids on the Huntingdon Frontier, 1866 and 1870.* Huntingdon, Quebec, 1967.

McInnis, E. W. *The Unguarded Frontier.* New York, 1942.

Middleton, J. E., and Landon, F. *The Province of Ontario: 1615-1927,* 4 vols. Toronto, 1927.

Moody, T. *The Fenian Movement.* Cork, 1968.

Morrison, N. F. *Garden Gateway to Canada: One Hundred Years of Windsor and Essex County, 1854-1954.* Toronto, 1954.

Morton, W. L. *The Critical Years: The Union of British North America, 1857-1873.* Toronto, 1964.

Neal, F. *The Township of Sandwich: Past and Present.* Windsor, 1909.

Nevins, A. *Hamilton Fish: The Inner History of the Grant Administration.* New York, 1936.

Ó Broin, L. *Fenian Fever: An Anglo-American Dilemma.* New York, 1971.

Phelan, J. *The Ardent Exile.* Toronto, 1951.

Read, D. B. *Lives of the Judges of Upper Canada and Ontario.* Toronto, 1888.

Ryan, D. *The Fenian Chief: A Biography of James Stephens.* Dublin and Sidney, 1967.

Shippee, L. B. *Canadian-American Relations: 1849-1874.* New Haven, 1939.

Shortt, A., and Doughty, A. G., eds. *Canada and Its Provinces: A History of the Canadian People and their Institutions,* vol. 7. Toronto, 1914.

Skelton, I. *The Life and Times of Thomas D'Arcy McGee.* Gardenvale, Quebec, 1925.

Skelton, O. D. *The Life and Times of Sir Alexander Tilloch Galt.* Toronto, 1920.

Slattery, T. P. *The Assassination of D'Arcy McGee.* Toronto and New York, 1968.

———. *They Got To Find Mee Guilty Yet.* Toronto, 1972.

Smith, J. P. *The Republican Expansionists of the Early Reconstruction Era.* Chicago, 1933.

Stacey, C. P. *Canada and the British Army, 1846-1871: A Study in the Practice of Responsible Government.* Toronto, 1963.

Stanley, G. F. G. *Canada's Soldiers, 1604-1954: The Military History of an Unmilitary People.* Toronto, 1960.

Strauss, E. *Irish Nationalism and British Democracy.* New York, 1951.

The Fenian Raids, 1866-1870, Missisquoi County. Missisquoi County Historical Society, Stanbridge East, Quebec, 1967.

Trotter, R. G. *Canadian Federation: Its Origins and Achievements.* Toronto and London, 1924.

Van Deusen, G. *William Henry Seward.* New York, 1967.

Waite, P. B. *The Life and Times of Confederation, 1864-1867.* Toronto, 1962.

Walker, M. *The Fenian Movement.* Colorado Springs, 1969.

Warner, D. F. *The Idea of Continental Union: Agitation for the Annexation of Canada to the United States, 1849-1893.* Louisville, Ky., 1960.

Winks, R. W. *Canada and the United States: The Civil War Years.* Baltimore, 1960.

Woodham-Smith, C. *The Great Hunger.* New York, 1962.

Articles and Theses

Ascher, E. "Number One Company, Niagara." *Niagara Historical Society* 27 (1915): 60-73.

Blegen, T. C. "A Plan for the Union of British North America and the United States, 1866." *Mississippi Valley Historical Review* 4 (1917-18): 470-83.

Brewster, N. "Recollections of the Fenian Raid." *WCHSPR* 2 (1926): 75-79.

Brusher, J. S. "The Fenian Invasions of Canada." Ph.D. dissertation, St. Louis University, 1943.

Callahan, J.M. "The Northern Lake Frontier during the Civil War." *American Historical Association Report* (1896): 337-59.

Cameron, J. M. "Fenian Times in Nova Scotia," *Collections of the Nova Scotia Historical Society* 37 (1970): 103-52.

Cassidy, M.A. "The History of the Fenian Movement in the United States, 1848-1866, And its Background in Ireland and America." M.A. dissertation, University of Buffalo, 1941.

Cooper, J. A. "The Fenian Raid of 1866." *CM* 10 (1897): 41-55.

Coyle, J. G. "General Michael Corcoran." *Journal of the American Irish Historical Society* 13 (1910): 109-26.

Creighton, D. G. "The United States and Canadian Confederation." *CHR* 39 (1958): 209-22.

Cruikshank, E. A. "The Fenian Raid of 1866." *WCHSPR* 2 (1926): 9-49.

Cuddy, H. "The Influence of the Fenian Movement on Anglo-American Relations." Ph.D. dissertation, St. John's University, New York, 1953.

Cumberland, B. "The Fenian Raid of 1866 and Events on the Frontier." *Proceedings and Transactions of the Royal Society of Canada,* 3rd ser. 4 (1910): 85-108.

Curran, C. "The Spy Behind the Speaker's Chair." *History Today* 18 (1968): 745-54.

Dafoe, J. W. "The Fenian Invasion of Quebec, 1866." *CM* 10 (1898): 339-47.

Davis, H. A. "The Fenian Raid on New Brunswick." *CHR* 36 (1955): 316-34.

Donovan, H. "Fenian Memories in Northern New York." *Journal of the American Irish Historical Society* 28 (1929/30): 148-52.

Duff, L. B. "Sam Johnston, Smuggler, Soldier, and Bearer of News." *WCHSPR* 2 (1926): 82-93.

Dunn, J. F. "Recollections of the Battle of Ridgeway." *WCHSPR* 2 (1926): 50-56.

Ellis, W. "The Adventures of a Prisoner of War." *CM* 13 (1899): 199-203.

"Fenianism—By One Who Knows," *Contemporary Review* 19 (1871-72): 301-16.

"Fenian Brotherhood." *Blackwood's Magazine* 190 (1911): 378-93.

"Force and Feebleness of Fenianism." *Blackwood's Magazine* 131 (1882): 454-67.

Gibson, J. A. "The Colonial Office View of Canadian Federation 1858-1868." *CHR* 35 (1954): 279-313.

Green, E. R. "The Fenians." *History Today* 8 (1958): 689-705.

Hamilton, C. F. "The Canadian Militia: The Fenian Raids." *Canadian Defense Quarterly* 6 (1929): 344-53.

Hoslett, S. D. "The Fenian Brotherhood." *Americana* 34 (1940): 596-603.

Hunter, C. "Reminiscences of the Fenian Raid." *Niagara Historical Society* 20 (1911): 3-22.

Jenkins, B. "The British Government, Sir John A. Macdonald, and the Fenian Claims." *CHR* 49 (1968): 142-59.

Johnson, R. P. "The Fenian Invasion of 1871." *Historical and Scientific Society of Manitoba,* ser. 111, no. 7 (1952): 30-39.

King, C. L. "The Fenian Movement." *University of Colorado Studies* 6 (1909): 187-213.

Landon, F. "The American Civil War and Canadian Federation." *Proceedings and Transactions of the Royal Society of Canada,* 3rd. ser. 21 (1927): 55-62.

Langan, M. "General John O'Neill, Soldier, Fenian, and Leader of Irish Catholic Colonization in America." M.A. dissertation, Notre Dame University, 1937.

Larmour, R. "Personal Reminiscences of the Fenian Raid of June, 1866." *CM* 10 (1898): 121-127.

———. "With Booker's Column." *CM* 10 (1898): 228-231.

Luvaas, J. "General Sir Patrick Macdougall: The American Civil War and Defence of Canada." *CHAR*, 1962, 44-54.

Lyne, D. C. "The Irish in the Province of Canada in the Decade Leading to Confederation, 1850-1867." M.A. dissertation, McGill University, 1962.

Macdougall, P. "Canada: The Fenian Raid and the Colonial Office." *Blackwood's Magazine* 108 (1870): 493-508.

Martin, C. "British Policy in Canadian Federation." *CHR* 13 (1932): 3–19.

——. "The United States and Canadian Nationality." *CHR* 18 (1937): 1–11.

McCallum, F. H. "Experiences of a Queen's Own Rifleman at Ridgeway." *Waterloo Historical Society Report,* no. 3 (1915): 24–29.

McGee, R. F. "The Toronto Irish Catholic Press and Fenianism, 1863–1866." M.A. dissertation, University of Ottawa, 1969.

Morton, W. L. "British North America and a Continent in Dissolution, 1861-1871." *History* 47 (1962): 139–56.

Neidhardt, W. S. "The Fenian Brotherhood and Southwestern Ontario." M.A. dissertation, University of Western Ontario, 1967.

——. "The Fenian Brotherhood and Western Ontario: The final years." *OH* 60 (1968): 149–61.

——. "The Abortive Fenian Uprising in Canada West: A Document Study." *OH* 61 (1969): 74–76.

——. "The American Government and the Fenian Brotherhood: A Study in Mutual Political Opportunism." *OH* 64 (1972): 27–44.

——. "The Fenian Brotherhood and Its Role in Canadian History." *The York Pioneer,* 1972, 2–13.

——. "We've Nothing Else to Do: The Fenian Invasion of Canada, 1866." *Canada: An Historical Magazine* 1, no. 2 (1973): 1–19.

——. "The Fenian Trials in the Province of Canada, 1866-1867." *OH* 66 (1974): 23–36.

O'Brien, W. "Was Fenianism Ever Formidable?" *Contemporary Review* 71 (1897): 680–93.

Pritchett, J. P. "The Origins of the so-called Fenian Raid on Manitoba." *CHR* 10 (1929): 23–42.

Quealy, F. M. "The Fenian Invasion of Canada West." *OH* 53 (1961): 37–66.

Reavley, A. W. "Personal Experiences in the Fenian Raid." *WCHSPR* 2 (1926): 66–74.

Robson, M. M. "The Alabama Claims and the Anglo-American Reconciliation, 1865-1871," *CHR* 42 (1961): 1–22.

Scott, F. R. "Political Nationalism and Confederation." *Canadian Journal of Economics and Political Science* 8 (1942): 386–415.

Senior, H. "Quebec and the Fenians." *CHR* 48 (1967): 26–44.

Severance, F. H. "The Fenian Raid of '66." *Buffalo Historical Society* 25 (1921): 263–85.

Sherk, M. G. "My Recollections of the Fenian Raid." *WCHSPR* 2 (1926): 60–65.

Smith, J. P. "American Republican Leadership and the Movement for the Annexation of Canada in the 1860's." *CHAR,* 1935, 67–75.

——. "A United States of North America: Shadow or Substance? 1815–1915." *CHR* 26 (1945): 109–18.

Stacey, C. P. "Fenianism and the Rise of National Feeling in Canada at the Time of Confederation." *CHR* 12 (1931): 238–61.

——. "The Garrison of Fort Wellington: A Military Dispute During the Fenian Troubles." *CHR* 14 (1933): 161–76.

——. "A Fenian Interlude: The Story of Michael Murphy." *CHR* 15 (1934): 133–54.

——. "British Military Policy in Canada in the Era of Federation." *CHAR,* 1934, 20–29.

——. "The Fenian Troubles and Canadian Military Development, 1865-1871." *CHAR,* 1935, 26–35.

——. "Britain's Withdrawal from North America, 1864-1871." *CHR* 36 (1955): 185–98.

Stanley, G. F. G. "L'Invasion Fénienne au Manitoba." *Revue d'Historique de l'Amérique Francaise* 17 (1963–64): 258–68.

Sweeny, W. M. "Brigadier-General Thomas W. Sweeny, United States Army." *Journal of the American Irish Historical Society* 27 (1928): 257–72.

Trémaudan, A. H. "Louis Riel and the Fenian Raid of 1871." *CHR* 4 (1923): 132–44.

Trotter, R. G. "Some American Influences upon the Canadian Federation Movement." *CHR* 5 (1924): 213–27.

———. "Canada as a Factor in Anglo-American Relations of the 1860's." *CHR* 16 (1935): 19–26.

Tucker, G. "The Famine Immigration to Canada, 1847." *American Historical Review* 36 (1931): 533–47.

Vesey, M. "When New Brunswick Suffered Invasion." *Dalhousie Review* 19 (1939/40): 197–204.

Vroom, J. "The Fenians on the St. Croix." *CM* 10 (1898): 411–13.

Wallace, W. S. "The Growth of Canadian National Feeling." *CHR* 1 (1920): 136–65.

Wells, G. "The Fenian Raid in Willoughby." *WCHSPR* 2 (1926); 57–59.

———. "A Romance of the Raid." *WCHSPR* 2 (1926): 80–81.

Wheeler, A. E. "Reminiscences of the Fenian Raids of '66." *York Pioneer and Historical Society Annual Report*, 1912, 17–19.

Winkler, L. "The Fenian Movement and Anglo-American Diplomacy in the Reconstruction Period." M.A. dissertation, New York University, 1936.

INDEX